ECKOPEDIA

The ECKANKAR *Lexicon*

Also by Harold Klemp

Animals Are Souls Too!
The Art of Spiritual Dreaming
Ask the Master, Books 1 and 2
Autobiography of a Modern Prophet
The Book of ECK Wisdom
The Call of Soul
Child in the Wilderness
Contemplation Seeds on the Temple of ECK
The ECKANKAR Soul Adventure Guidebook
ECK Essentials
ECK Masters and You: An Illustrated Guide
ECK Wisdom Temples, Spiritual Cities, & Guides: A Brief History
Is Life a Random Walk?
The Living Word, Books 1, 2, 3, and 4
A Modern Prophet Answers Your Key Questions about Life, Books 1, 2, and 3
Past Lives, Dreams, and Soul Travel
Soul Travelers of the Far Country
The Sound of Soul
Spiritual Exercises for the Shariyat, Book One
Spiritual Exercises for the Shariyat, Book Two
The Spiritual Exercises of ECK
The Spiritual Laws of Life
The Temple of ECK
Those Wonderful ECK Masters
The Wind of Change
Wisdom of the Heart, Books 1, 2, 3, and 4
Your Road Map to the ECK Teachings: ECKANKAR Study Guide, Volumes 1 and 2
Youth Ask a Modern Prophet about Life, Love, and God

The MAHANTA Transcripts Series

Journey of Soul, Book 1
How to Find God, Book 2
The Secret Teachings, Book 3
The Golden Heart, Book 4
Cloak of Consciousness, Book 5
Unlocking Your Sacred Puzzle Box, Book 6
The Eternal Dreamer, Book 7
The Dream Master, Book 8
We Come as Eagles, Book 9
The Drumbeat of Time, Book 10
What Is Spiritual Freedom?, Book 11
How the Inner Master Works, Book 12
The Slow Burning Love of God, Book 13
The Secret of Love, Book 14
Our Spiritual Wake-Up Calls, Book 15
How to Survive Spiritually in Our Times, Book 16
The Road to Spiritual Freedom, Book 17
Spiritual Lessons from Living, Book 18

The Immortality of Soul Series

The Awakened Heart
The Awakening Soul
HU, the Most Beautiful Prayer
The Language of Soul
Love—The Keystone of Life
The Loving Heart
The Spiritual Life
Touching the Face of God
Truth Has No Secrets

Stories to Help You See God in Your Life

The Book of ECK Parables, Volumes 1, 2, and 3
Stories to Help You See God in Your Life, ECK Parables, Book 4

Books by Paul Twitchell

ECKANKAR—The Key to Secret Worlds
The ECK-Vidya, Ancient Science of Prophecy
The Flute of God
Herbs: The Magic Healers
The Key to ECKANKAR
The Spiritual Notebook
Stranger by the River
The Tiger's Fang

A Selection of ECKANKAR Reference Books

The ECKANKAR Soul Adventure Guidebook
ECK Essentials
ECK Masters and You: An Illustrated Guide
ECK Wisdom Temples, Spiritual Cities, & Guides: A Brief History
The Shariyat-Ki-SUGMAD, Books One & Two*
Spiritual Exercises for the Shariyat, Book One
Spiritual Exercises for the Shariyat, Book Two
The Spiritual Exercises of ECK
The Spiritual Laws of Life
Those Wonderful ECK Masters
The Wonder within You (for youth)

* The ECKANKAR scriptures

New to ECK?

ECKANKAR's Spiritual Experiences Guidebook

The ECK Wisdom Series by Harold Klemp

ECK Wisdom on Conquering Fear
ECK Wisdom on Dreams
ECK Wisdom on Health and Healing
ECK Wisdom on Inner Guidance
ECK Wisdom on Karma and Reincarnation
ECK Wisdom on Life after Death
ECK Wisdom on Prayer, Meditation, and Contemplation
ECK Wisdom on Relationships
ECK Wisdom on Solving Problems
ECK Wisdom on Soul Travel
ECK Wisdom on Spiritual Freedom

ECKOPEDIA

The ECKANKAR *Lexicon*

HAROLD KLEMP

ECKANKAR
Minneapolis
Eckankar.org

ECKopedia: The ECKANKAR Lexicon

240215

Printed in USA

Cover photos by: Robert Huntley and Doug Kunin

Cover art by: Mary Ann Baxter, Stan Burgess,
Edith Freimanis, Magdalena Jurkowska, Jason Levinson,
Melony Mont-Eton, and Joan Ross

Second printing—2024

Library of Congress Cataloging-in-Publication Data

Names: Klemp, Harold, author.

Title: Eckopedia : the Eckankar lexicon / Harold Klemp.

Description: Minneapolis : Eckankar, [2023] | Portions of this book were previously published in ECKANKAR Dictionary, and in A Cosmic Sea of Words: The ECKANKAR Lexicon. | Includes bibliographical references. | Summary: "Author Harold Klemp, spiritual leader of Eckankar, offers the ultimate companion book for all Eckankar literature - an easy-to-use guide to spiritual terms and concepts"- - Provided by publisher.

Identifiers: LCCN 2023037243 | ISBN 9781570435515 (paperback)

Subjects: LCSH: Eckankar (Organization)- -Dictionaries.

Classification: LCC BP605.E3 K55389 2023 | DDC 299/.33- -dc23/eng/20231019

LC record available at https://lccn.loc.gov/2023037243

♾ This paper meets the requirements of ANSI/NISO Z39.48-1992 (Permanence of Paper).

Contents

Charts and Illustrations

Appendices

Foreword

Paul Twitchell reintroduced the ancient teachings of ECK to the world in 1965.

Early on there was a need to define or explain many terms and concepts, and in 1969 *A Dictionary of ECKANKAR Words and Terms* helped bring clarity to the ECK writings.

Reprinted and revised several times as the *ECKANKAR Dictionary*, this book was greatly expanded in 2009 and released as *A Cosmic Sea of Words: The ECKANKAR Lexicon*. By then, Sri Harold Klemp had been expanding and clarifying the ECK teachings, culture, and doctrines for over a quarter of a century.

The teachings of ECKANKAR are kept up to date by the Living ECK Master of the times. This latest volume, *ECKopedia*, features many of Sri Harold's newest updates and defines important principles and precepts more fully.

* * *

You will gain an ever greater understanding as you explore these ECK terms with the Inner Master in contemplation. Each is a portal to the MAHANTA's gift to you.

You will discover more than can ever be expressed in printed words.

Other Key Reference Books

ECK Essentials

The ECK-Vidya, Ancient Science of Prophecy

ECK Wisdom Temples, Spiritual Cities, & Guides:
A Brief History

The Spiritual Exercises of ECK

Usage Note

In the body of this book, terms set in "small caps" (SMALL CAPITAL LETTERS LIKE THESE) are cross-references—terms you can look up elsewhere in the book. Words set in "full caps" (e.g., *ECK* and *HU*) may also be terms you can look up.

Pronunciation Guide

The pronunciation keys in this book are based on the sounds of English words, as shown below. Note that the letter *h* in a pronunciation key for a vowel sound is silent. Stressed syllables are shown in all capital letters.

SOUND	AS IN	SPELLED AS	ECK EXAMPLE
Vowels			
short a	c**a**t	**a**	Askleposis *ask-leh-POH-sis*
ah sound	f**a**ther	**ah**	Banjani *bahn-JAHN-ee*
long a	d**a**y	**ay**	Akeviz *ah-KAY-veez*
short e	p**e**t	**eh**	Agam Des *AH-gahm DEHS*
long e	t**e**a	**ee**	Lai Tsi *lie TSEE*
long i	t**ie**	**ie**	Lai Tsi *lie TSEE*
short i	h**i**t	**i**	Askleposis *ask-leh-POH-sis*
long o	c**o**at	**oh**	Anami Lok *ah-NAH-mee LOHK*
ow sound	c**ow**	**ow**	Yaubl Sacabi *YEEOW-buhl sah-KAH-bee*
short u	m**u**g	**uh**	Tulsi Das *TUHL-see DAHS*
long u	r**u**le	**oo**	Fubbi Quantz *FOO-bee KWAHNTS*
Consonants			
b	**b**oy	**b**	Banjani *bahn-JAHN-ee*
ch	**Ch**ina	**ch**	Ju Chiao *JOO chee-AH-oh*

SOUND	AS IN	SPELLED AS	ECK EXAMPLE
d	**d**og	**d**	Gopal Das *GOH-pahl **D**AHS*
f	**f**at	**f**	Faqiti ***f**ah-KEE-tee*
hard g	**g**o	**g**	Gopal Das ***G**OH-pahl DAHS*
h	**h**at	**h**	Honardi ***h**oh-NAHR-dee*
soft g or j	**j**am	**j**	Banjani *bahn-**J**AHN-ee*
k	**k**eep	**k**	Katsupari ***k**aht-soo-PAH-ree*
l	**l**ily	**l**	Lai Tsi ***l**ie TSEE*
m	**m**an	**m**	Towart Managi *TOH-wahrt **m**ah-NAH-gee*
n	**n**o	**n**	Namayatan ***n**ah-mah-YAH-tah**n***
ng	si**ng**	**ng**	Sohang *SOH-hah**ng***
p	**p**at	**p**	Peddar Zaskq ***P**EH-dahr ZASK*
qu	**qu**ick	**kw**	Fubbi Quantz *FOO-bee **KW**AHNTS*
r	**r**ight	**r**	Rebazar Tarzs ***R**EE-bah-zahr TAH**R**Z*
s	**s**ay	**s**	Sakapori ***s**ah-kah-POHR-ee*
sh	**sh**ip	**sh**	Shariyat ***SH**AH-ree-aht*
t	**t**op	**t**	Tindor Saki ***T**IN-dohr SAH-kee*
th	**th**in	**th**	Thigala ***th**ee-GAH-lah*
v	**v**oice	**v**	ECK-Vidya *ehk-**V**EE-dyah*
w	**w**ay	**w**	Wu Tenna ***W**OO TEHN-nah*
x	e**x**it	**ks**	exoteric *e**ks**-oh-TEHR-ik*
y	**y**es	**y**	Yavata ***y**ah-VAH-tah*
z	**z**ipper	**z**	Shamus-i-Tabriz *SHAH-muhs-ee-tah-BREE**Z***

Abundant Fruits, Years of the *See* ERUTUA.

Accessible Realm The Eighth PLANE. *See* HUKIKAT LOK.

Acolyte *AH-koh-liet* One who has reached the FIRST INITIATION.

activity, supreme form of *See* SUPREME FORM OF ACTIVITY.

Adamic race *ah-DAH-mik* First of the ROOT RACES, the POLARIANS.

Adepiseka *ah-deh-pee-SEH-kah* One who has reached the TENTH INITIATION.

Adepts *a-DEHPTS* Another name for ECK MASTER(S).

Adhyatma *ah-DYAHT-mah* Another name for the supreme Spirit, the ECK.

adi karma *AH-dee KAHR-mah* *See* PRIMAL KARMA, one of the four types of KARMA.

The other types are DAILY KARMA, FATE KARMA, and RESERVE KARMA.

aditi *ah-DEE-tee* A word for the boundless; space; ether; that which has no beginning nor ending; eternity.

Adoni *ah-DAH-nee* A young ECK MASTER who serves among the nomadic tribes along the Indo-Asian divide. With dark and luminous eyes, he stands about five feet eight inches in height, is slender, and has quick and sure movements. His special interest is plants and herbs.

For a list of ECK Masters, see page 341.

Advaita *ah-DVAH-ee-tah* This is a term for the regions of the Nameless One, the true SPIRITUAL WORLDS, the universes of the God realm. The nonduality which lies beyond the worlds of duality.

Agam Des *AH-gahm DEHS* One of the ten SPIRITUAL CITIES on earth, located in the HINDU KUSH Mountains. It is the chief spiritual city and home to the Temple of GARE-HIRA. YAUBL SACABI is the spiritual leader of the city and GUARDIAN of the temple.

Agam Des has developed into a center of spiritual culture. Those who live here are called the Eshwar-Khanewale, or GOD-EATERS. Agam Des means "inaccessible world," and SOULS come here by invitation only.

The beings here are in charge of the secret forces of the cosmic energy which affects human history. The city is also a way station for spacecraft that pause here to acclimate travelers to the dense vibrations of earth.

The other nine spiritual cities are AKEVIZ, DAMCAR, KIMTAVED, MUMSAKA, NAMPAK, RAHAKAZ, SAT DHAM, SHAMBALLA, and ZEZIRATH. These all serve as outposts for Agam Des.

Agam Lok *AH-gahm LOHK* The Ninth PLANE (counting upward), the fifth of the pure, positive SPIRITUAL WORLDS. It is called the Inaccessible Plane, for few, if any, ever enter into this world.

Distinctions of the Agam Lok

HUK (with a short barking sound made deep in the throat) is the word, or CHANT, that one can sing in CONTEMPLATION to attune oneself to the VIBRATIONS of the Agam Lok or travel inwardly to a GOLDEN WISDOM TEMPLE or other places there.

An inner experience on this plane may include hearing the sound of the music of woodwinds.

The main Golden Wisdom Temple on this plane is KAZI DAWTZ, also called the TEMPLE OF AKASH; here AGNOTTI, the MAHAYA GURU, serves as GUARDIAN of the SHARIYAT-KI-SUGMAD. The ruler of the plane is the AGAM PURUSHA.

See also **The God Worlds Chart** on page 340; LOK.

Agam Purusha *AH-gahm poo-ROO-shah* The first limitation of SUGMAD upon Itself, brought into being by the ECK working through the ANAMI PURUSHA.

Through the Agam Purusha the HUKIKAT LOK came into being, along with the third lord, the HUKIKAT PURUSHA.

The Agam Purusha is ruler of the AGAM LOK and guardian of the ANAMI LOK. It is the duty of the Agam Purusha to see that all who enter into the Kingdom of God have passed beyond all FEAR.

See also **The God Worlds Chart** on page 340; PURUSHA.

Age of the ECK Missionary (1993–2005) *See* **Twelve-Year Cycles of the Master's Spiritual Mission** on page 352.

ages, four *See* FOUR CYCLES OF LIFE; YUGA(S).

Agnotti *ahg-NAHT-tee* The ECK MASTER in charge of the SHARIYAT-KI-SUGMAD in the Temple of Akash (KAZI DAWTZ) on the AGAM LOK. His title is the Mahaya Guru.

During the earliest times on earth, when man was in his most primitive stages of development, Agnotti served as the MAHANTA, the LIVING ECK MASTER and taught the sacred word *HU* in the DREAM STATE.

There is no way to tell what Agnotti's appearance might be, because he appears in different forms to different SOULS.

For a list of ECK Masters, see page 341.

Ahankar *ah-HAHN-kahr* One of the four faculties of MIND; the faculty of separating self and self-interest from all else; the I-ness, the faculty which executes orders. Exaggerated, it becomes VANITY, or ahankara.

The other faculties are BUDDHI, CHITTA, and MANAS.

ahankara *ah-HAHN-kah-rah* VANITY, one of the FIVE PASSIONS OF THE MIND.

ahanta *ah-HAHN-tah* The LITTLE SELF; the EGO.

Ahmad Qavani *AH-mahd kah-VAH-nee* The LIVING ECK MASTER during the reign of King John of England (AD 1199–1216).

Qavani worked behind the scenes to promote freedom, including SPIRITUAL FREEDOM, for the English people. In particular, he helped the barons assert their legal rights before King John. The result was the Magna Carta, and Ahmad Qavani was present at its signing in 1215.

For a list of ECK MASTERS, see page 341.

Ahrat *AH-raht* One who has reached the THIRD INITIATION. Sometimes called the Kurnai.

Ahura Mazda *ah-HOOR-ah MAHZ-dah* A name used in ancient Persia for the state of Godhood; ZOROASTER's name for God.

Akaha *ah-KAH-hah* The world of the SUGMAD; the unspoken, the name and location of which cannot be described in mortal language; the OCEAN OF LOVE AND MERCY.

Also called the Lamakan, the beyond-all which cannot even be termed a PLANE or region. This is the beginning and end of all worlds and circumscribes all worlds.

It is the love and power of this world which is vibrating in every place, by the force of its first principle.

In the beginning, the divine current emanates from this world and comes down in the form of the WORD, the ECK. This is the region of the Supreme ECK MASTERS.

Only the ECK Masters and their followers ever have the opportunity to reach the Akaha.

See also KINGDOM OF THE SUGMAD.

Akash, Temple of *See* KAZI DAWTZ.

Akasha *ah-KAHSH-ah* The primal matter force; the ether that composes all life. The ECK enters into the composition of all beings and things of life; It is the primary Sound of every world within the universes of the SUGMAD.

Also, a record of daily events in the BOOK OF LIFE that the LORDS OF KARMA examine.

Akash Bani *ah-KAHSH BAH-nee* HEAVENLY MUSIC; the WORD of God; SOUND CURRENT.

Akashic records *ah-KAH-sheek* The Akashic records are tally sheets of PAST LIVES spent on the PHYSICAL and ASTRAL PLANES. This book of records is stored on the CAUSAL PLANE. The Akashic records are the total accounting of your good and bad KARMA—how you stand with karma in your life today.

With training, those with the aptitude and interest can learn to read the Akashic records and see their past lives. In ECKANKAR, CHELAS access their own records via the MAHANTA's guidance, in the DREAM STATE or via SOUL TRAVEL.

Besides the Akashic records, there are two other

readings: the SOUL RECORDS and the ECK-VIDYA. The Soul reading is a fuller account of past lives spent in all the LOWER WORLDS, from the first incarnation to the present. The ECK-Vidya inspects the future through a minute-by-minute or day-by-day analysis that occurs in higher states of awareness.

Only the MAHANTA, the LIVING ECK MASTER has the training to read any of these records for others, although a few chelas do undergo the training to learn to read their own.

See also REINCARNATION.

Akeviz *ah-KAY-veez* One of the ten SPIRITUAL CITIES on earth, it is located in the highlands of Guatemala. Akeviz is one of the smaller communities of spiritual travelers who are still connected with the ancient civilization of the Mayans and promote the ancient mysteries of the once-powerful Mayans and AZTECS.

The other nine spiritual cities are AGAM DES, DAMCAR, KIMTAVED, MUMSAKA, NAMPAK, RAHAKAZ, SAT DHAM, SHAMBALLA, and ZEZIRATH.

Akivasha *See* ORACLE OF TIRMER; VOICE OF AKIVASHA.

Akshar *AHK-shahr* A name for the Supreme Deity, the SUGMAD; imperishable consciousness.

Akshar Realization This impersonal state lies beyond GOD-REALIZATION, which is of a more personal nature to the individual SOUL.

The Akshar state is not exclusive to itself. A Soul that has gone beyond God-Realization and is serving in the capacity of the MAHANTA, the LIVING ECK MASTER may also have attained the Akshar.

See also REALIZATION, LEVEL(S) OF.

Alakh Lok *ah-LAHK LOHK* The Sixth PLANE (counting upward), the second of the pure, positive SPIRITUAL WORLDS.

It is called the Invisible Plane, and those who reach this plane must have great determination to go beyond it, for they experience peace and happiness here.

Distinctions of the Alakh Lok

SHANTI (pronounced *SHAHN-tee*) is the word, or CHANT, that one can sing in CONTEMPLATION to attune oneself to the VIBRATIONS of the Alakh Lok or travel inwardly to a GOLDEN WISDOM TEMPLE or other places there.

An inner experience on this plane may include hearing the sound of the wind, sometimes roaring and sometimes gentle.

The main Golden Wisdom Temple on this plane is the TAMANATA KOP; here TOMO GESHIG, the SOKAGAMPO, serves as GUARDIAN of the SHARIYAT-KI-SUGMAD. Other ECK MASTERS working on this plane are CHU-KO YEN, HARI TITA, and HIPOLITO FAYOLLE. The ruler of the plane is the ALAKH PURUSHA.

See also **The God Worlds Chart** on page 340; LOK.

Alakh Purusha *ah-LAHK poo-ROO-shah* Ruler of the ALAKH LOK. Brought into being by the ECK working through the ALAYA PURUSHA, the Alakh Purusha became the fifth individual manifestation of the SUGMAD.

Through the Alakh Purusha, SAT NAM, the Sat Purusha, of the Atma Lok (SOUL PLANE) came into being.

See also **The God Worlds Chart** on page 340; PURUSHA.

Alaya Lok *ah-LAH-yah LOHK* The Seventh PLANE (counting upward), the third of the pure, positive SPIRITUAL WORLDS. It is called the Endless Plane, for it seems to have no end.

Distinctions of the Alaya Lok

HUM (pronounced *HYOOM*, like humming with the lips closed) is the word, or CHANT, that one can sing in CONTEMPLATION to attune oneself to the VIBRATIONS of the Alaya Lok or travel inwardly to a GOLDEN WISDOM TEMPLE or other places there.

An inner experience on this plane may include hearing the sound of deep humming.

The main Golden Wisdom Temple on the Alaya Lok is the ANAKAMUDI TEMPLE; here the ECK MASTER MESI GOKARITZ, the TSONG SIKHSA, serves as GUARDIAN of the SHARIYAT-KI-SUGMAD. The ruler of the plane is the ALAYA PURUSHA.

See also **The God Worlds Chart** on page 340; LOK.

Alaya Purusha *ah-LAH-yah poo-ROO-shah* The ruler of the ALAYA LOK, the Seventh PLANE.

Brought into being by the ECK working through the HUKIKAT PURUSHA, the Alaya Purusha became the fourth individual manifestation of the SUGMAD.

Through the Alaya Purusha, the ALAKH PURUSHA, ruler of the ALAKH LOK, came into being.

See also **The God Worlds Chart** on page 340; PURUSHA.

Alayi *ah-LAH-yee* A spiritually charged word attuned to the PHYSICAL PLANE. You can chant *Alayi* in CONTEMPLATION to visit GOLDEN WISDOM TEMPLES, meet ECK MASTERS, and have other experiences on this PLANE.

For an overview of the planes and their charged words, see **The God Worlds Chart** on page 340.

Aliva mind *ah-LEE-vah* The pure MIND, the highest type of all. It is next to the ECK Itself. Its dwelling place is in the ETHERIC PLANE, between the mind and SOUL PLANE.

See also KARAN MIND; NIJ MIND; PINDA MIND; SUKHSHAM MIND.

Aluk *ah-LOOK* A spiritually charged word attuned to the HUKIKAT LOK, the Eighth PLANE. You can chant *Aluk* in CONTEMPLATION to visit GOLDEN WISDOM TEMPLES, meet ECK MASTERS, and have other experiences on this plane.

For an overview of the planes and their charged words, see **The God Worlds Chart** on page 340.

Aluk, Temple of the *See* JARTZ CHONG.

"Amazing HU" This ECK song adapted from the public-domain song "Amazing Grace" (originally by John Newton) by SRI HAROLD KLEMP and his wife, Joan, was first presented by them at the TEMPLE OF ECK, on May 5, 1991.

It is sung to the traditional American melody of "Amazing Grace," and the song can be a PRAYER or spiritual exercise that opens your heart to love so you can hear God speak to you.

See page 336 for the lyrics.

Amdo *AHM-doh* The dialect of a tribe or community in northeastern Tibet, where ECK has been prominent and well known. FUBBI QUANTZ, REBAZAR TARZS, and YAUBL SACABI were originally of the Amdo people.

Amdo is also the Tibetan name of a large Chinese region.

Anahad Shabda *ah-NAH-hahd SHAHB-dah* Another name for the creative Sound; the great SOUND CURRENT; the still small voice; the voice of silence; the Voice that is that essence; the Holy Ghost, the Comforter, the Divine Spirit that gives life to all. The ECK.

Anakamudi Temple *ah-nah-kah-MOO-dee* The GOLDEN WISDOM TEMPLE on the ALAYA LOK, the Seventh PLANE.

Anami Lok *ah-NAH-mee LOHK* The Tenth PLANE (counting upward). This is the world of the Supreme Being; the mighty center of the universes, the very heart and core of all life and existence.

The sixth of the pure, positive SPIRITUAL WORLDS, it is called the Nameless (Anami) Plane, for there isn't anything to say about it; it is beyond the vocabulary of any human language.

This is the plane where SOULS are reproduced by the SUGMAD reacting upon Itself.

Distinctions of the Anami Lok

HU (pronounced *HYOO*)—the universal name of God, which is in the language of every living thing, everywhere, in everything—is the word, or CHANT, that one can sing in CONTEMPLATION to attune oneself to the VIBRATIONS of the Anami Lok or travel inwardly to a GOLDEN WISDOM TEMPLE or other places there.

An inner experience on this plane may include hearing the sound of the whirlpool.

The main Golden Wisdom Temple on this plane is the SATA VISIC PALACE; here an ECK MASTER with the title of PADMA SAMBA serves as GUARDIAN of the SHARIYAT-KI-SUGMAD. The ruler of the plane is the ANAMI PURUSHA.

See also **The God Worlds Chart** on page 340; LOK.

Anami Purusha *ah-NAH-mee poo-ROO-shah* Ruler of the Tenth PLANE, the ANAMI LOK, and the first individual manifestation of God.

Its very presence is beyond the imagination of man. All subsequent creations of life embodiments were carried on through this first individual manifestation.

The supreme creative ECK energy, working through the Anami Purusha, brought into being the second lord, ruler of the AGAM LOK, the AGAM PURUSHA.

See also **The God Worlds Chart** on page 340; PURUSHA.

Ancient One The MAHANTA.

Ancient Order of the VAIRAGI(s) *See* VAIRAGI(S), ANCIENT ORDER OF THE.

Ancient Science of Soul Travel (ASOST) A descriptive name for ECKANKAR. Used mainly in the time of PAUL TWITCHELL.

Anda *AHN-dah* The ASTRAL PLANE, second of three divisions of the LOWER WORLDS. The other two divisions are PINDA and BRAHMANDA.

Angel of Death The messenger who takes the uninitiated who die on the PHYSICAL PLANE to the region of the ASTRAL PLANE where the YAMA, the righteous judge, sits enthroned to judge every individual according to their KARMA.

See also TRANSLATION; YAMA DUTAS.

angels Any of the hosts of beings in the subtle region close to the earth who have great powers and are quite willing to serve people who live in harmony with them. These are beings above ordinary man in the SPIRITUAL HIERARCHY, and they serve him in many ways. Also called bhuts, devas, devtas, prets, etc.

People sometimes experience or describe an encounter with an ECK MASTER as a visit from their guardian angel.

anger One of the FIVE PASSIONS OF THE MIND. Also called krodha, it manifests as tantrums, fury, mental

carcinoma, slander, evil gossip, backbiting, profanity, faultfinding, jealousy, malice, impatience, resentment, mockery, destructive criticism, and ill will.

The antidote for anger is FORGIVENESS AND TOLERANCE, one of the FIVE VIRTUES.

anitya *ah-NEET-chah* In ECKANKAR, another word for CONTEMPLATION.

Anuga region *ah-NOO-gah* A place within the Atma Lok (SOUL PLANE) where the SOUL RECORDS are kept for those who have reached the SIXTH INITIATION.

The Soul records of the MAHDIS, those who have had the FIFTH INITIATION, are kept in the MEARP REGION. The ECK-NIDA REGION is where the Soul records of those who have received the SEVENTH INITIATION through TWELFTH INITIATION are kept.

Apollonius of Tyana *ap-uh-LOH-nee-uhs uhv TIE-uh-nuh* An ECK MASTER who was also a famous Greek teacher (known to history also as a mystic or neopythagorean philosopher) in the first century AD.

He was often seen in two places at the same time, and many miracles are attributed to him. Sentenced to death by a Roman tyrant, he escaped by suddenly disappearing from the courtroom, then appearing in a distant city a very short time later.

For a list of ECK Masters, see page 341.

Arahata *ah-rah-HAH-tah* One who has reached the SECOND INITIATION in ECKANKAR. Also, a teacher of ECK classes.

THE FOUR-STEP SPIRITUAL EXERCISE OF ECK uses "ECK Arahata" as a CHANT; *see* page 347.

See also ARAHATA MARG; TEACHING ARAHATA.

Arahata Marg *ah-rah-HAH-tah MAHRG* One of the SEVEN MARGS.

The Arahata Marg is the teaching order in ECKANKAR. Within this path the ECK INITIATE is able to work for the higher cause of ECK and give spiritual assistance by being a teacher of ECK to those who want to know more about it.

The single most important message you can ever give anyone is SOUL exists because God loves It. So the ARAHATA helps each person find their own relationship with Divine Spirit.

Arhirit *ahr-HEE-reet* The capital city of the ETHERIC PLANE and dwelling place of its ruler, LORD SOHANG.

In the center of this vast city of light is the DAYAKA TEMPLE, where the ECK MASTER LAI TSI serves as GUARDIAN of the SHARIYAT-KI-SUGMAD and supervises a school of divine WISDOM.

Arrians *ahr-REE-uhnz* A cruel ROOT RACE from Earth's arctic regions, which will take over the world about the year AD 3500, later spreading to Mars and Venus.

Aryans *AHR-ee-uhnz* Fifth ROOT RACE; present ruling race. The Aryans developed the magnificent UIGHUR EMPIRE in central Asia, which stretched from the Pacific Ocean to eastern Europe.

Asanga Kaya *ah-SAHN-gah KAH-yah* The title of the GUARDIAN of the SHARIYAT-KI-SUGMAD at the GOLDEN WISDOM TEMPLE of JARTZ CHONG on the HUKIKAT LOK. KADMON is currently the Asanga Kaya.

For a list of noted guardians, see **A Road Map for Spiritual Travelers** on page 343.

Ashta-dal-Kanwal *AHSH-tah-dahl-KAHN-wahl* The first region of the ASTRAL PLANE, where disciples of the MAHANTA, the LIVING ECK MASTER meet him in his RADIANT BODY.

This life-changing spiritual encounter begins the CHELA's travels through the INNER WORLDS. The MAHANTA greets the chela with great joy. From that moment on, the two are never separated.

"as if" principle An important spiritual principle, or technique, using the CREATIVE IMAGINATION.

This is the technique of imagining that you already are or have that which you desire, and then living from the state of the wish fulfilled. The Law of Attitudes and the Law of Facsimiles are keys to this principle.

See also ATTITUDES, LAW OF; FACSIMILES, LAW OF; FIFTEEN-TIMES SPIRITUAL EXERCISE.

Askleposis *ask-leh-POH-sis* The GOLDEN WISDOM TEMPLE on the ASTRAL PLANE, where GOPAL DAS, the great ECK MASTER, is the GUARDIAN of the fourth section of the SHARIYAT-KI-SUGMAD. REBAZAR TARZS also teaches here.

Description

Located in SAHASRA-DAL-KANWAL, Askleposis is a mammoth, octagon-shaped building of rose and white sandstone; with its huge columns, it has been likened to an ancient Egyptian or Indian temple. It towers high in the center of the city and is surrounded by a huge, green park.

Eight walks lead through the park to the temple, then up steps to gigantic brass doors which open into a majestic, circular room. In the center of this round hall, the Shariyat-Ki-SUGMAD is placed upon a spheroid mineral block. Adjacent to the temple is a huge library where some of the writings of the Shariyat are stored in an archival warehouse.

Asoki *ah-SOH-kee* An ECK MASTER born during the time of the UIGHUR EMPIRE and still living in the same body he inhabited some sixty thousand years before the advent of the Christian calendar. Living near the city of RETZ on Venus, he spreads the message of ECK throughout the planets of the physical world.

For a list of ECK Masters, see page 341.

ASOST An ECKANKAR acronym for ANCIENT SCIENCE OF SOUL TRAVEL.

aspects of the SUGMAD *See* THREE ASPECTS OF THE SUGMAD.

aspirant In ECKANKAR an aspirant is any disciple or

devotee of ECK—one who believes in ECK and follows ECKANKAR. The term *aspirant* sometimes refers to one who has not (yet) received the SECOND INITIATION.

The aspirant receives the full protection of the LIVING ECK MASTER's power and the Master's complete love.

When the student becomes an aspirant, he can expect the Master to become as much a part of him and guide him as much inwardly as he does for the highest CHELA in ECKANKAR.

Assumption, Law of One of the SPIRITUAL LAWS OF LIFE. It is only by living each moment in the assumption of one's divinity that an individual can bring his spiritual potential into the world. Also called the Law of Knowing.

We do not have to please God, we have to manifest Its presence.

Astik *ahs-TEEK* The first MONTH OF THE ECK-VIDYA, corresponding to January. Days of WISDOM. The month of the emerald.

In this journey of SOUL, the primary search is for courage for all future INCARNATIONS.

See also ECK-VIDYA WHEEL.

Astral body One of the BODIES OF SOUL (the others are the PHYSICAL BODY, CAUSAL BODY, MENTAL BODY, and ETHERIC BODY). The Astral body is a protective sheath SOUL uses for experience and expression on the ASTRAL PLANE.

It is lighter and finer than the Physical body. Also

known as the Emotional body, Light body, Light form, subtle body, and Nuri Sarup.

See also **The God Worlds Chart** on page 340; SOUL BODY.

astral cord *See* SILVER CORD.

astral form *See* ASTRAL BODY.

astral light The light which flows from and fills all the ASTRAL PLANE; extremely bright and starry in quality; often mistaken for the true LIGHT of God.

astral museum The great museum on the ASTRAL PLANE where prototypes of all past, present, and future inventions of Earth can be found.

Astral Plane The Second PLANE (counting upward) of the LOWER WORLDS. It is the plane of emotion and the source of all psychic phenomena—ghosts or spirits, ESP, etc. The first region of this plane, ASHTA-DAL-KANWAL, is where disciples of the MAHANTA, the LIVING ECK MASTER have a life-changing spiritual encounter with him in his RADIANT BODY.

Distinctions of the Astral Plane

KALA (pronounced *kah-LAH*) is a word, or CHANT, that one can sing in CONTEMPLATION to attune oneself to the VIBRATIONS of the Astral Plane or SOUL TRAVEL to the GOLDEN WISDOM TEMPLE or other places there.

An inner experience on this plane may include seeing a pink light or hearing the sound of a roaring sea.

The ASTRAL MUSEUM is located here, as is a vast library visited by many writers.

Within the capital city of SAHASRA-DAL-KANWAL is the Golden Wisdom Temple of ASKLEPOSIS; here GOPAL DAS, an ECK MASTER, serves as GUARDIAN of the SHARIYAT-KI-SUGMAD. Other ECK Masters working on this plane are ORI DIOGO (in charge of healing), YUONT-NA, and YU RANTGA. The Astral Plane is sometimes called Anda or Turiya Pad; its ruler is JOT NIRANJAN.

See also **The God Worlds Chart** on page 340.

astral projection A limited state of out-of-body travel not practiced in ECKANKAR; a phenomenon which splits off the sheath of the inner bodies to travel inwardly to the ASTRAL, or Second, PLANE just above the physical; an action which could lead to difficulties with PSYCHIC PHENOMENA, a source of delusion.

A safer and more far-reaching method of exploring the INNER WORLDS is SOUL TRAVEL.

See also **The God Worlds Chart** on page 340.

Astral world *See* ASTRAL PLANE.

astrology The study of the WHEEL OF THE EIGHTY-FOUR, the ZODIAC; uses unreliable mechanical means, such as charts, to foretell the future.

In ECKANKAR, the ECK-VIDYA is the higher approach to delving into the past, present, and future.

Asurati Lok *ah-soo-RAH-tee LOHK* The Desert World. The FAQITI MONASTERY, a supraphysical GOLDEN

WISDOM TEMPLE, is situated here, in the Gobi Desert. BANJANI serves there as GUARDIAN of the introduction to the SHARIYAT-KI-SUGMAD, which ECK CHELAS study here in the DREAM STATE or via SOUL TRAVEL.

See also LOK; PRITHVI LOK; SURATI LOK.

Atlantis *at-LAN-tis* A lost continent which existed long ago and had a history of tens of thousands of years. It was located in the Atlantic Ocean west of Gibraltar.

The long-lived and very extensive Atlantean civilization had been a land of science but also a selfish land where black MAGIC eventually brought about degeneration and destruction.

The People of Atlantis

The Atlanteans were the fourth ROOT RACE, the red race—an olive-skinned people who lived upon the continent of Atlantis.

They had some thirty thousand years to develop their civilization. In that time, they controlled the world and colonized most of it, as well as some other planets.

Tall and fair-haired, with good form and blue eyes, they wore light clothes similar to Roman togas. They developed herbal formulas, which were researched in formal government laboratories.

The Atlanteans developed science beyond anything known today, including exotic means of space travel for the colonization of nearby planets.

Destruction of Atlantis

Over the course of their long history, the Atlanteans turned from love and service to a grab for power and conquest. Their supreme deity was called Tat, and their king-priests were the Tat Tsoks. They unbalanced the cosmic energies, which brought a shower of asteroids and larger bodies down upon the earth. In the end, because of this moral corruption, Atlantis was destroyed by earthquakes and sank into the ocean.

Some escaped the destruction of their continent and fled to distant lands, including Europe, Africa, and the Americas. They took along the culture of their motherland, thus accounting for the similarity of architecture and customs found in widely scattered places like Egypt and Central America, both of which are sites of colossal pyramids.

ECK Masters in Atlantis

SUPAKU was the LIVING ECK MASTER during a high period of Atlantean civilization. He helped compile a number of the herbs, roots, seeds, and flowers which were researched in government health laboratories.

KASSAPA was the Living ECK Master during a period of Atlantis preceding its destruction.

CASTROG was the Living ECK Master who came to warn the people against the mixing of religion with black magic. He spoke from the gates of his own city, Devona, but was slain for his trouble.

DECATES was the MAHANTA, the Living ECK Master who lived in the Atlantean city of Sar-Kurteva. He warned people of the coming disaster

and led some followers to safety in the west, into a wilderness that would, centuries later, be called America.

Another ECK MASTER, **QUETZALCOATL**, left Atlantis just prior to its final destruction and went to what is now Mexico to establish the mysteries of ECK there.

Atma *AHT-mah* Another name for SOUL.

Atma Lok *AHT-mah LOHK* *See* LOK; SOUL PLANE.

Atma Sarup *AHT-mah sah-ROOP* *See* SOUL BODY.

Atma Sharir *AHT-mah shah-REER* *See* SOUL BODY.

attachment Being unduly influenced by affection, anxiety, procrastination, desires, or possessions. One of the FIVE PASSIONS OF THE MIND.

This is the state of being connected to the karmic conditions that hold one to the CONSCIOUSNESS of the LOWER WORLDS. Also called moha.

The antidote for attachment is DETACHMENT, one of the FIVE VIRTUES.

Attitudes, Law of The Law of Attitudes states that the power of IMAGINATION rules over will in the actions in this universe.

This is one of the spiritual laws of life; the fifth law of the physical universe (see **Seven Laws of the Physical Universe** on page 344). *See also* "AS IF" PRINCIPLE.

Audible Life Stream *See* SOUND CURRENT.

Aum *AHM or ah-UHM* A spiritually charged word attuned to the MENTAL PLANE, the Fourth PLANE. You can chant *Aum* in CONTEMPLATION to visit GOLDEN WISDOM TEMPLES, meet ECK MASTERS, and have other experiences on this plane.

For an overview of the planes and their charged words, see **The God Worlds Chart** on page 340.

aura *AHR-ah* Everything in nature generates its own aura, atmosphere, or magnetic field. The aura is a subtle extension of character, capable of both giving and receiving impressions.

It is often the thing people feel before they even get within hand-shaking or hugging distance; you either like someone or you don't, as it's a sense or INTUITION.

The aura changes as we change; for example, the aura may grow larger and brighter and change in color as the LIGHT of God cleanses SOUL. White in the aura indicates the true spiritual power; yellow is the color of Soul power; indigo, intuition; blue, WISDOM; green, energy; orange, health; red, life.

Avatar *AH-vah-tahr* The LIVING ECK MASTER is the Avatar of the world for all ECK followers. One is always present in the physical realm guiding the human race.

Avernus *ah-VEHR-nuhs* The dark realm of the ASTRAL PLANE—referred to as the seven worlds of Avernus, Hades, or HELL—where many SOULs who have

spent their earth lives in evil deeds must spend time.

While no one is purely good or purely evil, many who border on the edge of evil, or who are tainted with some evil, must spend time in this dark world. They later reincarnate into life again for the opportunity of regaining what has been lost in their SPIRITUAL UNFOLDMENT.

Once one has established himself and started working toward the good of existence, he will no longer spend time in these lower Astral planes or any of the underworld planes.

See also REINCARNATION; REMODELING OF SOUL.

Awagawan *ah-WAH-gah-wahn* Incarnating of SOUL; rebirth. Agelong cycles of life and death, transmigration and REINCARNATION; the wheel of life.

See also WHEEL OF THE EIGHTY-FOUR.

awakened Soul SOUL functioning in the SPIRITUAL WORLDS while still living in the physical state in Its PHYSICAL BODY.

awareness *See* CONSCIOUSNESS; TOTAL AWARENESS.

Awaz *ah-WAHZ* Another name for ECK, the SOUND CURRENT.

Ayur Vedha *AH-yoor VAY-dah* The ECK system for renewing the body's health and vitality. Not to be confused with ayurveda (the traditional system of medicine of India). An offshoot of Ayur Vedha is KAYA KALP.

See also SPIRITUAL HEALING.

Aztecs *AZ-tehks* One group of descendants of the race which once inhabited the sunken continent of ATLANTIS.

See also AKEVIZ; QUETZALCOATL.

Babla Mohenjo *BAH-blah moh-HEHN-joh* The LIVING ECK MASTER during the reign of Constantine I.

He had a small school for ECK CHELAS near Constantinople and was at the Council of Nicaea called by Constantine in Bithynia, Asia Minor, in AD 325.

It troubled him to see the church pronounce Christ an equal with God, yet he saw in the deification of Christ an inescapable direction for the Christian church. He did not interfere.

For a list of ECK MASTERS, see page 341.

baibek *BIE-behk* The third of four degrees of DISCRIMINATION, attained when SOUL has unfolded beyond SELF-REALIZATION, is freed of all coverings, and is able to operate by direct perception.

Baju *BAH-joo* A spiritually charged word attuned to the ETHERIC PLANE. You can chant *Baju* in CONTEMPLATION to visit GOLDEN WISDOM TEMPLES, meet ECK MASTERS, and have other experiences on this PLANE.

For an overview of the planes and their charged

words, see **The God Worlds Chart** on page 340.

Balance, Law of One of the SPIRITUAL LAWS OF LIFE. Underlying all in the great worlds of God is the Law of Balance. All is completely in balance in God's universal body. Balance is the principle of unity, of oneness. It is the stability which lies in the Godhead.

See also KARMA, LAW OF; MIDDLE PATH; POLARITY, LAW OF.

Bani *BAH-nee* The SOUND CURRENT; the HEAVENLY MUSIC; the ECK, which is the Audible Life Stream; the melody which is given by the SUGMAD through the ECK, the LIGHT AND SOUND.

Banjani *bahn-JAHN-ee* The ECK MASTER who teaches the introduction to the SHARIYAT-KI-SUGMAD and is GUARDIAN of the FAQITI MONASTERY, the GOLDEN WISDOM TEMPLE on the ASURATI LOK (Desert world) in the Gobi Desert.

He appears to be over one hundred years old and looks like an old sailor, with a wrinkled, ruddy face and a big smile. His voice is very high-pitched, yet filled with power and love.

For a list of ECK Masters, see page 341.

Baraka Bashad *bah-RAH-kah bah-SHAHD* Means "May the blessings be" and is often used as the ECK benediction.

Along with the HU CHANT, this ECK blessing is an example of the highest spiritual forms of PRAYER or worship. It is another way to say, "Thy will be done."

Beautiful Flowers, Years of the *See* YIGERTA.

Beautify Day One of the TRADITIONS OF ECK, celebrated every spring and fall (usually in May and September). These are key times for sprucing up and revitalizing ECK TEMPLES and ECK CENTERS around the world, as well as individual CONTEMPLATION spaces.

As an active spiritual exercise, CHELAS, individually or in groups, give special attention to renewal and cleanliness, finding ways to share their love of ECK and bring a shine to their part of the worldwide ECK community. Options include sponsored community cleanup projects.

beauty, days of *See* PARINAMA.

bhajan *BAH-jahn* The spiritual exercise of listening to the music of the ECK; that ability to listen to the HEAVENLY MUSIC within with the spiritual ears.

See also SPIRITUAL EXERCISES OF ECK.

Bhakti *BAHK-tee* Love which is inseparable from life itself; devotion to the LIVING ECK MASTER.

A Seventh Initiate in ECKANKAR is sometimes called the Bhakti or Shab.

> THE FOUR-STEP SPIRITUAL EXERCISE OF ECK uses "Bhakti" as a word to chant; *see* page 347.

See also DIVINE LOVE; SEVENTH INITIATION.

Bhakti Marg *BAHK-tee MAHRG* One of the SEVEN MARGS. This is the ECK order of love. One gives service by volunteering work in the works of ECK because of his great love for the MAHANTA, the LIVING ECK MASTER and the ECK Itself.

bilocation A term used by PAUL TWITCHELL, in the 1960s, for out-of-body travel. He found that people confused it with ASTRAL PROJECTION, so he replaced the term with *SOUL TRAVEL*.

Blessing, A Year of The seventh of the SPIRITUAL YEARS OF ECK.

For a description, see **The Spiritual Years of ECK** on page 354.

black magic *See* MAGIC.

Blue Light *See* MAHANTA.

Blue Star of ECK The six-pointed Blue Star of ECK is a manifestation of the MAHANTA usually seen by CHELAS before their FIFTH INITIATION, though HIGHER INITIATES may continue to see it too.

A six-pointed white star means the presence of the MAHANTA as it appears to an ECK INITIATE on the SOUL PLANE or higher.

In the TEMPLE OF ECK, the blue stained-glass star on the sanctuary ceiling represents the eternal presence of the MAHANTA with all SOULs at all times.

bodies of the MAHANTA *See* QUINTAN.

bodies of Soul The sheaths, or protective bodies, SOUL takes on when It operates in the LOWER WORLDS.

Each of us *is* Soul, and we *have* a physical body and inner bodies as well. Each body matches the VIBRATIONS of a particular PLANE, enabling Soul to have experiences and expression there. Besides the PHYSICAL

BODY, these sheaths include the ASTRAL BODY, CAUSAL BODY, MENTAL BODY, and ETHERIC BODY.

See also SOUL BODY; TEMPLE OF GOD.

body of glory *See* THREE ASPECTS OF THE SUGMAD.

Book of Life The Book of Records that the LORDS OF KARMA examine to determine the just merits due a person at the time of death.

See also AKASHIC RECORDS; KARMA; REINCARNATION.

Bountiful Earth, Years of the *See* SELTEA.

Bourchakoun *boor-chah-KOON* Another name for the VAIRAGI Adepts, the ECK MASTERS.

See also VAIRAGI(S), ANCIENT ORDER OF THE.

Brahm *BRAHM* The ruler of the three worlds (TRILOKI), usually called the LOWER WORLDS in ECKANKAR; the KAL NIRANJAN, or the negative power.

Brahmanda *brah-MAHN-dah* One of three divisions of the LOWER WORLDS; extends from just above the ASTRAL PLANE to just below the SOUL PLANE.

The other two divisions are ANDA and PINDA.

See also CAUSAL PLANE; MENTAL PLANE; ETHERIC PLANE.

Brahmanda, Hall of GOLDEN WISDOM TEMPLE on the MENTAL PLANE. SATO KURAJ is the GUARDIAN of the SHARIYAT-KI-SUGMAD there.

Located in the city of MER KAILASH, the Hall of Brahmanda is one of the largest of all the schools of WISDOM.

It is square in shape, with an overhanging roof supported by one hundred pillars; its style is similar to the ancient Temple of Diana (Artemis) and the Parthenon. It glitters white in the brilliant light of a sun a thousand times brighter than that of the PHYSICAL PLANE.

Inside the building is a long, flat block on which rests the Shariyat-Ki-SUGMAD, encased in a glasslike transparent material.

Brahmanda Lok *brah-MAHN-dah LOHK* *See* CAUSAL PLANE; LOK.

Brahm Lok *BRAHM LOHK* The MENTAL PLANE; sometimes designates the lower section of BRAHMANDA. It is the home of the UNIVERSAL MIND, and it is from this region that all individual MINDs are derived.

See also LOK.

Bright Snows, Years of the *See* GINTHE.

Brilliant Sun, Years of the *See* DORETI.

bronze age *See* FOUR CYCLES OF LIFE; MAHAYUGA; YUGA(S).

Brother(s) of the Leaf HIGH(ER) INITIATES. The Brothers of the Leaf are those who have reached the FIFTH INITIATION in ECKANKAR.

A band of people with strong spiritual ties, they act as one for all and all for one. They are like leaves on the same tree, the ECK. They have a secret "inner net" of communication with each other.

Each can also be said to have turned a new leaf, as one's view of living and of this world undergoes a complete transformation at the Fifth Initiation.

Buddhi *BOO-dee* One of the four faculties of the MIND; the intellect proper; chief instrument of thought, DISCRIMINATION, decision, and judgment.

The other faculties are AHANKAR, CHITTA, and MANAS.

Buddhi Sharir *BOO-dee shah-REER* *See* ETHERIC BODY.

Buddhi state The second of four degrees of DISCRIMINATION, not attained until SOUL has SELF-REALIZATION.

Buika Magna *Boo-I-kah MAG-nah* The remote mountain range in northern Tibet where the KATSUPARI MONASTERY is located.

Bytag, The *BIE-tahg* A collection of poems by FUBBI QUANTZ, the ECK MASTER at the KATSUPARI MONASTERY in Tibet.

Castrog *KAH-strahg* The LIVING ECK MASTER in ATLANTIS who came there to warn the people of the dangers of practicing black MAGIC and how this would lead to death and destruction under the waters of the sea. He was slain for his troubles.

For a list of ECK MASTERS, see page 341.

Causal body One of the BODIES OF SOUL (the others are the PHYSICAL BODY, ASTRAL BODY, MENTAL BODY, and ETHERIC BODY).

The Causal body is the protective sheath SOUL uses for experience and expression on the CAUSAL PLANE. Also known as the Karan Sarup, Karan Sharir, the memory body, and the seed body.

See also **The God Worlds Chart** on page 340; SOUL BODY.

Causal Plane The Third PLANE, counting upward, where memories and karmic patterns are stored—the past (including PAST LIVES) in visible records, and the future in seed form.

Distinctions of the Causal Plane

MANA (pronounced *mah-NAH* or *mah-NAY*) is a word, or CHANT, that one can sing in CONTEMPLATION to attune oneself to the VIBRATIONS of the Causal Plane or SOUL TRAVEL to a GOLDEN WISDOM TEMPLE or other places there.

An inner experience on this plane may include seeing an orange light or hearing the sound of tinkling bells.

The main Golden Wisdom Temple on this plane, in the city of HONU, is the Temple of SAKAPORI; here SHAMUS-I-TABRIZ, an ECK MASTER, serves as GUARDIAN of the SHARIYAT-KI-SUGMAD. Other ECK Masters working on this plane are ISMET HOUDONI, SARDAR LHUNPO, and VAJRA MANJUSHRI.

The Causal Plane is sometimes called the Brahmanda Lok; its ruler is RAMKAR.

See also **The God Worlds Chart** on page 340.

Cause and Effect, Law of *See* KARMA, LAW OF.

Cave of Fire An inner PURIFICATION each SOUL goes through in order to become a Coworker in the spiritual realms. The test of the Cave of Fire usually occurs early in a CHELA's time in ECKANKAR.

Its purpose is to weaken the hold of KARMA so that Soul gains a little more SPIRITUAL FREEDOM. Chelas may or may not remember this experience which helps them be more alert to the SOUND CURRENT and Its message.

See also CAVE(S) OF PURIFICATION.

cave(s) of purification This is an actual location on a number of PLANES. Its purpose is to provide a place for a rapid burn-off of KARMA.

The cave on the ASTRAL PLANE is in a mountainous area, and the mouth of the cave is tall enough to allow for twice the height of an average-sized man.

Some, but not all, Second Initiates are brought here in the DREAM STATE. The MAHANTA leads them into the cave where a brilliant white light burns away useless karmic burdens. The fire is white, but the flames throw no heat in the usual way. It is a fire that burns the atoms in one clean.

Sometime after this rite of PURIFICATION, the individual is cleared to pass into the CAUSAL PLANE.

See also CAVE OF FIRE.

celestial Light That LIGHT which surrounds any mystical or ESOTERIC vision that one might witness.

celestial Word *See* ECK.

censor *See* DREAM CENSOR.

ceremony, ceremonies *See* ECK CELEBRATIONS OF LIFE; INITIATION(S); PASSING OF THE ROD OF ECK POWER.

chaitanya *chie-TAHN-yah* A word for the embodiment of all attributes of life—of spiritual ENLIGHTENMENT, of vitality and vibrancy, of intelligence. The awakened CONSCIOUSNESS.

chakras *CHAH-krahz* The psychic centers which correspond with the nerve centers in the spine, neck,

and head of man; the microcosmic centers in the body of man which correspond to portions of the outlying universe or MACROCOSM.

The lower chakras used in the yoga systems are not part of the practice of ECKANKAR.

See also CROWN CHAKRA.

Change, Law of One of the SPIRITUAL LAWS OF LIFE.

We are changing, and we are changeless. The outer part of us (the PHYSICAL BODY, as well as the ASTRAL, CAUSAL, and MENTAL bodies) is always undergoing change, but the True Self, SOUL, is changeless.

Conditions in the worlds of time and space will always change at some point; there is no stability here, as the positive and negative streams are in a constant interplay.

Things ebb and flow in the universe all the time. This dynamic tension between the positive and negative forces is needed to stretch the individual beyond his present capacity.

Change is therefore not to be feared, but to be accepted as an integral part of life. Change strengthens Soul.

chant Repetition of a holy word or one of the holy names of God; often part of the SPIRITUAL EXERCISES OF ECK.

See also HU CHANT; MANTRA; ZIKAR.

charity The goodwill we give to all SOULS. Man does not have the capacity to give warm, personal love to all, so it is given to dear ones—friends and family.

But charity—detached love—can be given freely to everyone.

DETACHMENT does not mean lack of COMPASSION, but it resists interfering in somebody else's affairs.

A third kind of love, besides warm love and charity, is spiritual love; it is of the highest nature—the love of the individual for the MAHANTA, the LIVING ECK MASTER, who is the manifestation of God's love.

See also DIVINE LOVE; NONINTERFERENCE, LAW OF.

Charlemagne In the eighth and ninth centuries AD, Charlemagne was King of the Franks, King of the Lombards, and Holy Roman Emperor.

KETU JARAUL, the LIVING ECK MASTER of the time, taught Charlemagne the precepts of the ECK-VIDYA, the ancient science of prophecy. This ability to perceive the future was a priceless aid as he steered a course through the perilous times of his reign.

chastity Paired with HUMILITY, chastity is one of the FOUR DISCIPLINES OF ECK.

chela(s) *CHEE-lah* A chela is a student of ECKANKAR, a disciple (follower) of the LIVING ECK MASTER.

Formally, this is a spiritual student (ECKIST or member) who has enrolled in ECKANKAR'S SPIRITUAL LIVING COURSES. Chelas study under the LIVING ECK MASTER and become eligible for INITIATIONS. They can work within the SPIRITUAL HIERARCHY, serving the cause of ECK.

The laws and rules for the ECK chela are simple. These are to practice the FOUR DISCIPLINES OF ECK,

which give HARMONY, purity, and perfection of SOUL. This constitutes heaven while in the PHYSICAL BODY.

Chiad *chee-AHD* One who has reached the FOURTH INITIATION.

Chitta *CHEE-tah* One of the four faculties of the MIND; that function, or faculty, which takes cognizance of form, beauty, color, rhythm, harmony, and perspective, receiving its impressions mostly through the eyes.

The other faculties are AHANKAR, BUDDHI, and MANAS.

chosen one(s), chosen people Those who, through SELF-DISCIPLINE, have reached the STATE OF CONSCIOUSNESS whereby they are acting as godly instruments through which the ECK flows to the world and uplifts all life.

See also COWORKER(S) WITH GOD; COWORKER(S) WITH THE MAHANTA.

Christ consciousness JESUS'S STATE OF CONSCIOUSNESS and the CONSCIOUSNESS sought by Christians; also known as COSMIC CONSCIOUSNESS.

Chu-Ko Yen *CHOO-koh YEHN* The Chinese LIVING ECK MASTER who guided Confucius and advised him in his work. He is now a spiritual guide on the ALAKH LOK.

For a list of ECK MASTERS, see page 341.

circle(s) of initiation The stages, or levels, of INITIATION in ECKANKAR are often referred to as circles.

For a list of the initiations in ECK, see page 338.

clairaudience One of the THIRTY-TWO FACETS OF ECKANKAR. The psychic ability to hear sounds and voices regardless of distance.

clairvoyance One of the THIRTY-TWO FACETS OF ECKANKAR. The psychic ability to see and know, regardless of distance, in the LOWER WORLDS.

Clarion *KLAYR-ee-ahn* A planet where higher evolved SOULS are living to help carry on the work of God throughout the universe.

cleanliness of mind See FOUR DISCIPLINES OF ECK.

Clemains *kleh-MINZ* Twelfth of Earth's ROOT RACES. A ruthless race which will attempt to destroy everything of the former civilization in the years around AD 7000 and will try to set up a new religion based on the idea of priest-kings.

Cliff Hanger A God Seeker who hangs on the cliffs of the Mountain of God, above the crowd, knowing there are further heights to attain. PAUL TWITCHELL called himself a Cliff Hanger.

code of ethics *See* ETHICS, LAW OF.

communication with God Being aware of the value of the PRESENT MOMENT.

compassion Compassion is the way to WISDOM.

Compassion shrinks the walls between SOULS, for how could anyone not have compassion for another

Light of God in need of a smile, a kind word, or even a meal?

The compassion of the MAHANTA, the LIVING ECK MASTER knows no limit.

Compensation, Law of *See* KARMA, LAW OF.

connecting diamonds Events are like diamonds. Invisible lines connect them, a part of a divine plan.

The God lover learns to see and follow these lines, for they smooth his way. They lead over holy ground. It is there that the Holy Spirit does the wonders that help an individual do what he cannot do alone.

conscience The state of moral or ethical development which comes from SPIRITUAL UNFOLDMENT; the way the SUGMAD keeps man on the path of right conduct for the good of his fellow man.

See also DHARMA, LAW OF.

consciousness There are various degrees and STATES OF CONSCIOUSNESS far above and beyond the MIND. To raise one's consciousness is the ECK CHELA's purpose under the guidance of the MAHANTA.

We gradually learn to expand the consciousness so that we can hear the sweet whisperings of Divine Spirit as It is giving us answers in our everyday life. The further into the INNER WORLDS that SOUL travels, the higher the development of this consciousness.

Through SPIRITUAL UNFOLDMENT and the ECK INITIATIONS, the chela goes beyond the human and psychic levels of awareness to SELF-REALIZATION,

SPIRITUAL REALIZATION, and GOD-REALIZATION.

See also REALIZATION, LEVEL(S) OF.

Consciousness Five PAUL TWITCHELL's mission was to establish Consciousness Five, the spiritual CONSCIOUSNESS of the SOUL PLANE. This event was of great importance to the movement of ECKANKAR.

The event of Consciousness Five is the SELF-REALIZATION that occurs within each individual. Before he left this earthly theater in 1971, PAULJI set the stage for Consciousness Five, and this is the general area of the consciousness of the body of ECK today.

Yet Consciousness Five is still in the making, in that the body of ECK is trying to consolidate gains made since 1971. Then it can move into the level of Consciousness Six, become established there, and eventually make its way to CONSCIOUSNESS NINE.

Consciousness Nine SRI HAROLD KLEMP's mission is to establish Consciousness Nine, a high level of spiritual awareness. Each level is a turn higher on the spiral of CONSCIOUSNESS, as the waves of SOULs in ECK catch the returning tide home to the OCEAN OF LOVE AND MERCY.

As HARJI lays the foundation for Consciousness Nine, the result is the social, political, economic, and climatic changes of today.

Meanwhile the general level of the human race is Consciousness Two, which corresponds to the ASTRAL PLANE; humanity is struggling to come to grips with its emotions, after which it can progress to the level of the CAUSAL PLANE.

The body of ECK—which includes life on all PLANES, in all universes—is generally at CONSCIOUSNESS FIVE and trying to move to the level of Consciousness Six. Consciousness Six is a preliminary and necessary step of the overall spiritual level of Souls in ECK, as a body, on their way eventually to Consciousness Nine.

> The ECK teachings are for the individual. The group is incidental; it is only a reflection of the collective state of the individuals within it.

Consciousness, Law of One of the SPIRITUAL LAWS OF LIFE. We each choose our own STATE OF CONSCIOUSNESS. We make our own worlds. What we are today is the sum total of everything we have thought or been throughout the ages.

consciousness, seven principles of *See* INVISIBLE LAWS.

Consecration, A Year of The twelfth of the SPIRITUAL YEARS OF ECK.

For a description, see **The Spiritual Years of ECK** on page 354.

contemplation An essential spiritual exercise in ECKANKAR where the attention is focused upon some definite spiritual principle, thought or idea, or upon the LIVING ECK MASTER.

This is a conversation with the most secret, most genuine, and most mysterious part of oneself—a way to actively explore the INNER WORLDS of one's own being.

Contemplation is the process by which the know-

er and the known become one. Also known as TRUE CONTEMPLATION OF THE ECK WORKS, one of the FOUR FUNDAMENTALS OF ECK.

> This is a reciprocal relationship. As SOUL invests Itself in deeper realizations of TRUTH, Truth invests Itself in Soul.

The scope and form contemplation can take is infinite. The most direct is to sit for a session with the SPIRITUAL EXERCISES OF ECK for twenty minutes a day. As well, immersing oneself in any Soulful study or effort can result in communication with the GOD CURRENT, the ECK.

> Contemplation is a sacred act of PURIFICATION and upliftment, guided by the MAHANTA, the INNER MASTER. He is the desire for Truth that dwells in the contemplator's heart, and his devotion to Soul knows no equal.

See also NIRVIKALPA; RECIPROCITY, LAW OF; SAMADHI.

contemplation seed A short passage from one of the spiritual works of ECKANKAR, to be read aloud or silently and taken to heart, usually just before going into CONTEMPLATION.

contemplative order An area of service for the HIGH(ER) INITIATE who gives service to life quietly and privately as an individual in his community.

contentment Also called santosha, one of the FIVE VIRTUES; the peace of self which comes when one is rid

of desire; a step on the path to the FAR COUNTRY; the opposite of and remedy for lobha, or GREED.

See also FOUR DISCIPLINES OF ECK.

copper age *See* FOUR CYCLES OF LIFE; MAHAYUGA; YUGA(S).

cosmic altar of God The inner CONSCIOUSNESS shaped as needed in each individual case; that awareness or point at which the individual surrenders to the ECK.

cosmic consciousness A LEVEL OF REALIZATION; enlightenment of the intellectual senses on the MENTAL PLANE.

See also **The God Worlds Chart** on page 340.

cosmic principle The infinite in all life is at one with the infinite in man.

God is One, and this One is centered in each individual. Spirit is moving simultaneously in the macrocosm of the universe and in the microcosm of the individual, and the movement of the two harmonize.

They are that of the same Spirit.

See also MACROCOSM AND MICROCOSM.

Council of the Nine, the These nine unknown ECK MASTERS are the guardians of ECK and Its distribution in the LOWER WORLDS.

These Masters dwell on the ANAMI LOK. They are the close-knit brotherhood that took the ECK teachings underground during the time of GOPAL DAS. (The teachings publicly reemerged in the modern era, starting with PAUL TWITCHELL in 1965.)

Coworker(s) with God The destiny of every SOUL is to become one with the ECK and love as God loves.

As a Coworker with God, Soul decides upon Its final mission in eternity. Soul alone must make the choice of what It shall do for Its missionary assignment. This is the freedom of choice which the SUGMAD gives to all Souls.

The ECK MASTERS are Coworkers with God. The word *ECKANKAR* means Coworker with God.

See also COWORKER(S) WITH THE MAHANTA.

Coworker(s) with the MAHANTA One who is in training to be a COWORKER WITH GOD and an ECK MASTER. To give of oneself to bring the message of ECK to others is acting as a Coworker with the MAHANTA.

creation The LOWER WORLDS of energy, matter, space, and time created by the sound of HU—the WORD, the ECK Spirit—and sustained by It.

These are the finished worlds, established for the purpose of providing a training ground for SOUL. The original creation is within each Soul, and all is within the SUGMAD.

Each Soul saw it in the Golden Age and has since been trying to remember it.

See also FOUR CYCLES OF LIFE.

creative imagination The God-spark within you, also called the divine imagination. It is SOUL's peculiar talent for survival in every universe of CREATION. In the power of divine creativity, there is no limitation whatsoever.

The creative imagination is God in expression, manifesting Its creation in this world through our actions; it can lift us into truly becoming godlike beings.

A key to the SPIRITUAL EXERCISES OF ECK and a way to listen to God; the only faculty that makes one godlike.

See also "AS IF" PRINCIPLE.

creative power *See* RECIPROCITY, LAW OF.

Creativity, A Year of The ninth of the SPIRITUAL YEARS OF ECK.

For a description, see **The Spiritual Years of ECK** on page 354.

Creativity, Law of One of the SPIRITUAL LAWS OF LIFE. Every atom is striving continually to manifest more life; all are intelligent, and all are seeking to carry out the purpose for which they were created.

Creator SUGMAD, God, the Supreme Creator, the Originator of Life.

crown chakra The spiritual opening at the top of the head (the soft spot on a baby's head) and the easiest place to succeed with SOUL TRAVEL. Also called the SAHASRA-DAL-KANWAL or thousand-petaled lotus.

cycle(s) *See* ECK-VIDYA WHEEL; FOUR CYCLES OF LIFE; MAHAYUGA; TWELVE-YEAR CYCLE(S).

cycle, twelve-year *See* TWELVE-YEAR CYCLE(S).

daily karma One of the four types of KARMA. Karma which is made hour to hour and day to day; new karma created by actions during this life.

See also KARMA, LAW OF.

Dakaya technique *dah-KAH-yah* The first of two MASTER TECHNIQUES given in the ECK SPIRITUAL LIVING COURSES; the second is SUANG-TU. These techniques are used by the ECK MASTERS of the Order of the VAIRAGI for SOUL TRAVEL and can be used by CHELAS as well.

Damcar *DAHM-kahr* One of the ten SPIRITUAL CITIES, located in the Gobi Desert near the border between China and Mongolia. The beings living here help spread all religions for the enlightenment of mankind.

The other nine spiritual cities are AGAM DES, AKEVIZ, KIMTAVED, MUMSAKA, NAMPAK, RAHAKAZ, SAT DHAM, SHAMBALLA, and ZEZIRATH.

danda *DAHN-dah* SELF-DISCIPLINE; sometimes called the righteous law. It treats the divine rights of people as well as kings; works both ways, neither can trespass upon the other's rights.

dark night of Soul The season an individual thinks God has forsaken him, and that he is left to his own devices on the battlefield of life. An arid period through which every SOUL passes on Its way to SELF-REALIZATION and GOD-REALIZATION.

Behind the dark night of Soul is FEAR and ignorance, so the ECK INITIATE should ask, "What am I unwilling to face?"

Yet the day of understanding follows the night, always and ever—no matter how long or dark the night may be. Like the day, understanding will always defeat the night of ignorance.

Love and patience. And let God's holy name of HU be always on your lips.

Darshan *DAHR-shahn* The Darshan is the meeting with the Master, which can take place inwardly or outwardly. One form of the Darshan is the GAZE OF THE MASTER, or the Tiwaja, which has the power to uplift and heal all things.

There are two parts of the Darshan: meeting with the Master outwardly and being recognized by him, and meeting with him inwardly and traveling with him; seeing and being seen by him, and the ENLIGHTENMENT which comes with this act.

This is the gaze of love, the gaze that gives the love of God to people.

See also PRESENCE OF THE MASTER.

Daswan Dwar *DAHS-wahn DWAHR* The MENTAL PLANE. Also another name for the TENTH DOOR, the SPIRITUAL EYE.

Dayaka *dah-YAH-kah* The LIVING ECK MASTER who served in LEMURIA. Early on in Lemuria, there was no royalty. ECK Masters like GEUTAN and Dayaka gave direct spiritual guidance to the people. Later, as the land went into a decline of materialism, the ECK Masters went into hiding because of persecution by the kings and priests.

For a list of ECK MASTERS, see page 341.

Dayaka Temple *dah-YAH-kah* GOLDEN WISDOM TEMPLE in the city of ARHIRIT on the ETHERIC PLANE. LAI TSI is the GUARDIAN of the SHARIYAT-KI-SUGMAD there.

Dayaka is a great, round, towering temple that is shaped like a silo. It is more than a hundred stories high, with great windows that go around the whole structure. At the top is a spire, and upon it rests a shining golden ball whose brilliance is greater than that of any sun in the universe. Its rays reach out to the very edges of the Etheric Plane.

The Shariyat-Ki-SUGMAD itself rests on a lectern hundreds of feet below the golden ball of radiant light.

Day and Night of the SUGMAD (Day and Night of God) The two perpetually repeating periods of cosmic CREATION. Each Day of the SUGMAD is a MAHA-YUGA and is followed by a Night of the SUGMAD which is equal in length.

See also FOUR CYCLES OF LIFE; YUGA(S).

Decates *deh-KAH-tehz* The MAHANTA, the LIVING ECK MASTER of his time on the continent of ATLANTIS, in the city of Sar-Kurteva.

He was able to see the impending destruction that would result from the people having turned away from the worship of the SUGMAD to follow the false gods of black MAGIC. He led the few CHOSEN ONES—those who had experienced and accepted ECK as truth—west into a wilderness which would, centuries later, become known as America.

For a list of ECK MASTERS, see page 341.

dedication Devotion to something sacred. The devotion of CHELAS to the ECK and the LIVING ECK MASTER. The greatest asset of a chela.

déjà vu *DAY-jah VOO* A strong feeling of already having experienced something before. This can be bringing the memory of a dream into the present moment or a glimpse of past or future events. One of the THIRTY-TWO FACETS OF ECKANKAR.

Delphi *See* ORACLE OF DELPHI.

Desert world *See* ASURATI LOK.

desireless life, state *See* DETACHMENT.

Destiny, Law of One of the SPIRITUAL LAWS OF LIFE. SOUL comes into the world to accomplish an assortment of tasks; these assignments taken as a whole make up Its destiny.

detachment One of the FIVE VIRTUES and the remedy for ATTACHMENT. Also known as VAIRAG, this is the

release of undue attachments to worldly desires and possessions.

It means simply that you can have COMPASSION, you can enjoy life, but if sorrow comes, it does not burden you until the end of your days. You are able to see the hand of God in it. You will pick yourself up and have gratitude for what blessings you retain.

SOUL lives forever by giving, not by receiving. It is a state of being like the sun, shining upon all alike, yet asking nothing in return.

Detachment is the key to the SPIRITUAL WORLDS.

See also SELF-RENUNCIATION; SELF-SURRENDER.

Devona A city in ATLANTIS. CASTROG stood by the gates of this city and warned of an impending catastrophe which would result from the practice of black MAGIC.

Dharam Raya *DAHR-ahm RAY-ah* *See* YAMA.

dharma *See* DHARMA, LAW OF.

Dharma, Law of *DAHR-muh* One of the SPIRITUAL LAWS OF LIFE. The Law of Life; the righteousness of life; doing what is right; the code of conduct that sustains SOUL.

See also CONSCIENCE.

Dhun *DOON* HEAVENLY MUSIC; the melody of ECK; the BANI; Divine Spirit; the essence that gives life to all.

Dhunatmik *doo-NAHT-mik* The Sound which cannot be spoken; the ECK, the true WORD, or Voice, of the SUGMAD.

That part of the spiritual teachings that cannot be written or spoken. Nevertheless, it resounds within the CHELA. It is the cause of CONSCIOUSNESS in man.

Those who seek God always look for the one who is able to converse with the Dhunatmik—the MAHANTA, the LIVING ECK MASTER.

> The scriptures of the SHARIYAT-KI-SUGMAD can be spoken and written on the lower PLANES. But in the higher worlds it is only the heavenly white music.

See also VARNATMIK.

Dhyana *DYAHN-nah* The CHELA's perfect vision of the Master on the inner, when the very sight of him inspires tremendous affection; the technique which brings about the meeting with the Master on the inner and the ability to travel with him to the higher worlds. Also called the tassawar.

See also DARSHAN; PRESENCE OF THE MASTER.

dinta *DEEN-tah* Another word for the spiritual virtue of HUMILITY.

See FIVE VIRTUES.

Dionysus *die-uh-NIS-uhs* A Greek master who was taught by the Adepts of ECKANKAR. Also an ancient oracle and MYSTERY SCHOOL.

direct projection The instant, or direct, technique for SOUL TRAVEL; the ability to move out of the PHYSICAL BODY at will into any of the higher STATES OF CONSCIOUSNESS. Also called Saguna Sati.

disciplines of ECK *See* FOUR DISCIPLINES OF ECK; FIVE VIRTUES; SELF-DISCIPLINE.

discrimination Discrimination, also known as viveka, is one of the FOUR DISCIPLINES OF ECK. It is also one of the FIVE VIRTUES, the remedy for LUST.

There are four degrees of discrimination:

1. **Viveka**—The first step in ECKANKAR—being able to distinguish between what will be good for SPIRITUAL UNFOLDMENT and what would be wasting time.
2. The **Buddhi** state, not attained until SOUL has SELF-REALIZATION.
3. **Baibek**—attained when Soul has unfolded beyond Self-Realization, is freed of all coverings, and is able to operate by direct perception.
4. **Pratyahara**—attained only when Soul passes into the SPIRITUAL WORLDS, beyond all MIND and matter. It is the condition in which Soul is able to divert the attention away from all senses and objects of the senses, toward divine knowledge. The practice of complete withdrawal of CONSCIOUSNESS from the environment.

divine imagination *See* CREATIVE IMAGINATION.

divine love The unconditional, merciful love with which the SUGMAD looks upon all CREATION. God is love, and SOUL exists because God loves It.

In the infinite heart of all things, love and reality will be found to be one and the same.

> The purpose of life is to learn to give and receive divine love, to become a COWORKER WITH GOD. To love as God loves.

Inner experiences are important, but love and service to God stand above any inner experience. Service demonstrates love.

See also GRACE, LAW OF.

Divine Love, Law of *See* LOVE, LAW OF.

Divine Spirit *See* ECK.

doctrine of numbers Numbers are symbols of divine principles, sacred keys to the understanding of spiritual and physical realities. Explained in *The ECK-Vidya, Ancient Science of Prophecy*, by PAUL TWITCHELL.

Doreti *doh-RAY-tee* The third TWELVE-YEAR CYCLE of the ECK-VIDYA; the Years of the Brilliant Sun. Also the third year within a twelve-year cycle.

See also ECK-VIDYA WHEEL.

dream censor A part of the subconscious MIND that functions to keep SOUL in the LOWER WORLDS.

Its purpose is to maintain balance in your present STATE OF CONSCIOUSNESS by blocking out or scrambling dreams that it feels are not good for you to remember.

There is also a higher part of the Etheric (subconscious) mind—the translator function. This is the level at which the DREAM MASTER works. The Dream Master gives you an experience in another

world because there is a lesson for you to learn. Speech and objects in the other world are converted to something that makes sense to the HUMAN CONSCIOUSNESS.

There is a constant battle going on between the spiritual and the negative powers. So if there is a high spiritual truth coming through to you, the censor generally tries to scramble it and let it come through as a nightmare. The Dream Master must then try to undo the damage of this nightmare so you can receive and benefit from the spiritual message.

In summary, the lower part of the Etheric mind is the censor, and the higher part is a translator, or unscrambler. It unscrambles the incomprehensible and makes it something that your physical consciousness can accept.

dream discourses The second and third years of the ECK SPIRITUAL LIVING COURSES studied by CHELAS in ECKANKAR. Their focus is on SPIRITUAL UNFOLDMENT via dream experiences.

Dream Initiation *See* FIRST INITIATION.

Dream Master The MAHANTA, the LIVING ECK MASTER teaching in the CHELA'S DREAM STATE.

The Dream Master's help comes in three ways: (1) he uses the dream state to resolve KARMA that you need not undergo on the PHYSICAL PLANE, (2) he lets you study the SHARIYAT-KI-SUGMAD at GOLDEN WISDOM TEMPLES, and (3) he uses dreams to give you warnings or advice in regard to health, finances, or spiritual affairs.

He is a mentor, a trusted adviser, who can be a

great help to you in understanding the meaning of your dreams.

See also DREAMS, EIGHT TYPES OF; DREAM TEACHINGS.

dreams, eight types of There are eight types of dreams that can help advance one's spiritual understanding: (1) daydreams, (2) INITIATION dreams, (3) dreams of intrusion, (4) dreams of release from FEAR, (5) the WAKING DREAM, (6) the GOLDEN-TONGUED WISDOM, (7) dreams of understanding, and (8) dreams with the MAHANTA.

These eight types of dreams are further explained in *The Art of Spiritual Dreaming*, by HAROLD KLEMP.

dream state This is the realm of dream travel, a natural way for one to have experiences as SOUL when the PHYSICAL BODY is asleep. It is a spiritual state where you can meet the MAHANTA, the DREAM MASTER. The ECK MASTERS use this state to give the DREAM TEACHINGS and help CHELAS work off KARMA.

dream teachings These are deeper teachings of ECKANKAR that CHELAS can access in the DREAM STATE. Given by the DREAM MASTER or other ECK MASTERS, often at GOLDEN WISDOM TEMPLES, these teachings are customized to each SOUL's spiritual needs. The divine purpose of dreams is to give you experience in the LIGHT AND SOUND of God.

Dreaming is part of the CREATIVE IMAGINATION, a gift from God. It is the nature of immortal Soul to dream.

The dream teachings touch every level of our life. This is why your dreams, both in everyday life

and while asleep, are essential to Soul's SPIRITUAL UNFOLDMENT.

The study of dreams through the Dream Master is really a search to find your own hallowed ground.

dual consciousness This is being fully aware of the reality of some place in the INNER WORLDS (as during SOUL TRAVEL) and also being aware of your PHYSICAL BODY and environment at the same time.

dual(istic) worlds *See* LOWER WORLDS.

duodenary cycle The greater cycle of twelve years, a rotation into higher VIBRATIONS which affects men, nations, and planets.

See also ECK-VIDYA WHEEL; TWELVE-YEAR CYCLE(S).

Dwapara Yuga *dwah-PAH-rah YOO-gah* The Copper (or Bronze) Age.

See also FOUR CYCLES OF LIFE; MAHAYUGA; YUGA(S).

dying daily Saint Paul, speaking of resurrection in I Corinthians, says, "I die daily." Though little understood in modern Christianity, in ECKANKAR this refers to the natural movement of SOUL into the INNER WORLDS via the SPIRITUAL EXERCISES OF ECK.

See also SOUL TRAVEL.

Dzyani *DZYAH-nee* The ninth MONTH OF THE ECK-VIDYA, corresponding to September. The days of friendship. The month of the agate.

The journey of high success, power, achievement, and splendor.

See also ECK-VIDYA WHEEL.

Eagle-Eyed Adepts Another name for the ECK MASTERS.

Ebkia *EHB-kee-yah* The fourth MONTH OF THE ECK-VIDYA, corresponding to April. The days of hope. The month of the opal.

In this journey of SOUL the primary search is for peace.

See also ECK-VIDYA WHEEL.

ECK *EHK* The ECK is the Voice of God, the Audible Life Stream or SOUND CURRENT. It is the heartbeat and the pulse of God's creation.

It is all that is life. It encompasses all the teachings of religions and philosophies. It is the LIFE FORCE, or Holy Spirit, the GOD CURRENT we know as the source of our being. It is the fountain of love.

ECK is the thread—so fine as to be invisible, yet so strong as to be unbreakable—which binds together all beings in all the worlds of God, in all universes, throughout all time, and beyond time into eternity.

ECK is the eternal TRUTH and eternal paradox within all. It is the creator of all things, the essence of the SUGMAD, the LIVING WORD. The MAHANTA is the ECK, and the ECK is love.

The inner spiritual force, the ECK, is the God Force. It tries to direct us into better avenues of living, if we will allow It to. It will also show Itself through the humblest of Its creatures—if only we will be the humblest of Its creatures.

The ECK is the wave which SOUL must ride back home to God. The way to catch this wave is through the SPIRITUAL EXERCISES OF ECK.

We need the ECK, and the ECK needs us. The ECK is all-powerful, but It needs us in order to more fully express Its CONSCIOUSNESS, the higher realizations, GOD-REALIZATION, and ultimately even beyond that.

Why? So that this great expression of life can have ever-greater realization. As It does, we do; and as we do, It does. For this reason, when even one Soul unfolds, there is an upliftment in consciousness realized throughout the worlds of SUGMAD. This is why the INITIATIONS in ECK are so important.

The word *ECK* is also used as a short form of ECKANKAR.

See also LIGHT; LIGHT AND SOUND; MUSIC OF THE SPHERES; RECIPROCITY, LAW OF; SOUND CURRENT.

ECK Adepts *See* ECK MASTERS.

ECKANKAR *EHK-ahn-kahr* The word *ECKANKAR* means COWORKER WITH GOD—what all who follow this spiritual path aim to become.

ECKANKAR's purpose has always been to take SOUL by Its own path back home to God via SELF-REALIZATION and GOD-REALIZATION.

Known as the Path of Spiritual Freedom, ECKANKAR is the outer vehicle for the teachings of the MAHANTA, the LIVING ECK MASTER. It gives knowledge of both the LIGHT AND SOUND of God.

ECKANKAR redefines the experience of religion. It is a university for Soul's SPIRITUAL UNFOLDMENT.

The Living ECK Master provides a formal study program with the advanced SPIRITUAL LIVING COURSES that qualify a CHELA for ECK INITIATIONS. These lead to TOTAL AWARENESS and SPIRITUAL FREEDOM for Soul.

Six Spiritual Milestones in ECKANKAR

1. **recognition and acceptance** of the path
2. the **SECOND INITIATION**, which ends the need for any more physical INCARNATIONS
3. the **FIFTH INITIATION**, which sets Soul free from incarnations in all LOWER WORLDS
4. the **EIGHTH INITIATION**, the last outer initiation at the present time
5. the **NINTH INITIATION**, where one is accepted as an aspirant in the VAIRAGI ORDER
6. **GOD CONSCIOUSNESS**, one's admission into a realization of SUGMAD

ECKANKAR Organization

ECKANKAR's organization is hierarchical and headed by the MAHANTA, the Living ECK Master, who oversees the ECKANKAR SPIRITUAL CENTER (ESC).

The ESC, in turn, oversees the REGIONAL ECK SPIRITUAL AIDES (RESAs) around the world, who have been appointed by the Living ECK Master. The RESAs oversee the ECK SATSANG SOCIETIES within their regions. Regional service teams are staffed by volunteers.

Many ECK Satsang Societies maintain ECK CENTERS, and some have ECK TEMPLES.

ECKANKAR Organizational Chart

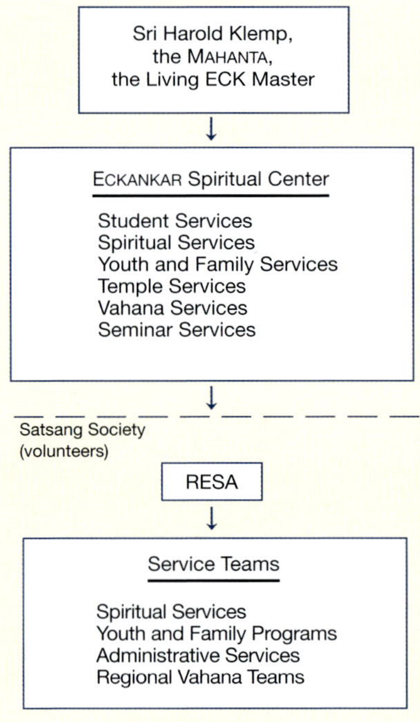

See also ECKANKAR SPIRITUAL CENTER; ECKANKAR SPIRITUAL PROGRAM; FIVE SPIRITUAL LEADERS OF MODERN-DAY ECKANKAR.

ECKANKAR Center *See* ECK CENTER(S).

ECKANKAR Founder's Day September 17, an ECKANKAR holiday honoring PAUL TWITCHELL and his mission to establish the modern-day teachings of ECKANKAR. It is a day of gratitude and thanksgiving observed on the anniversary of Twitchell's TRANSLATION.

ECKANKAR Spiritual Campus Located on 174 acres in Chanhassen, Minnesota, it is home to ECKANKAR. Sited on the campus are the TEMPLE OF ECK, the ECKANKAR SPIRITUAL CENTER, and the outdoor ECK CELEBRATIONS OF LIFE CHAPEL, surrounded by sacred CONTEMPLATION trails.

ECKANKAR Spiritual Center (ESC) Located on the ECKANKAR SPIRITUAL CAMPUS, the ESC serves as the worldwide administrative headquarters for ECKANKAR, a nonprofit organization.

At the direction of the LIVING ECK MASTER, the ESC brings ECK materials and programs to the world and, through the REGIONAL ECK SPIRITUAL AIDES, ensures the spiritual alignment of each region's ECK SATSANG SOCIETY.

ECKANKAR Spiritual Program The formal education and training program, provided by the LIVING ECK MASTER, that qualifies a spiritual student for ECK INITIATIONS and service in ECK.

For a visual overview of ECKANKAR's spiritual program, see page 337.

See also SPIRITUAL LIVING COURSES.

ECK celebrations of life These four ECK ceremonies—the ECK CONSECRATION CEREMONY, the ECK RITE OF PASSAGE, the ECK WEDDING CEREMONY, and the ECK MEMORIAL SERVICE—celebrate SOUL's journey through life. They are at the heart of the activities of mankind.

Each stage is a rite of passage, a way of coming into being, and these commemorative ceremonies celebrate how the LIGHT AND SOUND of God carry Soul to higher ground with each passage.

ECK Celebrations of Life Chapel Located on the ECKANKAR SPIRITUAL CAMPUS, this outdoor chapel can be used for any of the four ECK CELEBRATIONS OF LIFE, HU CHANTs, and other ECK activities.

ECK Center(s) A regional site for sharing the ECK teachings, open to the public as a place to find out more about ECKANKAR.

ECK Centers may offer events such as introductory talks and classes, ECK LIGHT AND SOUND SERVICES and SOUND OF SOUL EVENTS; also CHELA events, including ECK SATSANG CLASSES.

An ECK Center is a physical focal point for the LIGHT AND SOUND of God within an ECK SATSANG SOCIETY.

See also TEMPLE OF ECK.

ECK chela(s) *See* CHELA(S).

ECK cleric A HIGH INITIATE who has completed the required training and has been ordained into the ECK clergy.

An ECK cleric prepares the ground for others to meet the Master and experience the LIGHT AND SOUND of God. Sacerdotal functions of the cleric can include leading ECK LIGHT AND SOUND SERVICES, officiating the four ECK CELEBRATIONS OF LIFE, and serving in other spiritual capacities.

ECK Consecration Ceremony One of the four ECK CELEBRATIONS OF LIFE.

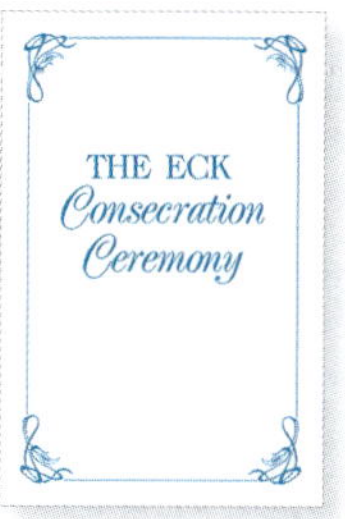

This ceremony celebrates new life and a new phase in SOUL's journey home to God. It also celebrates the commitment of the parent(s) or guardian(s) to bring a spiritual awareness into the home and the life of the child.

It is for infants and very young children. Older children can also have the service, but someone nearing age thirteen should instead prepare for the ECK RITE OF PASSAGE.

ECK discourses *See* SPIRITUAL LIVING COURSES.

ECK Initiate An ECK Initiate is a CHELA who has reached at least the FIRST INITIATION in ECKANKAR.

> The ECK works through him and becomes a part of everything he touches, entering into the environment and those within his sphere of influence. It makes changes for the better, because this is the hand of God at work, using the initiate as Its instrument.

Each ECK Initiate is a potential light to the world. *See also* COWORKER(S) WITH THE MAHANTA.

ECK initiation *See* INITIATION(S).

ECK Initiator An ECK CLERIC who has been appointed by the LIVING ECK MASTER to perform the ECK INITIATION ceremony.

An initiation is a most holy moment. Not only does the person getting the initiation walk into the presence of the Divine Spirit, but so does the Initiator. Both are standing in the circle of Divine Spirit, more so than they do ordinarily.

ECKist *EHK-ist* A CHELA, a spiritual student of ECKANKAR; a disciple of the LIVING ECK MASTER.

ECK leader(s) An ECK leader is a CHELA who lives the life of ECK and leads the way to the MAHANTA. This can be as a VAHANA or through any form of ECK service in daily life.

ECK Light and Sound Service A celebration of God's love for SOUL. The ECK community comes together to pass this love on to seekers and to each other.

The occasion serves as sacred ground for the experience of God's LIGHT AND SOUND. May include talks, creative arts, discussion, and a HU CHANT, as well as fellowship and refreshments.

ECK Marg *EHK MAHRG* One of the SEVEN MARGS. The secret path of the holy SOUND CURRENT; the path to the SUGMAD; the path of ECKANKAR.

ECK Master(s) The Adepts of the VAIRAGI, God-Realized SOULs and COWORKERS WITH GOD; also known as the Bourchakoun or Eagle-Eyed Adepts.

They are from all corners of the globe and eras in history. They can be male or female.

They serve under the direction of the MAHANTA, the LIVING ECK MASTER and work directly with students of the spiritual leader of ECKANKAR.

> ECK Masters are true agents of God and have the power to arouse an intense love for God in others. They are a self-fulfilling law of love, here to help every Soul gain SPIRITUAL FREEDOM in this lifetime.

See also COUNCIL OF THE NINE, THE; GUARDIAN(S); GOD-REALIZATION; MAHAVAKYIS; **Names of ECK Masters** (*list on page* 341); NINE SILENT ONES; VAIRAGI(S), ANCIENT ORDER OF THE; VOLAPUKS.

ECK Memorial Service One of the four ECK CELEBRATIONS OF LIFE. The ECK Memorial Service celebrates a loved one's life and passage to a new life in the spiritual worlds after TRANSLATION. The ceremony is conducted without remains present.

ECK Missionary, Age of the *See* AGE OF THE ECK MISSIONARY.

ECK Missionary, Year of the The fourth of the SPIRITUAL YEARS OF ECK.

For a description, see **The Spiritual Years of ECK** on page 354.

See also VAHANA.

ECK-nida region *EHK-NEE-dah* That area of the Atma Lok, or SOUL PLANE, where the records of the ECK INITIATES of the Seventh through Twelfth PLANES are kept.

The Soul records of the MAHDIS, those who have had the FIFTH INITIATION, are kept in the MEARP REGION. The ANUGA REGION is where the Soul records of those who have received the SIXTH INITIATION are kept.

ECK Rite of Passage One of the four ECK CELEBRATIONS OF LIFE. This ceremony is for youth on the threshold of becoming adults, at about age thirteen. It celebrates a personal commitment to the ECK teachings, to accepting the PRESENCE OF THE MASTER, and to becoming more aware of one's true spiritual nature.

ECK Satsang class(es) A small group of ECK CHELAS (up to twelve or so) who come together to review the ECK SPIRITUAL LIVING COURSES, share their experiences, and ask questions.

When one attends an ECK Satsang, he becomes refined in the presence of others and moves in grace toward becoming a COWORKER WITH GOD.

He becomes closer to the MAHANTA in spirit, and they can communicate secretly. The relationship be-

tween the two is of a love greater than words can express; it is the highest of any love.

See also SATSANG.

ECK Satsang Society A regional affiliate of ECKANKAR which functions under the guidance of a REGIONAL ECK SPIRITUAL AIDE. *See* the **ECKANKAR Organizational Chart** on page 64.

ECKshar *EHK-shahr* This is the ever-expanding state of SELF-REALIZATION.

See also REALIZATION, LEVEL(S) OF.

ECK Soul Adventure An ECKANKAR event which can help anyone explore ways to unlock the divine knowledge and creativity already within the heart.

A SOUL adventure is a spiritual experience that touches the very core of one's being—Soul, a unique, creative spark of God. Life is a Soul adventure!

ECK Spiritual Aide (ESA) The ESA is an ECK CLERIC appointed by the LIVING ECK MASTER to listen to an individual who wishes personal spiritual assistance. ESAs are listeners, quiet vehicles for the ECK, the Holy Spirit. In this way they provide spiritual aid, not counseling or therapy.

See also REGIONAL ECK SPIRITUAL AIDE (RESA).

ECK Spiritual New Year The ECK Spiritual New Year is celebrated on October 22, the date commemorating the PASSING OF THE ROD of ECK POWER.

The celebration signifies the high point, or spiritual harvest, in the year's cycle. It is the beginning of

a new, higher cycle for the next year. It marks the rebirth of the Golden Age for the coming year; a revitalization of the mission of the individual in the ECKANKAR organization to become an ever greater channel or instrument for the divine ECK.

Each new year in ECK carries a spiritual theme; *see* SPIRITUAL YEARS OF ECK, THE.

ECK spiritual year *See* SPIRITUAL YEARS OF ECK, THE.

ECK teacher *See* TEACHING ARAHATA.

ECK Teacher, Year of the The tenth of the SPIRITUAL YEARS OF ECK.

For a description, see **The Spiritual Years of ECK** on page 354.

ECK Temple(s) Any of the GOLDEN WISDOM TEMPLES, which include the TEMPLE OF ECK, or a regional ECKANKAR Temple maintained by an ECK SATSANG SOCIETY. Every Temple is a spiritual distribution center for the LIGHT AND SOUND of God to reach lovers of God.

ECK-Vidya *ehk-VEE-dyah* The ancient science of PROPHECY; the modus operandi of delving into the past, present, and future used by the ECK MASTERS.

The ECK-Vidya gives insights into the life cycles of men, nations, and planets. These are the cycles through which SOUL must pass in order to perfect Itself and return to Its heavenly home.

These life systems operate as an infinite series of wheels within wheels and cycles within cycles, all bound to the same center in the fashion of concentric circles.

ECK-Vidya: Life Cycles of Men, Nations, and Planets

The ECK-Vidya's doctrine of cycles takes into consideration the four seasons of the year, REINCARNATION, epochal changes on Earth and other planets, and more. Its scope is vast, and the more profound parts of this esoteric doctrine are still kept secret by the ECK MASTERS.

These secrets are revealed only during the higher INITIATIONS. The DREAM MASTER teaches CHELAS the ECK-Vidya in the DREAM STATE, and it can be a great help in understanding the meaning of one's dreams.

The prophecies of the ECK-Vidya are kept on the HUKIKAT LOK in the Temple of the Aluk (JARTZ CHONG) under KADMON, an ECK Adept high in the VAIRAGI ORDER. Anyone fortunate to rise to this spiritual elevation gets the entire overview during upheavals in a given region.

A reading of the ECK-Vidya is not absolute in its message about the future, because it lies within each of us to create a better future for ourselves through right spiritual action.

Each book of the SHARIYAT-KI-SUGMAD has a section devoted to a prophecy of men and nations.

The **GOLDEN-TONGUED WISDOM** and **WAKING DREAMS** are forms of the ECK-Vidya. The ECK-Vidya is presented in the book *The ECK-Vidya, Ancient Science of Prophecy*, by PAUL TWITCHELL.

THE FOUR-STEP SPIRITUAL EXERCISE OF ECK uses "ECK-Vidya" as a word to chant; *see* page 347.

THE ECK-VIDYA WHEEL

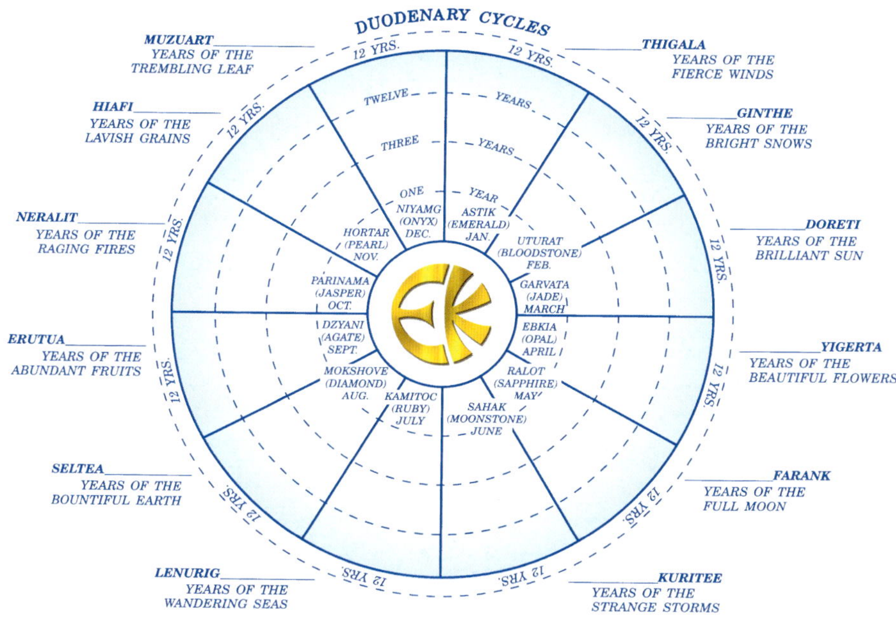

See also ECK-VIDYA WHEEL; FOUR CYCLES OF LIFE; MAHAYUGA; TWELVE-YEAR CYCLE(S); WHEEL OF THE EIGHTY-FOUR; YUGA(S).

ECK-Vidya wheel The TWELVE-YEAR CYCLES SOUL must experience in Its coming and going in the LOWER WORLDS to perfect Itself. It shows the yearly cycle of the ECK-VIDYA as well as the greater DUODENARY CYCLE of the WHEEL OF THE EIGHTY-FOUR.

ECK Wedding Ceremony One of the four ECK

CELEBRATIONS OF LIFE, this ceremony establishes the legal bond between two people (includes same-sex couples wherever permitted by law) as they celebrate their spiritual commitment to God and one another. It can also be a renewal of vows by a legally married couple.

A marriage of the heart lets each of the couple remain an individual, but the two are as one.

ECK Wisdom Temple(s) *See* GOLDEN WISDOM TEMPLE(S).

ECK-Ynari *EHK-yi-NAH-ree* A facet of ECKANKAR used by the ECK MASTERS as a way of understanding the unconscious. The ECK-Ynari is the secret knowledge of dreaming, the most ancient means used to judge the DREAM STATE.

THE FOUR-STEP SPIRITUAL EXERCISE OF ECK uses "ECK-Ynari" as a word to chant; *see* page 347.

See also DREAM DISCOURSES; DREAM MASTER; DREAMS, EIGHT TYPES OF; DREAM TEACHINGS.

Economy, Law of One of the SPIRITUAL LAWS OF LIFE. Using our resources to the fullest; making sure that whatever thought we have or action we take, it results in the most productive deed we can do as SOUL learning to become a COWORKER WITH GOD.

ego The HUMAN CONSCIOUSNESS; the personality; the mental self or LITTLE SELF; the I. Often struggles against the higher aspirations of SOUL.

Eighth Initiation This is the INITIATION of the HUKIKAT LOK, the Eighth PLANE, and is both an inner and outer ceremony.

The Eighth Initiate has directed his footsteps toward MASTERSHIP, and he can never turn back because life forces him on to the complete perfection of God.

He is the Gyanee, the pure disciple who serves the MAHANTA, the LIVING ECK MASTER with all his love and passion.

For a list of the ECK initiations, see page 338.

Eighth Plane *See* HUKIKAT LOK.

EK *EHK* A sacred symbol for ECK, the LIGHT AND SOUND of God. The EK symbol has appeared in many places in centuries past, from Greece to the Himalayas.

It is used in an essential spiritual exercise in this way: Along with the chanting of the word *ECK* or *E . . . C . . . K . . .*, the EK symbol can be held in the mind's eye.

This purges from the mind the dross of ignorance, and the human is transmuted into the divine by the spiritual alchemy of ECKANKAR.

Elam *EE-lahm* A minor god at the foot of the SPIRITUAL HIERARCHY. The ruler of the physical uni-

verse. His job is to carry out the directives that come from above, to serve people.

See also **The God Worlds Chart** on page 340.

elementals Near the bottom of the SPIRITUAL HIERARCHY are the four elementals: gnomes, salamanders, undines, and sylphs.

Gnomes, the earth creatures, are in charge of the earth elements—gold, silver, minerals, etc.

Next are the salamanders, the fire elementals, which live in the fire and look like small lizards or dragons and take care of the fire—sometimes destructively, sometimes for the good of man.

The undines, which are the water spirits, the mermaids of legends, live in the world of water and take care of that element.

Last are the sylphs, the air spirits, known in fables as fairies, which control the air elements. They look like graceful young women and are gentle until they are disturbed or become angry; storms are said to be the result of their rages.

Eleusinian mysteries *ehl-yoo-SIN-yehn* An ancient ECK MYSTERY SCHOOL which taught how to reach the divine Godhead. The Eleusinians gave their initiates hope about surviving the afterlife.

Eleventh Initiation This is the INITIATION of the Eleventh PLANE, the initiate's entrance into the SUGMAD world. It is only given through the inner channels.

This is the rebirth known as GOD-REALIZATION. The initiate enters into these high worlds in true humbleness.

It is only the MAHANTA, the LIVING ECK MASTER who can serve as the guide to lead the initiate into this world. The Eleventh Initiate is the Kevalshar.

For a list of the ECK initiations, see page 338.

Emotional body *See* ASTRAL BODY.

Endless Plane *See* ALAYA LOK.

Endless world *See* ALAYA LOK.

enlightenment The awakening of SOUL via INITIATION; also called illumination. It means becoming aware of God as an ever-present reality. Enlightenment is the result of SPIRITUAL UNFOLDMENT.

Key stages include SELF-REALIZATION, SPIRITUAL REALIZATION, and GOD-REALIZATION.

See also REALIZATION, LEVEL(S) OF.

Epictetus *eh-pik-TEE-tuhs* An ECK MASTER and a Greek stoic philosopher who taught ECK in Rome during the first century AD.

For a list of ECK MASTERS, see page 341.

Era of Stabilization (1981–93) *See* **Twelve-Year Cycles of the Master's Spiritual Mission** on page 352.

Erutua *ehr-oo-TOO-ah* The ninth TWELVE-YEAR CYCLE of the ECK-VIDYA; the Years of the Abundant Fruits. Also the ninth year within a twelve-year cycle.

See also ECK-VIDYA WHEEL.

ESA *See* ECK SPIRITUAL AIDE.

Eshwar-Khanewale *EHSH-wahr-KAH-neh-wahl* *See* GOD-EATERS.

esoteric The secret knowledge not obtainable by the uninitiated; the opposite of EXOTERIC.

Essenes *ehs-EENZ* A mystical group of teachers, in ancient times, who were influenced by ZADOK, an ECK MASTER.

Etheric body One of the BODIES OF SOUL (the others are the PHYSICAL BODY, ASTRAL BODY, CAUSAL BODY, and MENTAL BODY). The Etheric body is the highest aspect of the Mental body and is the protective sheath SOUL uses for experience and expression on the ETHERIC PLANE.

The Etheric body, or subconscious, acts as a communication link between MIND and Soul. It is very sensitive to impressions from Soul. (The Etheric body is also called the Buddhi Sharir.)

See also **The God Worlds Chart** on page 340; SOUL BODY.

Etheric Plane The top of the MENTAL PLANE, which is the Fourth PLANE (counting upward) of the LOWER WORLDS.

The Etheric Plane is the plane of the subconscious; the source of primitive thought; the very thin sheath between the MENTAL BODY and the Atma Sarup, the SOUL BODY.

Distinctions of the Etheric Plane

BAJU is a word, or CHANT, that one can sing in CONTEMPLATION to attune oneself to the VIBRATIONS of the Etheric Plane or SOUL TRAVEL to the GOLDEN WISDOM TEMPLE or other places there.

An inner experience on this plane may include seeing violet light or hearing a sound like the buzzing of bees.

Within the capital city of ARHIRIT is the DAYAKA TEMPLE, a GOLDEN WISDOM TEMPLE where LAI TSI, an ECK MASTER, serves as GUARDIAN of the SHARIYAT-KI-SUGMAD. Another ECK Master, JAGAT HO, also works there under Lai Tsi. Also on this plane is the city of URI.

The Etheric Plane is also known as the Saguna Lok; its ruler is LORD SOHANG.

See also **The God Worlds Chart** on page 340.

Ethics, Law of One of the SPIRITUAL LAWS OF LIFE. Doing that which is not selfish, which is good for the whole, which will not harm one and will do justice for all concerned. Actions for the benefit of all.

See also DHARMA, LAW OF.

Evolution, Law of *See* SPIRITUAL EVOLUTION, LAW OF.

exoteric That knowledge which is revealed to the physical eyes and ears; suitable for the uninitiated or outsiders; the opposite of ESOTERIC.

Eye of God This is sometimes seen in CONTEMPLATION. The individual who sees the single eye must at some time devote his entire life to the spiritual mission of being a COWORKER WITH GOD.

Facsimiles, Law of The Law of Facsimiles states that all effects in life are brought about by the thoughts and pictures in the MIND of the individual.

This is one of the SPIRITUAL LAWS OF LIFE; the sixth law of the physical universe (see **Seven Laws of the Physical Universe** on page 344).

See also "AS IF" PRINCIPLE.

faculties of the mind *See* MIND.

faith Faith is a starting point in ECK, but from here we go on—to knowledge, experience, and an awareness of the workings of the Holy Spirit, the ECK.

Faqiti Monastery *fah-KEE-tee* The GOLDEN WISDOM TEMPLE on the ASURATI LOK, or Desert World, in the Gobi Desert.

One of four SUPRAPHYSICAL Golden Wisdom Temples in the physical universe.

The temple is grey, rectangular, topped with a

broad dome. Wide steps lead to the main portal, which is flanked by high, square columns. BANJANI, an ECK MASTER, is the GUARDIAN of this temple and teaches the introduction to the SHARIYAT-KI-SUGMAD. Students come here in the DREAM STATE to learn their spiritual destiny.

Farank *FAH-rahnk* The fifth TWELVE-YEAR CYCLE of the ECK-VIDYA; called the Years of the Full Moon. Also the fifth year within a twelve-year cycle.

See also ECK-VIDYA WHEEL.

Far Country, the The vast INNER WORLDS lying beyond the PHYSICAL PLANE; a series of spiritual universes which are explored by SOUL on Its journey to the heart of God.

See also **The God Worlds Chart** on page 340.

fast(ing) *See* FRIDAY FAST.

fate karma One of the four types of KARMA. The sum of good and bad karma from a SOUL's account record which sets the conditions for Its next incarnation. Each lifetime of choices creates one's fate, or destiny, for subsequent lives.

See also KARMA, LAW OF; REINCARNATION.

fear A negative state of MIND; an emotion—along with ANGER, worry, sentimental emotionalism, and envy—which inhibits and poisons the consciousness of man, limiting SPIRITUAL UNFOLDMENT.

Love dispels fear. Where love exists, the lower things like fear, anger, shame, and doubt cannot exist.

feminine principle *See* PRINCIPLES, FEMININE AND MASCULINE.

Fierce Winds, Years of the *See* THIGALA.

Fifteen-Times spiritual exercise One of the key SPIRITUAL EXERCISES OF ECK. This technique is an open invitation to the ECK to bring the objects of your spiritual desire into your life.

> To learn how to do this exercise, see **Three Key Spiritual Exercises of ECK** on page 347.

Fifth Initiation At the Fifth INITIATION the CHELA receives a new SECRET WORD and is established above the PSYCHIC WORLDS in the first of the pure, positive GOD WORLDS, the SOUL PLANE. This is the state of SELF-REALIZATION.

> SOUL is no longer required to reincarnate into the LOWER WORLDS. He has become the Mahdis, a HIGH(ER) INITIATE.
>
> His life is one of inner and outer service in the name of the MAHANTA.

The MIND comes under control of SOUL, and the personality is illuminated by the SOUND CURRENT. This is sometimes referred to as the transfiguration.

The initiate is now eligible to enter advanced training under the MAHANTA, the LIVING ECK MASTER toward his goal of GOD-REALIZATION.

For a list of the ECK initiations, see page 338.

Fifth Plane *See* SOUL PLANE.

fifth root race *See* ARYANS; ROOT RACES.

Firdusi *feer-DOO-see* A great Persian poet during the eleventh century; taught by FUBBI QUANTZ.

First Grand Division *See* GRAND DIVISIONS, FIRST AND SECOND.

First Initiation The First INITIATION comes to a spiritual student in the DREAM STATE during the first year of enrollment in the ECK SPIRITUAL LIVING COURSES. It is given by the MAHANTA. This INITIATION corresponds to the PHYSICAL PLANE.

> Taking up the path of ECK allows the lower emotional and intellectual centers to come into contact with the higher ones. This is what the First Initiation is concerned with. This ECK INITIATE is the Acolyte—one who is at the stage of entering into the heart of life.

For a list of the ECK initiations, see page 338.

First of the Golden Years (2017–29) *See* **Twelve-Year Cycles of the Master's Spiritual Mission** on page 352.

first root race *See* POLARIANS; ROOT RACES.

Five Marching Men symbol This symbol depicts the illumined states that SOUL unfolds through in the LOWER WORLDS, until It reaches SELF-REALIZATION. It represents the PHYSICAL, ASTRAL, CAUSAL, MENTAL, and SOUL BODIES. It has long been used by ECKANKAR in its printed materials.

See also BODIES OF SOUL.

five passions of the mind The five passions of the MIND place the EGO between SOUL and heaven. They include all the dark moods of the mind and all other destructive mental states. They take possession when the mind is allowed to run wild.

To live in HARMONY with one's self, one must be disciplined—able to allow the spiritual impulses of the ECK to influence and guide the mind.

The five passions are LUST (kama), ANGER (krodha), GREED (lobha), VANITY (ahankara), and ATTACHMENT (moha). When any of these passions gets out of control, it limits one's SPIRITUAL UNFOLDMENT and binds Soul to the LOWER WORLDS.

For antidotes to the the five passions of the mind, see FIVE VIRTUES.

See also SELF-DISCIPLINE.

Five Spiritual Laws of This World These are just five of the many spiritual laws of this world. They are important especially when looking at political and religious fields.

1. The beginning of human life is when breath comes into the fetus.
2. Love is the first and great commandment; also called the rule of spiritual law: love God, love your neighbor, and love yourself.
3. Work for your food. This deals with the welfare system and our responsibility to make our own way as much as we can in this world.
4. Give tribute to God and Caesar. This relates to our duty to the government regarding taxes.

5. Reward the laborer. This is about the government's duty to the people.

See also MAYBURY'S TWO LAWS; PHYSICAL UNIVERSE, LAWS OF THE; SPIRITUAL LAWS OF LIFE.

five spiritual leaders of modern-day ECKANKAR

Here is a sketch of the first five spiritual leaders of modern-day ECKANKAR and their missions:

1. **PEDDAR ZASKQ** (PAUL TWITCHELL). At his appointment to the spiritual duties, he was immediately the MAHANTA, the LIVING ECK MASTER. His job was to get the ECK teachings up and running. Time was of no concern.
2. **DAP REN** (*see* GROSS, DARWIN). A Living ECK Master whose duty was to maintain the teachings and keep the ECK CHELAS together.
3. **WAH Z** (HAROLD KLEMP). His job, like that of Peddar Zaskq, is to be highly innovative, breaking into new fields of spiritual endeavor. A bridge between the public and secret teachings, the basic and advanced, the old and new, this third stage marks enormous change.

   It is longest in terms of actual spiritual advances and is the keystone to the Golden Age of ECK. He also came in as the MAHANTA, the Living ECK Master.
4. **The fourth Master is still in training.** His skills will keep the ECK teachings pure and the ECK followers together.

It will take supreme wisdom to fill the fourth slot, a season of consolidation. There will then be much back and forth in the plans and goals in ECKANKAR: a period of extreme testing. Many original chelas will doubt the ECK, wondering about the validity of the Living ECK Master. However, many more will find ECKANKAR.

See below for an update to this fourth position.

5. **The fifth ECK MASTER** will serve in the sunset of this initial golden age of ECK.

He will come into his duties as the MAHANTA, the Living ECK Master, because this entire first cycle is an extraordinary time in the annals of human history. He will display an exceptional gift of imagination.

His task is to prepare chelas for the dark days to follow his term of office, when the KAL will regain more control over the spiritual affairs of mankind.

Known or unknown, the ECK Masters are here to uplift the human race.

Update: The fourth of the five spiritual leaders needs a further word. Rather than being a person, it is more accurate to call it a stage, or position.

This position may be filled by five or more successive ECK Masters (twelfth circle of ECK INITIATIONS) before the next MAHANTA, the Living ECK Master (fourteenth circle) comes to fill the fifth position.

The reason? The coming of the next MAHANTA of the fourteenth circle depends on spiritual need. All SOULS, in all universes, determine that need, for as the GROUP ENTITY their spiritual progress is the final key.

Will this group entity stay on the fast track to God or stop along the path to rest?

It has chosen to rest.

Free will allows the group entity, and all the individuals within it, to go at their own speed. Earth is a reflection of the universal group entity. Current events since then have seen a gradual slowdown of people's spiritual drive as evidenced in a renewed interest in social welfare and warfare. Until these Souls are ready to shoulder their own responsibilities again, they'll rest.

So five to seven Living ECK Masters of the twelfth circle will serve successively in the fourth spiritual leadership stage, or position, until the time is right. After that comes the next MAHANTA, the Living ECK Master of the fourteenth circle.

See also PASSING OF THE ROD OF ECK POWER.

For a list of the ECK initiations, see page 338.

five virtues Practicing the five virtues of ECK is a way to develop the spiritual intelligence of SOUL. These virtues protect you from the snares of MAYA, or illusion, and lead you to higher states of Coworkership with Divine Spirit.

Each of the five virtues is an antidote for one of

the FIVE PASSIONS OF THE MIND.

Discrimination, also known as **viveka**, is one of the FOUR DISCIPLINES OF ECK. It is the remedy for LUST.

Discrimination is the first step in ECKANKAR—being able to distinguish between what will be good for SPIRITUAL UNFOLDMENT and what would be wasting time.

See also DISCRIMINATION on page 55.

Forgiveness and tolerance, also known as **kshama**, is the antidote for ANGER.

Forgiveness and tolerance are two qualities to help keep one's flash point in check. They eliminate the need to blame others when correcting a mistake. It is another way of saying "Do unto others as you would have them do unto you."

Contentment, also called **santosha**, is the opposite of and remedy for GREED.

Contentment is the peace of self which comes when one is rid of desire. This is a step on the path to the FAR COUNTRY.

Humility, also called **dinta**, is the antidote for VANITY. Paired with chastity, humility is one of the FOUR DISCIPLINES OF ECK.

The highest goodness in man is characterized by humility.

It compels one to be self-effacing, like the ECK—pure in heart, never distracted from the way of ECK. Such a person loves unselfishly, wields virtue, and understands all, while denying himself. He puts life into others without trying to own them.

Dignity and sweet humility are the twin traits in the ECK CHELA.

Detachment, also known as **vairag**, is the antidote for ATTACHMENT.

Detachment is the release of undue attachments to worldly desires and possessions.

SOUL lives forever by giving, not by receiving. It means simply that you can have COMPASSION, you can enjoy life, but if sorrow comes, it does not burden you until the end of your days. You are able to see the hand of God in it. You will pick yourself up and have gratitude for what blessings you retain.

It is a state of being like the sun, shining upon all alike, yet asking nothing in return.

Detachment is the key to the SPIRITUAL WORLDS.

See also SELF-DISCIPLINE; SELF-RENUNCIATION; SELF-SURRENDER.

flute of the SUGMAD With the ECK comes the Sound of the flute of the SUGMAD. This is what SOUL is, and none can deprive Soul of It once It has been experienced.

It is something beyond words and sounds, symbols and signs.

See also FLUTE, SINGLE NOTE OF A.

flute, single note of a A sound of ECK that can be heard on the SOUL PLANE.

forgiveness and tolerance Also called kshama, one

of the FIVE VIRTUES, the remedy for ANGER. Another way of saying, Do unto others as you would have them do unto you.

Founder's Day *See* ECKANKAR FOUNDER'S DAY.

Four Cycles of Life There are four cycles of manifestation, based on four ages of cosmic history: the golden age, silver age, copper (or bronze) age, and iron age. See descriptions below.

> This sequence of cycles repeats and subdivides infinitely, right down to each minute of your life.

If you are aware of these cycles operating in every part of your life, you can uplift yourself spiritually to at least soften the effect of change.

With the power of ECK you can re-create or instill a new golden age almost at will. Sometimes the divine law may simply allow a cycle to run its course, but the silver, copper, and iron ages can pass very quickly to bring you to a new golden age.

The Four Ages

Golden Age First of the four cycles of manifestation. A period of HARMONY, TRUTH, peace, beauty, and goodness, bringing love and a simplicity of heart.

The Satya (or Krita) Yuga is the golden age of cosmic history—first of the four YUGAS that comprise a MAHAYUGA.

Silver Age The second cycle of manifestation. A period when everything starts to go amiss and every pleasure has some anxiety attached; less righteous than the preceding golden age.

The Tretya Yuga is the silver age of cosmic history—second of the four yugas that comprise a mahayuga.

Copper (or Bronze) Age The third cycle of manifestation. A period when forces of light and darkness, good and evil, pleasure and pain are equally balanced.

The Dwapara Yuga is the copper age of cosmic history—third of the four yugas that comprise a mahayuga.

Iron Age The fourth cycle of manifestation. In this period of darkness and unhappiness, illusion reigns. Characterized by strife, discord, quarreling, and contention, it marks the lowest ebb in individual and social degeneration.

The Kali Yuga is the iron age of cosmic history—last of the four yugas that comprise a mahayuga. It is the age we are in today, and it lasts 432,000 years. The Kali Yuga, or Iron Age, is key, as it gives SOUL the opportunity to be tempered to Its final purity so that It can become a COWORKER WITH GOD. In that sense, the Kali Yuga is the age of high spirituality, the true golden age.

A Day and a Night of the SUGMAD

At the end of each mahayuga, the LOWER WORLDS are destroyed, and Souls are drawn up from there

to the SOUL PLANE to sleep throughout a period sometimes called a Night of the SUGMAD, which lasts as long as a mahayuga (4,320,000 years). They will find themselves in a state of original unity and bliss, in a life of total peace, while the formation of a new universe occurs in the bosom of the SUGMAD.

Then the grand cycle starts again: there follows a new Day of the SUGMAD—a new CREATION and a new mahayuga, beginning with its golden age—and the Souls in need of experience are returned to the new worlds of matter for a fresh start.

four disciplines of ECK The spiritual disciplines the CHELA practices that give HARMONY, purity, and perfection of SOUL. These disciplines are as listed below.

(*See also* FIVE VIRTUES.)

1. ***Cleanliness of Mind*** Let no words which would pollute the air enter into your MIND. Look upon everyone as creatures of God, for they, like yourself, are temples who shall eventually become COWORKERS WITH GOD.

   Fast continuously from all KAL (negative) thoughts which could infect your mental state and CONSCIOUSNESS.

   Through this you learn the powerful awareness of the presence of the LIVING ECK MASTER, who is with you constantly.

2. ***Patience*** This is the greatest discipline of all the spiritual works of ECK. By patience you can

endure life, hardships, karmic burdens, slander, and the pricks of pain and disease.

Keep your mind steadfastly upon the LIGHT of God, never swerving, never letting up on your attention to the goal of GOD-REALIZATION.

3. ***Humility and Chastity*** As you come to know these attributes in your life, you learn all your responsibility belongs to God, not to anyone nor anything within this physical realm.

   Your loved ones, family, and relatives are images of God, mirrored in this worldly life and embodiment to serve the SUGMAD, the Supreme Deity.

   Realize that humility is opposite to the EGO. Do not let a false concept of your worth to the Master and to the SUGMAD stand in your way to reach the heavenly states. Know that VANITY is only a trap of the negative power, the KAL NIRANJAN, and you will become a fool if you let yourself be enslaved by the Kal.

4. ***Discrimination*** Learn to discriminate between all things, recognizing that there is no good nor evil, no beauty nor ugliness, and there is no sin. These are all concepts of the mind, the dual forces in the matter worlds.

   Once you recognize and understand this, you will then be free of Kal traps. You will be ready to enter into the Kingdom of God, the OCEAN OF LOVE AND MERCY.

   You will be the ECK, of Itself.

See also PURIFY OR POLLUTE.

four ECK celebrations of life *See* ECK CELEBRATIONS OF LIFE.

Four Fundamentals of ECK The four basic principles behind the practice of ECKANKAR: (1) practicing the SPIRITUAL EXERCISES OF ECK, (2) TRUE CONTEMPLATION OF THE ECK WORKS, (3) TOTAL RELIANCE ON THE INNER MASTER, and (4) SELF-DISCIPLINE.

Four Precepts of ECK The precepts which the CHELA must have imprinted on his heart and MIND:

1. There is but one God, and Its reality is the SUGMAD.
2. The MAHANTA, the LIVING ECK MASTER is the messenger of the SUGMAD in all worlds, be they material, psychic, or spiritual.
3. The faithful, those who follow the works of ECK, shall have all the blessings and riches of the heavenly kingdom given unto them.
4. The SHARIYAT-KI-SUGMAD is the holy book of those who follow ECKANKAR, and there shall be none above it.

four states of the High Initiate Having reached the FIFTH INITIATION, it is the duty of the HIGHER INITIATE to improve, to spiritualize himself by CONTEMPLATION.

He is supposed to pass through the four following states:

First is **Salokiam**, which signifies the only tie with the lower worlds. In this state SOUL seeks to lift Itself, with the assistance of the MAHANTA, the LIVING ECK MASTER, to the true SPIRITUAL WORLDS and to take Its place in the presence of Divinity Itself; It holds communication with those Souls who have gone before into the regions of eternity and makes use of the body left on earth as an instrument to transcribe, under the permanent form of writing, the sublime teachings It receives in these worlds of true spirituality.

Second is **Samipiam**, which signifies proximity. By the exercises of contemplation and the disregard of all earthly objects, the knowledge and idea of the SUGMAD becomes familiar to It. It becomes farseeing and begins to witness marvels which are not of this world.

Third is **Souaroupiam**, which signifies resemblance. In this state Soul gradually acquires a perfect resemblance to the ECK and participates in all Its attributes. It reads the future and the universe has no secrets for It.

Fourth is **Sayodiyam**, identity. Soul finally becomes closely united to the MAHANTA, the Living ECK Master. This last transformation takes place only through the death of the PHYSICAL BODY, that is to say, the entire disruption of all material ties by TRANSLATION.

Four-Step Spiritual Exercise of ECK, The One of the key SPIRITUAL EXERCISES OF ECK. This exercise will help you remember the special purpose you had in mind before coming into this present life.

To learn how to do this exercise, see **Three Key Spiritual Exercises of ECK** on page 347.

Fourteenth Initiation The Fourteenth Initiate is the MAHANTA.

For a list of the ECK INITIATIONS, see page 338.

Fourth Initiation The Fourth INITIATION is both an inner and outer ceremony where the chela receives a new SECRET WORD to assist him in working through the MENTAL PLANE.

This is where Soul is concerned with the spiritual evolution of intelligence. The Fourth Initiate, the Chiad (sometimes called the Bhakta), recognizes the limits of acquired knowledge and begins to cast off the influence of the psychic worlds. He allows the ECK to work within him beyond the reach of MIND since neither reason nor logic offer the way to truth.

This leads to entering into a full trust of his inner senses. He becomes a more potent channel for the MAHANTA.

For a list of the ECK initiations, see page 338.

Fourth Plane *See* MENTAL PLANE.

fourth root race *See* ATLANTIS; ROOT RACES.

four Zoas *ZOH-ahz* The four Zoas (laws) of ECKANKAR for the MAHDIS, the Initiates of the Fifth Circle, are key to their spiritual advancement.

The Four Zoas

1. The Mahdis shall not use alcohol, tobacco, or drugs; gamble; or be gluttonous in any way. No Mahdis shall be existent on the animal level.

   He is a leader, and he must fix his attention above the psychology of the brute.

2. The Mahdis shall not speak with tongue of VANITY or deceit or unhappiness, criticize the actions of others, blame others for wrongdoings, quarrel, fight, or inflict injury.

   He shall at all times be respectful and courteous to his fellow man and show great COMPASSION and happiness.

3. The Mahdis shall have HUMILITY, love, and freedom from all bonds of creeds. He shall be free from the laws of KARMA which snare him with boastfulness and vanity.

   He shall have love for all people and all creatures of the SUGMAD.

4. The Mahdis must preach the message of ECK at all times, and prove to the world that he is an example of PURITY and happiness. He must show that the disciple in the human body must have a Master in the human body.

See also HIGH(ER) INITIATE (HI).

Francis of Assisi, Saint This Christian saint served as a vehicle for ECK in the late twelfth and early thirteenth century.

freedom, days of *See* KAMITOC.

freedom, spiritual *See* SPIRITUAL FREEDOM.

free will The power and right each SOUL has to decide what path to take. Soul has the free will to open a way between Itself and the WORD of God. *See* SOUL, LAW OF.

Freticrets *FREHT-i-krehts* The last ROOT RACE before the end of the Kali Yuga, or Iron Age (*see* YUGA(S)), who will be dealers in black MAGIC. A desperate and ruthless race from the world of Pluto, they will control Earth and most of the planets throughout the universe.

Friday fast ECK INITIATEs of the Second Circle and above use the spiritual practice of fasting on Fridays to help develop the discipline to reach GOD-REALIZATION.

The recommended fast for today is the mental fast—keeping the thoughts on the MAHANTA all day or putting every negative thought into the ECK stream.

friendship, days of *See* DZYANI.

Fubbi Quantz *FOO-bee KWAHNTS*

The MAHANTA, the LIVING ECK MASTER during the time of Buddha, about 500 BC.

He completed his mission, then immortalized his body, and is now the GUARDIAN of the SHARIYAT-KI-SUGMAD at the KATSUPARI MONASTERY in northern Tibet.

A teacher of FIRDUSI, the Persian poet, he was also

the spiritual guide for Christopher Columbus and encouraged his voyage to the Americas in order to revitalize the depleted nutrition of the Europeans.

Description

Fubbi Quantz appears as a tall, elderly man with a lantern jaw, white hair and beard, and a gentle smile. Good humor gleams in his eyes. He appears to spiritual students in a white robe that reaches well below the knees.

He has a knowingness about him. It seems to those who sit in his SATSANG that he knows all about them, yet it is a knowledge that he never holds over them as a control factor. He has the spiritual presence to accept people for what they are: Souls groping through life, endeavoring to find their way home to the SUGMAD. He is often seen to reflect deeply upon the observations of the students in his class, for he, too, is still learning more about the grandeur of life.

Fubbi Quantz is ever aware that the humblest chela in class might have a jewel of insight that no one else has ever been able to express before.

Many students come to him in the DREAM STATE to study when they first begin on the path of ECKANKAR. All who attend his classes on the Shariyat are fortunate indeed, for he passes on the LIGHT and Music of God to all who are there.

For a list of ECK MASTERS, see page 341.

Full Moon, Years of the *See* FARANK.

Gakko *GAHK-koh* A state of relative perfection within the SOUL PLANE, where all or most of the ECK MASTERS live who are not doing duty in the other PLANES and worlds. The world of being; a STATE OF CONSCIOUSNESS.

Gakko is also the name attributed to the first ECK Master who came out of the heart of God into this world about six million years ago. The whole line of ECK Masters has descended from him in an unbroken lineage.

For a list of ECK Masters, see page 341.

Gare-Hira *GAH-ray-HEE-rah* This GOLDEN WISDOM TEMPLE is located in the spiritual city of AGAM DES, home of the Eshwar-Khanewale, the GOD-EATERS.

The Temple of Gare-Hira is a white structure that looks somewhat like an Islamic mosque. It is a sturdy building with a white dome topped by a cupola.

Classrooms ring the main sanctuary, and the second section of the SHARIYAT-KI-SUGMAD is displayed on the altar of the inner sanctum. This section is called "The Records of the Kros." (*See also* RECORDS OF THE KROS.)

The ECK MASTER YAUBL SACABI is the GUARDIAN here, and students come nightly in their SOUL forms to study the WISDOM of God.

This is one of the four SUPRAPHYSICAL Golden Wisdom Temples in this material universe. The others are the FAQITI MONASTERY, the HOUSE OF MOKSHA, and the KATSUPARI MONASTERY.

Garvata *gahr-VAH-tah* The third MONTH OF THE ECK-VIDYA, corresponding to March. The days of joy. The month of the jade. During this journey, SOUL is restless and has a great sense of urgency.

See also ECK-VIDYA WHEEL.

Gaze of the Master The Gaze of the Master, one form of the DARSHAN, has the power to uplift and heal all things. Also called the Tiwaja.

See also PRESENCE OF THE MASTER.

Geutan *geh-OO-tahn* An ECK MASTER who served the people of LEMURIA and, as the MAHANTA, the LIVING ECK MASTER, warned them of the coming destruction of their continent.

For a list of ECK Masters, see page 341.

ghata *GAH-tah* Act of opening the CONSCIOUSNESS; sometimes called SATORI or ENLIGHTENMENT.

giana *gee-AH-nah* A word chanted in a spiritual exercise to pass through the window of the SPIRITUAL EYE.

giani *gee-AH-nee* A learned CHELA; one who practices or walks the path of WISDOM.

See also GIANI MARG.

Giani Marg *gee-AH-nee MAHRG* One of the SEVEN MARGS. The path of ESOTERIC wisdom; the path of studying at the GOLDEN WISDOM TEMPLES.

In this order of WISDOM, the ECK INITIATE gives his services by writing, painting, and other forms of creative arts for and about ECKANKAR. He gains himself while at the same time giving of himself to others through the creative forms.

THE FOUR-STEP SPIRITUAL EXERCISE OF ECK uses "Giani Marg" as a chant; *see* page 347.

gift-waves Waves of energy sent forth from the MAHANTA to stimulate spiritual development and greatly assist the ASPIRANT seeking the ECKSHAR, the ENLIGHTENMENT.

The LIVING ECK MASTER assists in the granting of these waves, otherwise known as the conferring of power, which constitutes the true spiritual INITIATION.

Ginthe *GIN-theh* The second TWELVE-YEAR CYCLE of the ECK-VIDYA; the Years of the Bright Snows. Also the second year within a twelve-year cycle.

See also ECK-VIDYA WHEEL.

Giving, The Year of The sixth of the SPIRITUAL YEARS OF ECK.

For a description, see **The Spiritual Years of ECK** on page 354.

gnomes *See* ELEMENTALS.

gnothi seauton *GNOH-thee seh-ah-oo-TAHN* An ancient Greek aphorism that means "Know thyself." This is written over the doors of ancient temples, as man's first duty is to know himself.

See also SELF-REALIZATION.

God *See* SUGMAD.

God, Law of One of the SPIRITUAL LAWS OF LIFE. Everything has its origin in SPIRIT; divine truth is one and unchanging.

God Consciousness *See* GOD-REALIZATION.

God Current The essence of the SUGMAD (God).

See ECK.

God-Discovery Another term for GOD-REALIZATION.

God-Eaters These are the ECK MASTERS who partake of cosmic energy instead of material food and live to great ages beyond the normal span of human life. They are also known as the Eshwar-Khanewale.

ECKANKAR was brought to Earth from Venus by the Eshwar-Khanewale. Many of the God-Eaters now live in the spiritual city of AGAM DES.

God Force *See* ECK.

Godman The MAHANTA; he has attained the highest STATE OF CONSCIOUSNESS known to mankind. Often refers to the LIVING ECK MASTER.

God-Realization The state of being a COWORKER WITH GOD. Also called God Consciousness. The knowledge of God; the uniting of the human and divine natures.

The realization of God begins as SOUL makes the transition between the Eighth and Ninth INITIATIONS, increases through the Ninth and Tenth, and reaches fulfillment in the Eleventh.

God-Realization is a state of wonder, bliss, and being beyond words. It's Soul's destiny to love as God loves.

Tips on Reaching God-Realization

1. Do everything in the name of the MAHANTA.
2. Do even the smallest act with love and attention to detail.
3. Above all, give others the right to find their own way to God.

See also REALIZATION, LEVEL(S) OF.

Gods of Eternity *See* NINE UNKNOWN GODS OF ETERNITY.

God Sound *See* HU.

God State *See* GOD-REALIZATION.

God Worlds Every universe and PLANE; all that exists in the SPIRITUAL WORLDS and LOWER WORLDS.

See **The God Worlds Chart** on page 340.

golden age *See* FOUR CYCLES OF LIFE; MAHAYUGA; YUGA(S).

Golden Contract, the Every encounter, without exception, is there to move SOUL along spiritually on Its way back home to God.

golden heart, the The loving heart, the open heart. The golden heart is full of the love for God and has COMPASSION for those who are lost in the darkness of the HUMAN CONSCIOUSNESS.

See also HEART CENTER.

Golden-tongued Wisdom Guidance or insight from the ECK via a nudge, an intuitive connection to spoken or written words, or even a direct message from the INNER MASTER. Can also come via a dream or WAKING DREAM. The Golden-tongued Wisdom is a form of the ECK-VIDYA, the Ancient Science of Prophecy.

Golden Wisdom Temple(s) Also called Temples of Golden Wisdom, these are situated throughout the various PLANES.

Many Temples hold a section of the SHARIYAT-KI-SUGMAD. Spiritual students regularly visit these temples, often in the DREAM STATE or via SOUL TRAVEL, to acquire divine knowledge or receive SPIRITUAL HEALING.

There are fifteen main temples, each headed by an ECK MASTER, but also many branch temples.

The fifteen main temples are as follows:

PHYSICAL PLANE: TEMPLE OF ECK, FAQITI MONASTERY, KATSUPARI MONASTERY, Temple of GARE-HIRA, HOUSE OF MOKSHA

ASTRAL PLANE: Temple of ASKLEPOSIS

Causal Plane: Temple of Sakapori

Mental Plane: Namayatan Temple

Etheric Plane: Dayaka Temple

Soul Plane: Param Akshar Temple

Alakh Lok: Tamanata Kop Temple

Alaya Lok: Anakamudi Temple

Hukikat Lok: Jartz Chong Temple

Agam Lok: Kazi Dawtz Temple

Anami Lok: Sata Visic Palace

See also **A Road Map for Spiritual Travelers** on page 343.

Golden Years

See **Twelve-Year Cycles of the Master's Spiritual Mission** on page 352.

Gopal Das *GOH-pahl DAHS*

The Mahanta, the Living ECK Master in Egypt, around 3000 BC, who founded the mystery schools of Osiris and Isis. He is now the guardian of the fourth section of the Shariyat-Ki-Sugmad on the Astral Plane. He teaches at the Golden Wisdom Temple there.

A rather tall, spare man with light yellow-golden hair, he is sometimes mistaken for Christ by people with a Christian background. He often appears in a snow-white robe, but mostly favors the maroon robe of the Vairagi Order.

See also ASKLEPOSIS.

For a list of ECK MASTERS, see page 341.

Grace, Law of We live in a time of unequaled spiritual opportunity. The daily struggles that life presents are opportunities to cultivate spiritual grace.

Graceful living is to realize everything that comes into your life is for the good. It is having the grace to accept God's will as it appears.

In a God-created universe, the secret of life is no power.

> When we come to the Kingdom of God, we find there is no power, only grace. It is by this divine grace that we survive in all universes, and no power of any kind can operate against us, in us, or through us.

This puts us in a very humble position. We must acknowledge that we, of ourselves, do nothing. We have become a channel for divine grace.

See also DIVINE LOVE.

Graceful Living, The Year of The eleventh of the SPIRITUAL YEARS OF ECK.

For a description, see **The Spiritual Years of ECK** on page 354.

Grand Divisions, First and Second In ECKANKAR literature referring to two grand divisions, the First Grand Division is the PLANES of the LOWER WORLDS. The Second Grand Division is the SPIRITUAL WORLDS of the SUGMAD.

See also **The God Worlds Chart** on page 340.

grand paradox SOUL lives forever by giving, not by receiving.

Gratitude, Law of One of the SPIRITUAL LAWS OF LIFE. Abundance flourishes in a grateful heart; gratitude is the secret of love.

greed Also called lobha, one of the FIVE PASSIONS OF THE MIND. Preoccupation with material gain. Miserliness, lying, hypocrisy, perjury, misrepresentation, robbery, bribery, and trickery of all sorts.

> The antidote for greed is CONTENTMENT, one of the FIVE VIRTUES.

Gross, Darwin PAUL TWITCHELL named Darwin Gross to succeed him and serve as an interim LIVING ECK MASTER. Gross served in this capacity for a ten-year period after Paul's TRANSLATION in 1971.

In October 1981, the ROD OF ECK POWER was passed again, and Gross announced HAROLD KLEMP as the new Living ECK Master. But Gross failed to accept that he himself was no longer the spiritual head of the teachings. He was discharged from ECKANKAR and dismissed from the VAIRAGI ORDER in late 1983.

SRI Harold writes about the spiritual lessons to be learned from this period of ECKANKAR's history in his book *Soul Travelers of the Far Country*, chapter 11.

See also FIVE SPIRITUAL LEADERS OF MODERN-DAY ECKANKAR; PASSING OF THE ROD OF ECK POWER.

group entity A number of SOULs, like a family or a community, tied together by a commonality; an entity in which the members act and react upon one another as they unfold spiritually. A group thought form. There's a group entity for ants, dogs, cats, birds, and everything else.

guardian(s) In the works of ECKANKAR, certain ECK MASTERS are referred to as guardians of GOLDEN WISDOM TEMPLES or of the SHARIYAT-KI-SUGMAD. This guardianship is one and the same.

For a list of noted guardians, see **A Road Map for Spiritual Travelers** on page 343.

The Temples of Golden Wisdom, here and there, operate as an expression of love for SUGMAD. It's a very matter-of-fact universe.

Assistants

Though in many cases it sounds like a one-man show, the ECK Master in charge is like the chief executive officer (CEO) of a modern organization. He runs an entire staff. It includes the assistance of other ECK Masters who help him with the normal duties one would expect in a spiritual and administrative center.

Some ECK Masters at a Temple of Golden Wisdom serve in more than one capacity. For example, a keeper of records may double as an ARAHATA, while a master gardener may be equally adept as one who specializes in teaching a course in spiritual ethics.

Roles for ECK Initiates

There are also other ECK INITIATES on staff who carry out things that need doing. Yes, someone even

cleans the floors. Another initiate is an expert at inventory control. And there are receptionists and secretaries, as well as those who prepare food.

Some who hear of these daily workings may think such duties are unspiritual. Be that as it may. But remember that earth is a reflection of what is above. So look around. The interests and pursuits of things around us have a model on the higher PLANES.

guru *GOO-roo* A common title for a teacher of spiritual works.

See also SAT GURU.

Gyanee *gie-YAH-nee* One who has reached the EIGHTH INITIATION.

Habu Medinet *HAH-boo mehd-ee-NEHT* The LIVING ECK MASTER around the fifth century BC. The ancient beginnings of Mithraism developed from his teachings. Many ECKists of today once studied under him and took part in what later became the initiations of Mithraism.

During the Battle of Marathon, in 490 BC, Habu Medinet publicly prophesied the Persian defeat.

He is now serving the SUGMAD on the MENTAL PLANE in the GOLDEN WISDOM TEMPLE in the city of MER KAILASH, under TOWART MANAGI.

For a list of ECK MASTERS, see page 341.

Hafiz *hah-FEEZ* Famous fourteenth-century poet of Persia who was a follower of ECK.

Hall of Brahmanda *See* BRAHMANDA, HALL OF.

Hamsa *HAHM-sah* Among the many images of God is the Hamsa, the divine bird, which lays the world in the form of an egg. The syllables *ham-sa* may also be heard as *sa-ham* or *sa-aham*, which is to say, "I am THAT," or "THAT SOUL"—what each and every being *is*.

Hari Tita *HAH-ree TEE-tah* The MAHANTA, the LIVING ECK MASTER during the Trojan period of Greek history; he now works in the ALAKH LOK, the Sixth Plane.

For a list of ECK MASTERS, see page 341.

Harji *HAHR-jee* A respectful name of affection for SRI HAROLD KLEMP.

See also WAH Z; Z.

Harji dinner HARJI dinners are a combined spiritual and social function in the ECK community; occasions for thanksgiving. A congenial setting of good food and company, where principles of ECK can be discussed with visitors in an informal way; bonds ECK INITIATES together.

See also TRADITIONS OF ECK.

Harmonics, Law of *See* VIBRATIONS, LAW OF.

harmony There is something more important than being right; the higher path is to work in harmony with every living thing on all PLANES. It requires real insight to develop this ability. The path of ECK is one of harmony and balance.

The ECK MASTERS, in their mission to serve the SUGMAD, work in harmony, nurturing the plus factor, the building element, in all they do.

See also PROGRESSIVE CONTINUATION, LAW OF.

Harold Klemp

SRI Harold Klemp is the present-day MAHANTA, the LIVING ECK MASTER, the spiritual leader of ECKANKAR.

He received the ROD OF ECK POWER in 1981 and is the latest in an ancient line of ECK MASTERS who have served throughout history in every culture of the world. His spiritual name is WAH Z, or Z, and he is also known as HARJI. For ECK CHELAS, he serves as the INNER AND OUTER MASTER as he leads SOUL by Its own path home to God.

A Pioneer

Known as a pioneer of today's focus on "everyday spirituality," Sri Harold's extensive talks and writings present the SPIRITUAL EXERCISES OF ECK as the essential route to higher states of awareness and freedom. He continues to expand, update, and clarify ECK doctrine and culture. Every book, talk, and article shines with this unchanging message: Soul exists because God loves It.

Much of his teaching is given in story form, as parables and in sharing the accounts of ordinary people having profound spiritual experiences in everyday life. Each story contains a seed of transformational truth and is a part of the LIVING SHARIYAT.

With humor and compassion he offers practical tools, creative techniques, and loving guidance as aids to Soul's journey toward SELF-REALIZATION and GOD-REALIZATION.

Mission

As Soul, each person has the God knowledge within him. The Master's main job is to awaken the knowledge and the love for the divine things that are already in one's heart.

Sri Harold's overall mission is to establish CONSCIOUSNESS NINE. He has laid the foundation for this, and the result can be seen in the social, political, and climatic changes of today. Each level is a turn higher on the spiral of CONSCIOUSNESS as the waves of Souls in ECK catch the returning tide home to the center of God's love and mercy.

As we move into this golden age of spirituality, a creative fountain has been opened, and many more people will be able to manifest that which is of the higher worlds.

Sri Harold's mission was destined to be highly innovative, breaking into new fields of spiritual endeavor. A bridge between the public and secret teachings, this era has marked enormous change. It is the longest in terms of actual spiritual advances and is the keystone to the Golden Age of ECK.

Key Advances

A key facet has been the building of the TEMPLE OF ECK in Chanhassen, Minnesota, and establishing it as ECKANKAR'S SEAT OF POWER. The GOLDEN WISDOM TEMPLE is situated on the ECKANKAR SPIRITUAL CAMPUS, which also houses the ECKANKAR SPIRITUAL CENTER.

Early on he also saw the need to align the administrative hierarchy with essential spiritual principles and so formed a network of REGIONAL ECK SPIRITUAL AIDES around the world. This has included decades of innovations for the spiritual education and training of chelas, ECK LEADERS, HIGH INITIATES, and ECK CLERICS.

Autobiography

Sri Harold's memoir, *Autobiography of a Modern Prophet,* details the story of his personal journey into the heart of God. In this groundbreaking account, he pulls back the curtain on spiritual realities known only to ECK Masters and seasoned travelers of the GOD WORLDS.

It tells of the extensive inner and outer training he underwent to accept his role as the spiritual leader. Lifetimes of training had already been invested in his spiritual education. This lifetime was the final polishing.

Sri Harold's purpose in telling this story is to inspire any serious student to their own spiritual MASTERSHIP.

Life Overview

He was born in Wisconsin and grew up on a small farm. He attended a two-room country schoolhouse before going to high school at a religious boarding school in Milwaukee, Wisconsin.

Leaving behind his preministerial studies, he joined the US Air Force, where he trained as a language specialist, then as a radio intercept operator.

It was during a two-year stint in Japan, in the late 1960s, that he first learned of the teachings of ECKANKAR. He answered an ad in *Fate* magazine which had been placed by PAUL TWITCHELL. It was a momentous occasion, and yet by then Harold had already spent lifetimes preparing for his role as spiritual leader of ECKANKAR.

On October 22, 1981, he became the MAHANTA, the Living ECK Master.

* * *

As head of the Ancient Order of the VAIRAGI, Sri Harold Klemp continues to serve as the SUGMAD's representative on earth, making it possible for willing Souls to make their way home to the OCEAN OF LOVE AND MERCY.

See also FIVE SPIRITUAL LEADERS OF MODERN-DAY ECKANKAR; VAIRAGI(S), ANCIENT ORDER OF THE.

For a list of ECK Masters, see page 341.

healing *See* SPIRITUAL HEALING.

heart center The heart center is the point at which the part meets with the whole, the finite becomes the infinite, the uncreated becomes the created, the universal becomes individualized, and the invisible becomes visible.

See also GOLDEN HEART.

heaven Heaven exists in all persons, and all persons have access to it.

See also INNER WORLDS.

heavenly music The PRIMAL SOUND, the ECK; the Voice of the SUGMAD, the DHUNATMIK; cannot be spoken or written; the original music, the heavenly white sound; the WORD of the worlds; the SOUND CURRENT.

heavenly worlds *See* GOD WORLDS.

hell A part of the LOWER WORLDS in one corner of the ASTRAL PLANE; a mock-up by the citizens of the earth world, manifested by religions to control their members through the priests.

See also AVERNUS.

Helvidius Priscus *Hehl-VID-ee-uhs PRIS-kuhs* An ECK MASTER who was a Roman senator during the time of Vespasian, who reigned from AD 69 to 79.

For a list of ECK Masters, see page 341.

Heraclians *heh-RAH-klee-ahnz* A future ROOT RACE prophesied to conquer and control the world. Fair and just, they will rule around the year AD 6025, and the civilization will last from five hundred to one thousand years.

HI, HIs Initialism for HIGH(ER) INITIATE(S).

Hiafi *hee-AH-fee* The eleventh TWELVE-YEAR CYCLE of the ECK-VIDYA; called the Years of the Lavish Grains. Also the eleventh year within a twelve-year cycle.

See also ECK-VIDYA WHEEL.

hierarchy See SPIRITUAL HIERARCHY.

High(er) Initiate (HI) A CHELA of the Fifth Circle (SOUL PLANE) or above in ECKANKAR; sometimes referred to as a MAHDIS or BROTHER OF THE LEAF.

The HI has attained the ECKshar, SELF-REALIZATION, and is able to work as a COWORKER WITH THE MAHANTA in the first five PLANES, as a distributor of the ECK power.

See also FOUR STATES OF THE HIGH INITIATE; FOUR ZOAS.

Hindu Kush *HIN-doo KOOSH* Mountain range along the border of northern Afghanistan and Pakistan, to the west of the Himalayas.

AGAM DES, TIRICH MIR, and REBAZAR TARZS's hut are all in the Hindu Kush.

Hipolito Fayolle *hee-POH-lee-toh fay-OHL* LIVING ECK MASTER who served during the eighteenth century. Born near Dresden, Germany, he lived to the age of ninety-seven and lifted many ECK CHELAS into the higher worlds. Most of his outer works concerned European and American political figures.

Upon TRANSLATION, he went into the INNER WORLDS to work on the ALAKH LOK, the Sixth PLANE.

For a list of ECK MASTERS, see page 341.

historical MAHANTA *See* THREE ASPECTS OF THE SUGMAD.

Hittites *HIT-tiets* A people who existed during the Dwapara Yuga, or the Copper Age (see YUGA(S)). They

used copper for making weapons and were among the first to make the sword. They were also among the first known conquerors in the history of mankind.

Most of us had PAST LIVES as Hittites. Our gods controlled the weather, fertility, health, and the raising of crops.

Myths still linger from the ancient religions of the Atlanteans and the Hittites. Priests then had already created a Divine Being both vengeful and good. Wrenching people's emotions back and forth between FEAR and love, they beat down the FAITH and spirit of man. Broken in will, man meekly accepted outer authority and the chains of spiritual bondage.

In contrast, ECK MASTERS encourage initiates to acquire and live by the highest attributes of total SPIRITUAL FREEDOM, TOTAL AWARENESS, and self-responsibility.

holy fire The burning love for all things, all people, and all life. This is the love of God stirring SOUL to find Itself and give up all the mental qualms, emotions, and attachments to anything in the material PLANE.

The love of all because life is God. This is the only path to SPIRITUAL FREEDOM.

Holy Spirit *SEE* ECK.

Honardi *hoh-NAHR-dee* A spiritual community of ECK Adepts on the Atma Lok, the SOUL PLANE, where many ECK MASTERS maintain a residence.

Honu *HOH-noo* A city on the CAUSAL PLANE, site of the TEMPLE OF SAKAPORI.

hope, days of *See* EBKIA.

Hortar *HOHR-tahr* The eleventh MONTH OF THE ECK-VIDYA, corresponding to November. The days of wealth. The month of the pearl.

In this journey, SOUL begins to see liberation.

See also ECK-VIDYA WHEEL.

House of Imperishable Knowledge *See* PARAM AKSHAR.

House of Moksha *MOHK-shah* The House of Liberation; the GOLDEN WISDOM TEMPLE in the city of RETZ on the planet Venus where RAMI NURI is in charge of the SHARIYAT-KI-SUGMAD. One of four SUPRAPHYSICAL Golden Wisdom Temples in the physical universe.

Description

This temple is similar to an old English cathedral, with a peaked roof and a spire. It's made from some kind of stone, so old that it looks ancient and weathered. One enters by going up steps to the huge doors, which are opened by heavy rings, into a foyer, and then into a long nave where many rows of seats are found. There is a podium from which the Master, Rami Nuri, gives instructions to the students who are brought there to study.

The third section of the Shariyat-Ki-SUGMAD is kept in an enclosure cut out of the wall and protected by a sheet of glasslike fiber. Students can look through the fiber material, but none can touch it.

The building described above stands within a large temple complex with other striking features, notably the translucent dome at one end, where Rami Nuri also teaches.

HU *HYOO* HU is an ancient, sacred name for God—a carrier of love between God and SOUL. It does not belong to any language; no language can help belonging to It. And no people or religion can claim It as their own.

HU is the Sound behind all sounds, woven into the language of life. It is everywhere, in everything. In this mantric sound all the positive and forward-pressing forces of the human, which are trying to blow up its limitations and burst the fetters of ignorance, are united and concentrated on the ECK, like an arrow point.

When sung or chanted with love, HU opens the lines of communication to the most sacred part of yourself. It acts as a tuning fork, aligning Soul with higher states of love, creativity, healing, and awareness. It is the clear Voice of God, with the power to transform the lead of HUMAN CONSCIOUSNESS into the gold of an enlightened Soul. HU will prepare you to accept the full love of God in this lifetime.

The ancient brotherhood of ECK MASTERS chose

the present age to bring knowledge of HU to the modern world.

HU is the audible whisper of God's love stirring in your very atoms—a proof that Soul exists because God loves It.

Sing *HU* every day. You will begin to vibrate in tune with the SOUND CURRENT. Once you enter the rhythm of life, you *become* the Song of HU itself.

See also ANAMI LOK; **The God Worlds Chart** on page 340; HU, LAW OF; HU, A YEAR OF; HU CHANT; MANTRA.

HU, Law of The Law of HU states that Spirit is the all-penetrating power, the forming power of the universes. The Voice of HU has one great quality, and that is to create effect.

This is one of the SPIRITUAL LAWS OF LIFE; the first law of the physical universe (see **Seven Laws of the Physical Universe** on page 344).

HU, A Year of The fifth of the SPIRITUAL YEARS OF ECK.

For a description, see **The Spiritual Years of ECK** on page 354.

HU Chant Also HU Song. A gathering of like-hearted SOULs who come together to chant the ancient love song to God, the HU. It is simply for the spiritual upliftment of those who come and is not directed to any other purpose.

See also HU.

Huk *HOOK* A spiritually charged word attuned to the AGAM LOK, the Ninth PLANE.

You can chant *Huk* (ends in a short barking sound made deep in the throat) in CONTEMPLATION to visit GOLDEN WISDOM TEMPLES, meet ECK MASTERS, and have other experiences on this plane.

For an overview of the planes and their charged words, see **The God Worlds Chart** on page 340.

Hukikat Lok *hoo-kee-KAHT LOHK* The Eighth PLANE (counting upward), the fourth of the pure, positive SPIRITUAL WORLDS. It is the threshold of GOD-REALIZATION, where SOUL learns God knowledge; the highest state Soul generally reaches.

Distinctions of the Hukikat Lok

ALUK (pronounced *ah-LOOK*) is the word, or CHANT, that one can sing in CONTEMPLATION to attune oneself to the VIBRATIONS of the Hukikat Lok or travel inwardly to a GOLDEN WISDOM TEMPLE or other places there.

An inner experience on this plane may include hearing the sound of a thousand violins.

The main Golden Wisdom Temple on this plane is JARTZ CHONG, also called Temple of the Aluk. The prophecies of the ECK-VIDYA are kept here under KADMON, the ASANGA KAYA, who serves as GUARDIAN of the SHARIYAT-KI-SUGMAD. The ruler of the plane is the HUKIKAT PURUSHA.

See also **The God Worlds Chart** on page 340; LOK.

Hukikat Purusha *hoo-kee-KAHT poo-ROO-shah* The ruler of the HUKIKAT LOK, the Eighth PLANE. Brought into being by the ECK working through the AGAM PURUSHA, the Hukikat Purusha became the third individual manifestation of the SUGMAD.

Through the Hukikat Purusha, the ALAYA PURUSHA, ruler of the ALAYA LOK, came into being.

See also **The God Worlds Chart** on page 340; PURUSHA.

Hum *HYOOM* A spiritually charged word attuned to the ALAYA LOK, the Seventh PLANE.

You can chant *Hum* (like humming with the lips closed) in CONTEMPLATION to visit GOLDEN WISDOM TEMPLES, meet ECK MASTERS, and have other experiences on this plane.

For an overview of the planes and their charged words, see **The God Worlds Chart** on page 340.

human consciousness The CONSCIOUSNESS SOUL assumes when It takes on a human body for Its spiritual education on the PHYSICAL PLANE.

This education comes via the clash between the material and spiritual forces. The SPIRITUAL EXERCISES OF ECK and ECK INITIATIONS take Soul beyond the human consciousness into SELF-REALIZATION and higher levels of realization.

See also REALIZATION, LEVEL(S) OF.

humility The highest goodness in man is characterized by humility, also known as dinta.

It compels one to be self-effacing, like the ECK—

pure in heart, never distracted from the way of ECK. He loves unselfishly, wields virtue, and understands all, while denying himself. He puts life into others without trying to own them.

Paired with chastity, humility is one of the FOUR DISCIPLINES OF ECK. It is also one of the FIVE VIRTUES, the opposite of VANITY (ahankara) and the remedy for it.

Dignity and sweet humility are the twin traits in the ECK CHELA.

HU Song *See* HU CHANT.

Hyperboreans *hie-pehr-BOHR-ee-ahnz* The second ROOT RACE of mankind. This root race established the Melniboran empire in Africa under the VARKAS kings.

hypnotism A sleeplike condition psychically induced. Self-hypnotism cannot lead to SPIRITUAL UNFOLDMENT and is not a part of ECKANKAR. Yet ECKANKAR does recognize that clinical hypnosis by trained health professionals can achieve certain therapeutic goals.

illumination Another word for ENLIGHTENMENT.

illusion *See* MAYA.

imagination *See* CREATIVE IMAGINATION.

imaginative body *See* ASTRAL BODY.

imaginative technique *See* SPIRITUAL EXERCISES OF ECK.

impatience One of the manifestations of ANGER.

Inaccessible Plane *See* AGAM LOK.

inaccessible world *See* AGAM DES.

incarnations The cycles of births and deaths in the LOWER WORLDS.

See also REINCARNATION.

individuality Individuality is the necessary complement of the Spirit. Until actualized and distributed by SOULS, the ECK, the GOD CURRENT, is undifferentiated.

Soul is an individual; It retains Its individuality beyond all time, beyond all universes. But It retains Its individuality to be a COWORKER WITH GOD, helping others find their way to the LIGHT AND SOUND. Each Soul will realize an individual mission in service to the SUGMAD.

See also RECIPROCITY, LAW OF.

initiate *See* ECK INITIATE.

initiate report ECKISTS of the SECOND INITIATION and above are asked to write a monthly initiate report to the LIVING ECK MASTER. They have the privilege of putting their thoughts, hopes, dreams, burdens, and FEARS down on paper, thus releasing them to the MAHANTA. Whether or not to mail the report is between them and the INNER MASTER.

The initiate report is about surrender. It is a personal assessment and serves as an aid in working out KARMA.

In turning your concerns over to the Master, you break their hold on you.

See also SELF-SURRENDER.

initiation(s) An ECK initiation is a sacred rite that increases the power and love of ECK in your life. TRUTH is instilled in your heart, and your ability to solve your own problems increases.

Each initiation is a state of SOUL in Its embodiment of truth.

During the SECOND INITIATION, the LIGHT GIVER, the MAHANTA, the LIVING ECK MASTER links Soul with the returning wave of the SOUND CURRENT.

The ECK initiations are steps toward GOD-REALIZATION, and each one imbues Soul with a greater amount of LIGHT AND SOUND.

For deeper insights on each initiation, see chapter 12, "The Circles of ECK Initiations," in *THE SHARIYAT-KI-SUGMAD*, Book Two.

For a list of the ECK initiations, see page 338.

See also REALIZATION, LEVEL(S) OF.

Initiator *See* ECK INITIATOR.

Inner and Outer Master Two different aspects of one being—the MAHANTA, the LIVING ECK MASTER.

It is the role of the Outer Master to keep the sacred teachings of LIGHT AND SOUND available and attuned to the spiritual needs and CONSCIOUSNESS of the people of the day.

The INNER MASTER, the MAHANTA, customizes the path to exactly fit the spiritual needs of each individual. This is done via DREAM TEACHINGS, inner guidance, SOUL TRAVEL, and one's CONTEMPLATION. The Inner Master is Divine Spirit Itself.

See also INNER TEACHINGS; PRESENCE OF THE MASTER.

inner ear The faculty within by which one can hear the SOUND CURRENT, the ECK.

inner eye *See* SPIRITUAL EYE.

inner initiation The inner INITIATION may come years before the outer initiation.

The FIRST INITIATION is an inner initiation given in

the DREAM STATE by the DREAM MASTER. Sometimes the CHELA is fully conscious and can remember everything about it; it prepares the chela for the linkup with the SOUND CURRENT, the Audible Life Stream.

The SECOND INITIATION through EIGHTH INITIATION occurs both inwardly and outwardly. The outer ceremony is necessary for the initiation to be completed.

All initiations above the Eighth are inner initiations only.

For a list of ECK initiations, see page 338.

Inner Master LIGHT AND SOUND blended; the highest form of all love; the inner form of the LIVING ECK MASTER.

See also INNER AND OUTER MASTER; MAHANTA; TOTAL RELIANCE ON THE INNER MASTER.

inner teachings The secret teachings of ECKANKAR come directly from the MAHANTA to each SOUL. These are the greater teachings and are tailored to each individual. They are often held in silence by the CHELA so as not to diminish their power.

These teachings are given by the MAHANTA or the ECK MASTERS via the inner channels—in CONTEMPLATION, in the DREAM STATE, or during SOUL TRAVEL at the GOLDEN WISDOM TEMPLES on the various inner PLANES.

See also SECRET DOCTRINE; SILENCE, LAW OF.

inner vision That seeing which does not use the body's eyes but sees with the SPIRITUAL EYE.

inner voice The voice of the ECK or the INNER MASTER,

or what some call the still small voice within. That which guides, protects, offers insight to, and enlightens the spiritual student.

inner worlds Your own worlds of being; the PLANES of CONSCIOUSNESS within you; sometimes called the FAR COUNTRY. You cannot become lost in these worlds, because it is your own personal universe.

intuition Intuition is actually Spirit giving us the gentle guidance to make our life better. The power of knowing without knowing; an innate, instinctive knowledge.

Invisible Laws Below are seven principles of CONSCIOUSNESS which are among the SPIRITUAL LAWS OF LIFE.

Invisible Laws

1. ***Appreciation*** of the teacher
2. ***Sincerity*** in seeking higher LEVELS OF REALIZATION
3. ***Unselfishness,*** the willingness to sacrifice the LITTLE SELF to the greater
4. ***Idealism,*** the faculty of perceiving spiritual values through a perfect pattern
5. ***Devotion,*** to fill the heart with love and aspiration and align oneself with the will of God
6. ***Personal effort,*** the spiritual motivating force which is within all
7. ***Attainment,*** the reward for spiritual effort

Invisible Plane *See* ALAKH LOK.

iron age *See* FOUR CYCLES OF LIFE; MAHAYUGA; YUGA(S).

Is it true? Is it necessary? Is it kind? A simple ECK code for spiritual living; three questions to ask oneself when in doubt about an action.

Unless the answer is yes for all three, you would do well to reconsider your intended action.

Ismet Houdoni *EES-meht hoo-DOH-nee* The MAHANTA, the LIVING ECK MASTER during the reign of King James I of England. He served as an adviser to the king.

He also inspired the poet Henry Vaughan and arranged for Lancelot Andrewes to head the group of religious scholars that produced the King James version of the Bible in 1611.

After Ismet Houdoni's TRANSLATION, at age 135, he entered into the CAUSAL PLANE to work for the cause of ECK.

For a list of ECK MASTERS, see page 341.

Ism-i-Azam Another name for the ECK, the SOUND CURRENT.

Jagat Giri *jah-GAHT GEE-ree* Jagat Giri is the title of the GUARDIAN of the SHARIYAT-KI-SUGMAD at the PARAM AKSHAR Temple on the SOUL PLANE. This position is currently held by TINDOR SAKI.

For a list of noted guardians, see **A Road Map for Spiritual Travelers** on page 343.

Jagat Ho *jah-GAHT HOH* The LIVING ECK MASTER in China during the years 490–438 BC. He is now serving under LAI TSI as a COWORKER WITH GOD in the DAYAKA TEMPLE on the ETHERIC PLANE.

For a list of ECK MASTERS, see page 341.

Jalal ad-Din ar-Rumi *jah-LAHL ahd-DEEN ar-ROO-mee* *See* Rumi.

Janos Moneta *JAH-nohs moh-NEH-tah* The LIVING ECK MASTER who lived near Stockholm, Sweden, and had a deep spiritual influence on the early eighteenth century, helping break up old, established forms of religion, music, and art.

He was a friend of Swedenborg, who studied ECK.

Much of Swedenborg's life and writings shows the influence of this ECK MASTER.

When Janos Moneta passed on, he went into the MENTAL PLANE to work.

For a list of ECK Masters, see page 341.

Jartz Chong *JAHRTS CHOHNG* The GOLDEN WISDOM TEMPLE on the Eighth PLANE, or HUKIKAT LOK, also called Temple of the ALUK.

Jesus *JEE-zuhs* The embodiment of the CHRIST CONSCIOUSNESS. He once was an ECK CHELA under ZADOK, the ECK MASTER in Judea, who gave him the basic fundamentals of ECK. Out of this knowledge came what is known today as Christianity.

Jewels of ECK, The SOUL is always in eternity, It is always in the present now, It is always in the heavenly state of the SUGMAD, and It exists because of God's love for It.

Jivan Mukti *JEE-vahn MOOK-tee* Another name for SPIRITUAL FREEDOM.

Jivatma *jee-VAHT-mah* Another word for SOUL.

Jot Niranjan *JAHT nee-RAHN-jahn* The ruler of the ASTRAL PLANE; the powerhouse of the physical universe, the PINDA world. Also called Jehovah.

See also **The God Worlds Chart** on page 340.

joy, days of *See* GARVATA.

Joyti Basji *joh-EE-tee BAHS-jee* The LIVING ECK MASTER in Mexico during the extension of the Mayan empire from the Yucatan and Guatemala into the heart of Mexico.

For a list of ECK MASTERS, see page 341.

Ju Chiao *JOO chee-AH-oh* The ECK MASTER in charge of the Temple of PARAM AKSHAR, the GOLDEN WISDOM TEMPLE on the SOUL PLANE.

Ju Chiao had been a young fisherman who, restless for an understanding of life, took up the call and became a warrior under Hannibal during the Punic Wars between Rome and Carthage. He learned that his search for life lay beyond this and followed VAITA DANU, who initiated him.

Upon departing from this world, Vaita Danu passed the spiritual mantle of LIVING ECK MASTER to Ju Chiao. Hannibal, however, did not like the teachings of Ju Chiao and had him killed.

For a list of ECK Masters, see page 341.

Kabir *kah-BEER* A weaver and mystic poet in the fifteenth and sixteenth centuries, in India.

He was a direct descendant in RAMA's spiritual mastership and was the first to bring the mysteries of SOUL TRAVEL out into the open. Those who were followers of the science of Soul Travel knew he was wrong to try to reveal such truth at that time.

A Muslim by birth, Kabir hoped his poems would unite the Muslims and Hindus; however, it was the wrong time, and he ended up being hounded by both factions.

Among his band of followers was Guru Nanak, founder of Sikhism, which carried elements of the LIGHT AND SOUND to India.

Kadath Inscriptions *KAH-dahth* Ancient records which show the history of the LIVING ECK MASTERS throughout the ages; kept in the KATSUPARI MONASTERY in northern Tibet.

Kadmon *KAD-mahn* The ECK MASTER in charge of the Temple of the ALUK, or Temple of JARTZ CHONG, on the HUKIKAT LOK, the Eighth PLANE, where the sacred writings of the SHARIYAT-KI-SUGMAD are found.

One of the highest of the ECK Adepts in the VAIRAGI ORDER, he was on earth during the infancy of man and served as the MAHANTA, the LIVING ECK MASTER. As GUARDIAN of the Shariyat-Ki-SUGMAD in Jartz Chong, he bears the title of Asanga Kaya.

For a list of ECK Masters, see page 341.

Kai-Kuas *kie-KOO-ahs* Served as the LIVING ECK MASTER during the time of the powerful, fierce, and ruthless VARKAS kings. He lived in secret and countered the psychic forces by teaching ECK to the chosen few who could understand him. He was discovered in hiding, captured, and put to death.

For a list of ECK MASTERS, see page 341.

Kailash *KIE-lahsh* One of three mountain peaks on the MENTAL PLANE. The other two are MER and SUMER.

See also MER KAILASH.

Kaishvits *KIE-shvits* A ROOT RACE from Mars who will conquer Earth and all the major planets after a major catastrophe spares only Mars. They will be in power for about five thousand years.

Kal *KAL* The negative power. The word *Kal* is also used to denote the KAL NIRANJAN. This power is confined to the LOWER WORLDS of duality.

It is the purpose of the Kal power to temper each SOUL in the art of life so that It can come to the MAHANTA as a CHELA.

Kala *kah-LAH* A spiritually charged word attuned to the ASTRAL PLANE, the Second PLANE. You can chant *Kala* in CONTEMPLATION to visit GOLDEN WISDOM TEMPLES, meet ECK MASTERS, and have other experiences on this plane.

For an overview of the planes and their charged words, see **The God Worlds Chart** on page 340.

Kalam *kah-LAHM* Another word for the SOUND CURRENT; a spiritual word you can CHANT to experience the Sound.

Kalam-i-Illahi *KAH-lahm-ee-ee-LAH-hee* One of the many names for the WORD of God, the SOUND CURRENT.

Kali Yuga *KAH-lee YOO-gah* The Iron Age.

See also FOUR CYCLES OF LIFE; MAHAYUGA; YUGA(S).

Kal Niranjan *KAL nee-RAHN-jahn* The KAL. The personification of the negative power, known outside of ECKANKAR as Satan or the devil. Lord of the LOWER WORLDS.

The Kal's job is to keep SOULS in the worlds of matter, yet the negative power is always working, as part of the SPIRITUAL HIERARCHY, for the divine cause. It provides education in the lower worlds that leads to the PURIFICATION of Soul.

kalpa *KAHL-pah* *See* MAHAYUGA.

kama *KAH-mah* *See* LUST.

kamit *KAH-mit* *See* SILENCE, LAW OF.

Kamitoc *KAH-mee-tahk* The seventh MONTH OF THE ECK-VIDYA, corresponding to July. The days of freedom. The month of the ruby.

In this journey of SOUL, freedom comes through knowledge.

See also ECK-VIDYA WHEEL.

Kangra Sambha *KAHN-grah SAHM-bah* More often called TRANSLATION in ECKANKAR, the Kangra Sambha is the passing of SOUL from the PHYSICAL BODY upon the death of that temple of clay.

kani *KAH-nee* The EGO, or opposite of HUMILITY.

Karan mind *KAH-rahn* The MIND operating on the CAUSAL PLANE. Also called the Nij mind, Nij Manas, or inner mind. It carries the seeds of all mental actions within itself, and it also carries the SANSKARAS (impressions of all former lives). A function of the UNIVERSAL MIND force.

See also ALIVA MIND; PINDA MIND; SUKHSHAM MIND.

Karan Sarup *See* CAUSAL BODY.

Karan Sharir *See* CAUSAL BODY.

karma This is the principle of individual responsibility for every thought, word, and deed. It is an educational process for SOULs gaining experience in the LOWER WORLDS.

Karma is cause and effect, action and reaction, reaping what one sows, balancing the scales of justice. It is a system of credits (good karma) and debits (bad karma) overseen by the LORDS OF KARMA. The purpose

is to purify Soul.

A way to sidestep making new karma is to do all things in the name of the MAHANTA.

For the uninitiated, at the end of each life, the Lords of Karma examine the individual's karmic balance in the BOOK OF LIFE and assign that Soul to the conditions It has earned for Its next incarnation. This process continues for countless lifetimes.

When an ECK CHELA receives the SECOND INITIATION in ECKANKAR, the MAHANTA, the LIVING ECK MASTER takes over his or her karma and gives it back to the individual to work off in an orderly, forward-moving manner. That Soul will not have to reincarnate on the PHYSICAL PLANE again. When an ECK chela receives the FIFTH INITIATION, that Soul no longer needs to reincarnate anywhere in the lower worlds.

All karma can be worked off in this lifetime.

The Four Types of Karma

1. **Primal karma**, karma not earned by the individual Soul—that which was established to begin Soul's journey in the lower worlds, also called adi karma or seed karma. It could be any positive or negative quality.
2. **Daily karma**, which is made hour to hour and day to day; new karma created by actions during this life.
3. **Fate karma**, the sum of good and bad karma from Soul's account record which sets the conditions for Its next incarnation; each lifetime of choices creates one's fate, or destiny, for subsequent lives.

4. **Reserve karma**, a surplus of credits and debits from PAST LIVES, issued to a Soul in Its present incarnation at the behest of the Lords of Karma.

   When a person experiences sudden fortune or misfortune in life (such as winning the lottery or suffering a catastrophic loss), it indicates reserve karma: That person is reaping credits or paying debts incurred in a past life.

See also KARMA, LAW OF; KARMALESS ACTION; KARMA MARG; PAST LIVES; REINCARNATION; WHEEL OF THE EIGHTY-FOUR.

Karma, Law of *KAHR-mah* One of the SPIRITUAL LAWS OF LIFE. A facet of the Law of Love, it purifies people by holding them responsible for their thoughts and deeds, both to themselves and others.

One of the great laws by which the universes are sustained. Also called Law of Cause and Effect, the Law of Returns, or the Law of Universal Compensation.

See also KARMA; LOVE, LAW OF.

karmaless action To live the karmaless life—to act without creating further KARMA—is to do everything in the name of God, in the name of the MAHANTA, in the name of Divine Spirit. Do this from your heart.

Karma, Lords of *See* LORDS OF KARMA.

Karma Marg *KAHR-mah MAHRG* One of the

SEVEN MARGS. The way of KARMA as a path to God; the approach to God through selflessness and harmonious deeds. Similar to the BHAKTI MARG, but a more personal path of service to God.

Kassapa *kah-SAH-pah* The LIVING ECK MASTER before the destruction of ATLANTIS.

For a list of ECK MASTERS, see page 341.

Kata Daki *KAH-tah DAH-kee*

An ECK MASTER in the Ancient Order of the VAIRAGI Adepts, who is a woman.

Although her true age is beyond belief, she appears to be in her mid-twenties to early thirties. She is five and a half feet tall. Her light-brown (honey-blond) hair often falls to her shoulders, but she changes hairstyles to fit her duties.

Like all the ECK Masters, she serves SUGMAD (God) by helping others find the MAHANTA, the LIVING ECK MASTER. Her pet project is to help people get back on their feet during hardship.

See also LONGEVITY.

For a list of ECK Masters, see page 341 .

Katsupari Monastery *kaht-soo-PAH-ree* An ECK monastery and GOLDEN WISDOM TEMPLE in the BUIKA MAGNA mountain range of northern Tibet, near the VALLEY OF SHANGTA.

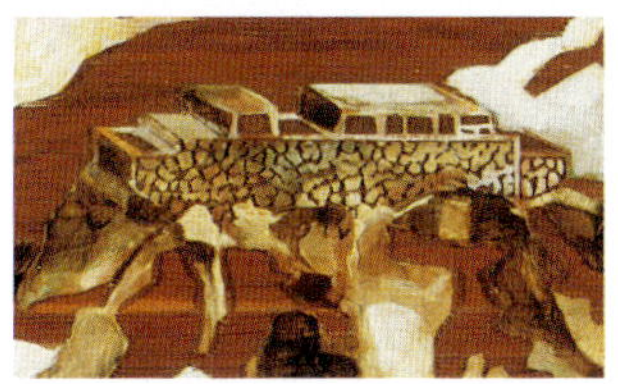

One of four SUPRAPHYSICAL Golden Wisdom Temples in the physical universe, it was founded by RAMA and is now under the GUARDIANship of FUBBI QUANTZ.

The temple is a weathered, dark-colored building squatting on craggy heights, and it commands a view of perhaps a hundred miles during clear weather. Although fifty monks in dark maroon robes live in this seventy-five-room castlelike structure, only three are responsible for guarding the holy book there.

With permission of the abbot, Fubbi Quantz, many spiritual students come here in the DREAM STATE or via SOUL TRAVEL to study, after taking up the path of ECKANKAR.

Legend has it that JESUS once came to the monastery during his "silent years" and met Fubbi Quantz.

Chief among the writings in the Katsupari Monastery is the first section of the SHARIYAT-KI-SUGMAD, "The Chronicles of ECK." The KADATH INSCRIPTIONS are also found here, as well as the RECORDS OF THE KROS. Years before the Chinese invasion of Tibet, intrepid travelers sometimes came to Katsupari for the KAYA KALP treatments of physical rejuvenation.

Kaya Kalp *KAH-yah KAHLP* A system of renewing the health and youth of the PHYSICAL BODY; an offshoot of AYUR VEDHA.

THE FOUR-STEP SPIRITUAL EXERCISE OF ECK uses "Kaya Kalp" as a chant; *see* page 347.

See also SPIRITUAL HEALING.

Kazi Dawtz *KAH-zee DAHTS* The GOLDEN WISDOM TEMPLE on the AGAM LOK, the Ninth PLANE, or the fifth of the SPIRITUAL WORLDS; also called the Temple of Akash. There is a community of ECK MASTERS nearby.

Ketu Jaraul *KEH-too ja-RAHL* A LIVING ECK MASTER who was the secret adviser for CHARLEMAGNE, teaching him the secrets of ECK and helping with his spiritual training.

Ketu Jaraul's training allowed Charlemagne to become a prince of ECK instead of merely the king of an earthly realm. He has been called the father of Europe, and his reign is today regarded as a golden age in a time of otherwise great spiritual darkness in the West.

For a list of ECK MASTERS, see page 341.

Kevalshar *KEHV-ahl-shahr* One who has reached the ELEVENTH INITIATION.

Khara Khota *KAH-rah KOH-tah* The capital city of the ancient UIGHUR EMPIRE in central Asia in the Gobi Desert, home of the fifth ROOT RACE, the ARYANS.

RAMA, an ECK MASTER, preached ECKANKAR there but was hounded out of the empire, went to Tibet, and founded the KATSUPARI MONASTERY.

YUONT-NA, another ECK Master, also once taught in Khara Khota.

The city now lies buried deep beneath the desert sands.

Kimtaved *keem-TAH-vehd* One of the ten SPIRITUAL

CITIES on earth to help this world.

It is located in South America, high in the Andes Mountains between Venezuela and Colombia. The beings here are descendants of the Incas. They keep watch over the planetary spirits and keep check on the dark forces of this world.

The other nine spiritual cities are AGAM DES, AKEVIZ, DAMCAR, MUMSAKA, NAMPAK, RAHAKAZ, SAT DHAM, SHAMBALLA, and ZEZIRATH.

Kingdom of the SUGMAD This is the ultimate, the highest, of all the imperishable SPIRITUAL WORLDS. It is the ANAMI LOK, the nameless region; the beginning and ending of all worlds. From here the love and power of the SUGMAD, the first principle, vibrates throughout all the worlds.

See also AKAHA.

King of the Dead *See* YAMA.

Kitai *kee-TIE* One who has reached the SECOND INITIATION in ECKANKAR, more often called the ARAHATA. This is the enlightened one; the second stage of INITIATION on the path of ECK.

Kita Sorgi *KEE-tah SOHR-gee* An ECK MASTER during the time of Alexander the Great, who went with him to visit the Oracle of Ammon in Egypt.

For a list of ECK Masters, see page 341.

Klemp, Harold *See* HAROLD KLEMP.

Knowing, Law of *See* ASSUMPTION, LAW OF.

Koji Chanda *KOH-jee CHAHN-dah* The title of the GUARDIAN of the SHARIYAT-KI-SUGMAD on the PAR BRAHM Lok, the Fourth, or MENTAL, PLANE, at the NAMAYATAN GOLDEN WISDOM TEMPLE in the city of MER KAILASH.

The Koji Chanda is currently TOWART MANAGI.

For a list of noted guardians, see **A Road Map for Spiritual Travelers** on page 343.

Krita Yuga Another name for the Satya Yuga, the Golden Age.

See also FOUR CYCLES OF LIFE; MAHAYUGA; YUGA(S).

kriyaman karma *KREE-yah-mahn KAHR-mah* DAILY KARMA, one of the four types of KARMA.

The other types are FATE KARMA, PRIMAL KARMA, and RESERVE KARMA.

krodha *KROH-dah* *See* ANGER.

Kros, Records of the *KROHS* *See* RECORDS OF THE KROS.

kshama *KSHAH-mah* Another word for the spiritual virtue of FORGIVENESS AND TOLERANCE.

See FIVE VIRTUES.

kundalini *koon-dah-LEE-nee* A lower-world force which is better left asleep; not part of ECKANKAR or the SPIRITUAL EXERCISES OF ECK.

See also PSYCHIC PHENOMENA.

Kundun *KOON-DOON* *See* PRESENCE OF THE MASTER.

Kuritee *koo-REE-tee* The sixth TWELVE-YEAR CYCLE of the ECK-VIDYA; called the Years of the Strange Storms. Also the sixth year within a twelve-year cycle.

See also ECK-VIDYA WHEEL.

Kurnai *KEHR-nie* One who has reached the THIRD INITIATION. More often called the Ahrat.

Lady of ECK *See* SIMHA.

Lai Tsi *lie TSEE*

The Chinese ECK MASTER who is the GUARDIAN of the SHARIYAT-KI-SUGMAD on the SAGUNA LOK, the ETHERIC PLANE, at the GOLDEN WISDOM TEMPLE in the city of ARHIRIT. He once served as the MAHANTA, the LIVING ECK MASTER.

Description

Lai Tsi is a slender man of medium height with a long beard and mustache. He usually wears his hair in a single braid to his shoulders. Luminous dark eyes and a wide, smiling mouth speak of his benevolence and good humor. His hands taper, with straight, polished nails.

Sometimes he wears a heavy maroon robe and a high, brimless hat which is ornamented with many mysterious symbols.

The light around him is silvery, and he appears

to many in the lower worlds as a silver light with a humming sound like that of bees.

Biographical Sketch

As a young man in ancient China, Lai Tsi studied religion and became a revered doctor of divinity. But he came to understand that GOD-REALIZATION could never be gained from books, and he set out to find God in nature and solitude, retiring to a mountain cave.

There, two ECK MASTERS—TOMO GESHIG and YAUBL SACABI—came to visit him in the SOUL BODY for a period of seven years. As a result, Lai Tsi was lifted out of his PHYSICAL BODY and into the high worlds of God. In his illumination, he beheld the SUGMAD.

After this experience, a handful of the chosen few gathered and became his disciples. Thus began his mission as Living ECK Master.

Lai Tsi's Prayer

A short CONTEMPLATION SEED that ECK MASTER LAI TSI found in himself upon returning from the heavenly worlds. He says, "Should anyone be in distress or need to reach the great SUGMAD, use this CONTEMPLATION; repeat it slowly, and it certainly brings results." It goes as follows:

Show me Thy ways, O SUGMAD;

Teach me Thy path.

> Lead me in Thy truth, and teach me;
> On Thee do I wait all day.
> I remember, O Beloved, Thy guiding light
> And Thy loving care.
> For it has been ever Thy will,
> To lead the least of Thy servants to Thee!

Lai Tsi's prayer is recorded in *THE SHARIYAT-KI-SUGMAD*, Book Two, in the chapter titled "The Visions of Lai Tsi."

For a list of ECK Masters, see page 341.

Lamakan *LAH-mah-kahn* *See* AKAHA.

Lamotta *lah-MAHT-tah* The MAHANTA, the LIVING ECK MASTER who accepted the ROD OF ECK POWER in 1000 BC. He served his mission in the time of King David and tried to spread ECK throughout the world.

He had few followers, however, and did not have much success in reviving the secret teachings of ECK. The fault was not his, but that of his disciples, who did not have the spiritual vision to appreciate the gifts he offered them.

Lamotta was hunted down and slain by bands of Assyrians. After his TRANSLATION, he took up the duty of assisting RAMI NURI on Venus, teaching the SHARIYAT-KI-SUGMAD to those who come there to learn.

For a list of ECK MASTERS, see page 341.

Lao-tzu *low-TSOO* Lao-tzu was a sixth-century BC

Chinese holy man. Years after his passing, his teachings developed into the philosophy of Taoism. The *Tao-te Ching* is ascribed to Lao-tzu but may have actually been compiled by others.

Lao-tzu's Mission

The SPIRITUAL HIERARCHY had assigned a mission to Lao-tzu: to take news of the Tao, ECK (Holy Spirit) to people. He'd gone a long way in his SPIRITUAL UNFOLDMENT, having traveled into the first of the true SPIRITUAL WORLDS. He gladly came to earth at the behest of the spiritual hierarchy.

His mission was vastly different than that of his contemporary Confucius. Lao-tzu was to teach people about the Life Stream of God. Yet the nearest he could describe It to them was to call It the Way.

However, his audience was of quite a low STATE OF CONSCIOUSNESS, and the spiritual WISDOM didn't stick.

Feeling he had failed in his mission, Lao-tzu nearly gave up. Fortunately, the ECK intervened, and a lowly gatekeeper prevailed upon him to stay and set his teachings into writing. Due to the gatekeeper, this world is a far richer place today.

Lavish Grains, Years of the *See* HIAFI.

laws, spiritual *See* SPIRITUAL LAWS OF LIFE.

Lemuria *leh-MOOR-ee-ah* Lemuria, the lost continent also known as Mu, existed some fifty thousand

years ago and developed over the course of many centuries. It was located in the midst of the Pacific Ocean and stretched into what is now China. Lemuria formed colonies around the globe.

It was a remarkable land said to belong to the golden age of mankind's history. The RECORDS OF THE KROS tell us that Lemuria was where the legendary paradise of man, thought of as the Garden of Eden, was located. Lemuria became the greatest civilization known to the world and was called the Empire of the Sun.

A tropical country of vast plains, low rolling hills, and a soft, pleasant climate, Lemuria seemed invincible to change. There were no mountains. The valleys and plains were covered with rich grazing grass and tilled fields.

On the continent of Mu were seven major cities, centers of religion, science, and education. There were also many other large cities for trading and industry. Mu came to be known as the center of the world, where all came for learning and commerce.

The ECK MASTERS DAYAKA and GEUTAN served their missions in Lemuria.

The People of Lemuria

The lost continent of Mu, or Lemuria, was home to the third ROOT RACE, the Lemurians.

The people of Mu were highly civilized and enlightened. They were gentle and peaceful and lived together without savagery. They practiced the Law of the One, which simply said to help your neighbor help himself, for he is of the same essence as you.

The citizens of this great empire were under the protection of Mu, the motherland of the earth. The Lemurians' reverence for their deity was so great they never spoke Its name; even in prayer It was addressed always through a symbol. Ra, the sun, was used as a collective symbol for all the deity possessed.

The Lemurians also believed in the immortality of SOUL, which eventually returned to the Source from whence It came.

The ruling race was fairly tall and slender, with brown or olive skin, dark eyes, and straight black hair. There were also other races—the yellow, brown, and black people. Ten tribes made up the bulk of citizens, all under an emperor named Ra Mu, who was the representative of the Supreme Deity but was not worshipped.

Advancements

Besides being exemplars of moral behavior, the Lemurians were also a technologically advanced people. They sailed the seas and discovered new lands, establishing colonies around the globe. They built great temples, stone palaces, and gigantic carved monuments.

They practiced a system of agriculture which could feed thousands upon thousands, and they

protected the terraced fields from cyclones by setting up stations (some three hundred miles apart) with many crystals in each.

They could also prevent earthquakes, and they constructed buildings by precisely cutting massive blocks of stone and transporting them through the air before dropping them into place.

The Destruction of Lemuria

When it was time for its long life to end, seismic upheavals made it clear that Lemuria's days were numbered. Missionaries went to colonies around the world, including Atlantis. There they hid their writings to ensure that Lemuria's history would live on in the annals of mankind.

The destruction of Lemuria and its colonial empire came about due to gas pockets under the crust of the earth that had formed hundreds of thousands of years before. Earthquakes and tidal waves caused most of the continent to go down under the seas.

After the fall of Lemuria, one of its surviving provinces developed into ATLANTIS. Another province of Lemuria would much later become the location of the UIGHUR EMPIRE. Some Pacific islands of today are remnants of ancient Lemuria.

Lenurig *leh-NOO-reeg* The seventh TWELVE-YEAR CYCLE of the ECK-VIDYA; called the Years of the Wan-

dering Seas. Also the seventh year within a twelve-year cycle.

See also ECK-VIDYA WHEEL.

level(s) of realization *See* REALIZATION, LEVEL(S) OF.

Lhokhor *LOH-kohr* The cycle of the ECK-VIDYA which is divided into twelve years is called the Lhokhor.

Twelve is the number of completion or perfection. It takes one through the INITIATIONS into the highest PLANE, that of the SUGMAD, the OCEAN OF LOVE AND MERCY.

The twelve-year cycle of Lhokhor, being the great cycle, takes in all the inner cycles of threes. It is also the beginning of the greater cycles which culminate in the number sixty (*see* RABJUNG).

> The MAHANTA, the LIVING ECK MASTER, the embodiment and expression of the SUGMAD, is the expression and completion of the number twelve.

See also RABJUNG; TWELVE-YEAR CYCLE(S).

liberation, spiritual *See* SPIRITUAL FREEDOM.

life cycles *See* FOUR CYCLES OF LIFE.

Life Force The essence of the SUGMAD (God). *See* ECK.

Life, Law of *See* DHARMA, LAW OF.

Life Stream *See* SOUND CURRENT.

Light Along with the SOUND CURRENT, one of the twin pillars of God's love and a mainstay of the ECK

teachings. The reflection of the spiritual atoms moving in space, as the ECK, the manifestation of the SUGMAD in the LOWER WORLDS, flows from the SUGMAD into them and returns.

See also LIGHT AND SOUND.

light, days of *See* MOKSHOVE.

Light and Sound God's love in action. The LIGHT and Sound are the Voice of God, the ECK (Holy Spirit).

All SOULs are made of Light and Sound. The Light and Sound contain the totality of all teaching emanating from God.

One can make contact via the SPIRITUAL EXERCISES OF ECK, where one may see an inner or outer light and hear an inner or outer sound. This brings PURIFICATION of Soul.

See also ECK; SOUND CURRENT.

Light and Sound Service *See* ECK LIGHT AND SOUND SERVICE.

Light and Sound, The Year of The first of the SPIRITUAL YEARS OF ECK.

For a description, see **The Spiritual Years of ECK** on page 354.

Light body *See* ASTRAL BODY.

Light form *See* ASTRAL BODY.

Light Giver The MAHANTA; the VI-GURU; the GODMAN;

the LIVING ECK MASTER.

The MAHANTA is called the Light Giver because of the LIGHT that is showered upon the individual at the ECK INITIATION. Additionally, SOUL is illuminated by this inner side of the LIVING ECK MASTER as he gives talks and performs other outer duties.

Lightning Worlds Along with the MOON WORLDS and SUN WORLDS, these are subplanes which lie between the PHYSICAL PLANE and the true ASTRAL PLANE.

lila *LEE-lah* Singing and dancing made up of sound, silence, motion, and rest which SOUL does as a result of GOD-REALIZATION. The play of Soul.

little self The limited, human STATE OF CONSCIOUSNESS; the EGO; that which strives only to see that it exists. SOUL rises above the pull of this little self via the SPIRITUAL EXERCISES OF ECK and practice of the FIVE VIRTUES.

See also HUMAN CONSCIOUSNESS.

Living ECK Master The MAHANTA, the Living ECK Master is the spiritual leader of ECKANKAR, the VI-GURU, the GODMAN, the LIVING WORD.

He is the ECK personified, the living embodiment of all that is spiritual—the spirit of life that lies dormant in others. The Living ECK Master transcends time, space, and causation, holding the past, present, and future in the palm of his hand.

The sole purpose of the MAHANTA, the Living ECK Master is to help SOUL find Its way home to God.

The world is never without a Living ECK Master.

The MAHANTA can only be embodied in the Living ECK Master. The MAHANTA, the Living ECK Master is the spiritual head of the Ancient Order of the VAIRAGIS.

Two Sides of the Master

The two sides of the Living ECK Master are known as the INNER AND OUTER MASTER. The Outer Master provides the outer teachings such as the ECK SPIRITUAL LIVING COURSES and books.

Yet the greater part is the INNER MASTER, the MAHANTA. Like the air you breathe, he is everywhere. As the ECK, he can easily be with all his CHELAS at the same time.

The Inner and Outer Master are manifestations of the ECK force in the individual's life. The combination of the two releases the power of DIVINE LOVE, which begins like a small flame that grows until it consumes the whole heart.

Lineage

All Living ECK Masters trace their lineage to the first ECK MASTER, GAKKO. Some have been married, others single. They serve the ECK faithfully, giving their lives to It. A Soul in training for the role of the MAHANTA, the Living ECK Master enters this life as a male due to the arrangement of atoms.

Each Living ECK Master appoints his successor, and the transition is marked by the PASSING OF THE ROD OF ECK POWER.

For a list of ECK Masters, see page 341.

living Quintan *See* QUINTAN.

living Shariyat The SHARIYAT is the holy book of the VAIRAGI ADEPTS, a record of spiritual evolution on every PLANE of God.

The living Shariyat refers to the action of the ECK, the Holy Spirit, as it occurs in CREATION, before it is recorded in a book.

> This is the dynamic influence of the LIGHT AND SOUND of ECK in our daily lives. Every experience in our life that teaches something of God's love for SOUL—and Soul's love for It—is a part of the living Shariyat.

From the SOUL PLANE on up, the MAHANTA may teach one by direct experience with the Sound and LIGHT, which is also the living Shariyat.

See also SHARIYAT-KI-SUGMAD.

living truth The LIGHT AND SOUND of God as It manifests fully in all who have had GOD-REALIZATION.

See also TRUTH.

living water Another term for the ECK, Divine Spirit.

See also ECK.

Living Word The ECK, the WORD of God, as It comes through the MAHANTA, the LIVING ECK MASTER.

The true source of the ECK teachings beyond any books or discourses. The Living Word is always at the head of ECKANKAR as the Living ECK Master.

lobha *LOHB-hah* *See* GREED.

Logos *LOH-gohs* The WORD of God, NAM; inner reality; the Divine Spirit which gives life to all.

See also ECK.

lok *LOHK* Another word for world or PLANE.

longevity Living in a human body far beyond what is considered to be the normal life span.

Many ECK MASTERS of the Order of the VAIRAGI have remained on earth for hundreds of years for the purpose of assisting the LIVING ECK MASTER in his mission in this universe.

The GOD-EATERS are known for living to great ages by consuming cosmic energy. ECK MASTERS ISMET HOUDONI, HIPOLITO FAYOLLE, SUDAR SINGH, and SUTO T'SING lived well beyond the average life span of their day.

Other ECK Masters who have been granted longevity include KATA DAKI, LAI TSI, and REBAZAR TARZS.

Three who have immortalized their physical bodies and are still living in them on earth are FUBBI QUANTZ, REBAZAR TARZS, and YAUBL SACABI.

See also SPIRITUAL HEALING; VAIRAGI(S), ANCIENT ORDER OF THE.

Lords of Karma *KAHR-mah* The distributors of KARMA, responsible for the allocation of PRIMAL KARMA to SOULS first entering this world and for adding and subtracting karma in the records of Souls in the LOWER WORLDS.

There are layers upon layers of lords, with a council of about twelve lords at the top of the pyramid; a single lord presides over the council and answers to the KAL NIRANJAN.

Individuals on the path of ECKANKAR are not subject to the Lords of Karma. When one first steps onto the ECK path, the LIVING ECK MASTER takes over that Soul's karma, arranges it, and provides guidance to help the CHELA work off karma and gain SPIRITUAL FREEDOM.

For more, see article 23, "How the Lords of Karma Work," in *Wisdom of the Heart*, Book 4.

See also AKASHIC RECORDS; BOOK OF LIFE; REINCARNATION.

Lord Sohang *See* SOHANG, LORD.

love *See* DIVINE LOVE.

love, days of *See* UTURAT.

Love, Law of One of the SPIRITUAL LAWS OF LIFE.

It is the great law of life: SOUL exists because God loves It. Everything revolves around love. To get love, you must give love; and Do unto others as you would have them do unto you.

The Law of Love supersedes KARMA. This is part of the SECRET DOCTRINE of ECK. The Law of Love alone can carry you to God.

See also DIVINE LOVE; GOLDEN CONTRACT, THE.

lower planes *See* LOWER WORLDS.

lower worlds The PLANES below the SOUL PLANE; from lowest to highest, the PHYSICAL, ASTRAL, CAUSAL, MENTAL, and ETHERIC PLANEs. Also called the lower planes, dualistic planes, or psychic planes (worlds), these are schools of experience for SOUL. The worlds of energy, matter, time, and space.

Each successive plane beyond the Physical has a higher proportion of Spirit to matter.

See also ECK-VIDYA WHEEL; **The God Worlds Chart** on page 340; SPIRITUAL WORLDS.

lust Also called kama, one of the FIVE PASSIONS OF THE MIND which bind SOUL to the LOWER WORLDS.

This is self-indulgence, overindulgence in anything; the degradation of sex; abnormal desires which includes drugs, alcoholic drinks, tobacco, or foods eaten only for taste.

The antidote for lust is DISCRIMINATION, one of the FIVE VIRTUES.

macrocosm and microcosm GOD-REALIZATION is attained by those who care about the little things. They know that the little things, the microcosm, contain the secrets of the macrocosm.

By learning the lessons of the little things at hand, we can develop the skills and talents to handle the greater scope of the Godhead.

Man is a microcosm of the vast macrocosm comprising all of CREATION. The action of Spirit is moving simultaneously in the macrocosm of the universe and in the microcosm of the individual.

The movement of the two harmonize because they are that of the same Spirit.

The bodies of each individual are a microcosm in which the macrocosm dwells. Each PLANE has both the universal and individual aspects which are both within us and without.

Man, the individual, the microcosm, is capable of reproducing all the qualities of God, the univer-

> sal, the macrocosm. Man learns that he is SOUL, a divine spark of God.

See also RECIPROCITY, LAW OF.

Magi *MAY-jie* A mystical order of the Zoroastrian religion, one of the ancient groups which secretly studied ECK and practiced It six hundred years before Christ. PYTHAGORAS was well versed in the mysteries of the Magi.

See also RAMA.

magic A psychic practice that is to be avoided in ECKANKAR. Magic includes any attempt to direct the ECK (Divine Spirit), whether through rituals, thought, word, or PRAYER.

Trying to change somebody else's life or way of thinking, without that person's permission, is a violation of spiritual law.

White magic involves the intent to do good, while black magic, at its darkest, seeks to harm or control others. Both forms of magic result in KARMA for the practitioner.

> An ECK INITIATE can practice KARMALESS ACTION by doing everything in the name of the MAHANTA, the LIVING ECK MASTER, for the good of the whole.

See also NONINTERFERENCE, LAW OF; PSYCHIC PHENOMENA.

maha *MAH-hah* A Sanskrit word meaning great.

Maha Kal *MAH-hah KAL* Another name for KAL NIRANJAN.

Maha Kal Brahm Another name for RAMKAR.

Maha Kal Lok *MAH-hah KAL LOHK* Another name for the MENTAL PLANE.

See also LOK.

Maha Nada *MAH-hah NAH-dah* Another name for the great music of the ECK, the life current.

See also ECK; NADA BINDU; SOUND CURRENT.

MAHANTA *mah-HAHN-tah* The MAHANTA, the LIVING ECK MASTER is the spiritual leader of ECKANKAR.

He makes the actual linkup between SOUL and the returning wave of the SOUND CURRENT via the ECK INITIATION. He can also release Soul from the WHEEL OF THE EIGHTY-FOUR.

The MAHANTA is an expression of the Spirit of God that is always with you. Sometimes he is seen as a Blue Light or Blue Star.

The MAHANTA can change one's fate. He is the Soul of all beings and the sole agent of God. In all things is his face, and in all life is he the divine seed.

He is the good that dwells in the heart of every mortal creature and loves Soul more than Soul loves Its defilements.

Also called the LIVING WORD, the Wayshower, the VI-GURU, and the LIGHT GIVER, this special incarnation of the SUGMAD makes an appearance once every five to a thousand or more years, depending on the part he is to play in a major upliftment of CONSCIOUSNESS on every PLANE.

The title of MAHANTA is transferred from one Living ECK Master to another, in an unbroken line, via the PASSING OF THE ROD OF ECK POWER.

When the MAHANTA, the Living ECK Master is a Fourteenth Initiate, the full force of the ROD OF ECK POWER and the Mantle of the MAHANTA are embodied directly in him. If the successor (a Twelfth or Thirteenth Initiate) is only appointed to carry the Rod of ECK Power instead of inheriting the crown, he still takes on the spiritual title of MAHANTA.

> The words of the MAHANTA alone can change the world, completely and irrevocably.

See also INNER AND OUTER MASTER; MAHANTA CONSCIOUSNESS; MAHANTAS, ORDER OF THE; QUINTAN.

MAHANTA, historical *See* THREE ASPECTS OF THE SUGMAD.

MAHANTA, primordial *See* THREE ASPECTS OF THE SUGMAD.

MAHANTA Consciousness The spiritual body of the MAHANTA is always with all people at all times.

> He has been the spiritual head of the world since its creation, manifesting physically to different races

at different periods of human history as the vehicle for the SUGMAD in the form to which they are most accustomed and by the name familiar to them.

If the people were Hindu, he has appeared as Krishna, Buddha, or Vishnu so they would know him. He was Zeus to the Greeks; Jupiter to the Romans; Osiris, Amun, Re, and Aton to the Egyptians; Jehovah to the old Judeans; Ishtar to the Babylonians; Varuna to the Aryans; Jesus to the Christians; and Allah to the Muslims.

He has appeared to all in every age of this world. He is the secret force behind world historical events. None can escape the SUGMAD, and none can be higher in this world and other worlds than the MAHANTA, the Divine One, who is the manifestation in body form of the eternal MAHANTA.

See also MAHANTA; THREE ASPECTS OF THE SUGMAD.

MAHANTA Maharai *mah-HAHN-tah MAH-hah-rie* One who has reached the THIRTEENTH INITIATION. He knows his relationship to the MAHANTA CONSCIOUSNESS.

MAHANTAS, Order of the A loosely knit brotherhood of all who once served as the MAHANTA, the LIVING ECK MASTER.

The members of this order exist to serve life. They obey the SUGMAD's bidding. This spiritual service to all living things is the reason for their being. They are also in a hierarchy; the longer they have served, the greater is their compassion and love for all creatures and beings of God.

See also MAHARAJ; VAIRAGI(S), ANCIENT ORDER OF THE.

Maharaj *mah-hah-RAHJ* These are the ECK INITIATES of the Ninth through Eleventh Circles. These ancient ones are the Brotherhood of ECK MASTERS, subordinate to the MAHANTA, the LIVING ECK MASTER who holds the ROD OF ECK POWER.

Maharaji *mah-hah-RAH-jee* One who has reached the TWELFTH INITIATION.

Mahavakyis *mah-hah-VAHK-yeez* The silent travelers; Silent Ones; agents of the SUGMAD who are responsible only to It. They are in command of the great SOUND CURRENT, and give aid and comfort to the SUGMAD in Its eternal home, as well as being in charge of the mechanical phases of the lower universes.

> All SOULS within all universes are within their orbit of affairs. Their duties are to see that every Soul, regardless of Its spiritual status, has the opportunity to enter into the Kingdom of God here and now.

It makes little difference which PLANE the Soul is on. It depends on the individual Soul to do what It will with the opportunity presented to It.

The Mahavakyis are part of a larger body of Silent Ones which includes the VOLAPUKS; they run the clockworks of the spirito-material worlds and come and go like shadows.

See also NINE SILENT ONES.

Mahaya Guru *mah-HAH-yah GOO-roo* The title of the GUARDIAN of the holy book, the SHARIYAT-KI-SUGMAD, on the AGAM LOK, the Ninth PLANE, at the KAZI DAWTZ GOLDEN WISDOM TEMPLE; this is currently AGNOTTI.

For a list of noted guardians, see **A Road Map for Spiritual Travelers** on page 343.

mahayuga *mah-hah-YOO-gah* The grand cycle of cosmic history, lasting 4,320,000 years. Also known as a Day of the SUGMAD. Sometimes called a kalpa or manvantara. It consists of four ages (YUGAS):

1. The **Satya Yuga,** the Golden Age, 1,728,000 years, or four-tenths of the cycle.
2. The **Tretya Yuga,** the Silver Age, 1,296,000 years, or three-tenths of the cycle.
3. The **Dwapara Yuga,** the Copper Age, 864,000 years, or two-tenths of the cycle.
4. The **Kali Yuga,** the Iron Age, 432,000 years, or one-tenth of the cycle.

At the end of each mahayuga, the LOWER WORLDS are destroyed, and SOULS are drawn up to the SOUL PLANE. There they find themselves in original unity and bliss, in a life of total peace. This period is sometimes called a Night of the SUGMAD and lasts as long as a mahayuga. Then the grand cycle starts again, and the Souls in need of experience are returned to the new worlds of matter for a fresh start.

For more about Soul's journey through these ages, see FOUR CYCLES OF LIFE.

Mahdis *MAH-dees* One who has reached the FIFTH INITIATION. Sometimes used as a generic term for all HIGH INITIATEs in ECK.

Malati *mah-LAH-tee* The first ECK MASTER of record among the POLARIANS who was sent by the SUGMAD to give man his first spiritual knowledge of God. ECK Masters, like Malati, introduced sign language to combat the linguistic turmoil of early man.

For a list of ECK Masters, see page 341.

Mana *MAH-nah* Often chanted as *mah-NAY* or *mah-NAH*. A spiritually charged word attuned to the CAUSAL PLANE, the Third PLANE.

You can chant *Mana* in CONTEMPLATION to visit GOLDEN WISDOM TEMPLES, meet ECK MASTERS, and have other experiences on this plane.

For an overview of the planes and their charged words, see **The God Worlds Chart** on page 340.

Manas *MAH-nahs* One of the four faculties of the MIND. Manas has the power to receive feeling, taste, smell, and hearing.

The other faculties are AHANKAR, BUDDHI, and CHITTA.

mantra *MAHN-trah* A word or phrase which is chanted in order to link up with Divine Spirit, the ECK.

It can be described as a sacred prayer-song which, when repeatedly chanted, gradually converts the devotee into a living center of spiritual vibration which is attuned to some other center of vibration vastly more powerful than his own.

Chanting a mantra produces a series of spiritual effects, mainly that of love. When one concentrates the MIND on the mantra, a deep sense of peace and love arises. Mantra chanting focuses the mind to a sharp point that is capable of penetrating through the ordinary thoughts to the deeper layers of Soul which lie beneath.

To the ordinary man, the mantra would appear to be nonsensical. Nevertheless, it is a powerful instrument of love and DETACHMENT for that ECK CHELA who practices it regularly.

He reaches out to people whom he will never know and changes the course of their lives from the KAL forces which might be gripping them to the ECK, which will lead them to God.

Few, if any, will ever learn what has happened, but the mantra built up by the ECKists, either individually or collectively, will bring about a change in the worlds: first the world of man and then that of the spiritual heavens where necessary.

Knowledge of the creative word lives deeply in the heart of every ECK INITIATE.

It is the LIVING ECK MASTER who brings the opportunity of love via the mantra to the chela. He gives the secret mantra to those who deserve it, and thereafter the responsibility lies in the hands of the chela, who can make the best of it if he is at all spiritually observant and energetic.

The essential mantra in ECKANKAR is HU.

See also HU; HU CHANT; SECRET WORD; ZIKAR.

manvantara *mahn-vahn-TAH-rah* Another word for MAHAYUGA.

marg *MAHRG* *See* SEVEN MARGS.

Marpa *MAHR-pah* Known as Marpa, the Translator. Teacher to MILAREPA, Marpa was secretly an ECK MASTER.

> Once, when Milarepa and other disciples approached Marpa and offered to help carry some of his spiritual load, Marpa at first said no. Then, when the disciples asked again, he put a little of the load on a heavy oak door.
>
> The oak door split, and the disciples learned that each individual is given, or earns, his share of the LIGHT AND SOUND, the blessings of ECK.

For a list of ECK Masters, see page 341.

masculine principle *See* PRINCIPLES, FEMININE AND MASCULINE.

Masnavi *mahs-NAH-vee* A book of poems or couplets written by RUMI, the Persian poet and mystic, to express the glory and love of God.

Master *See* ECK MASTERS; INNER AND OUTER MASTER; LIVING ECK MASTER.

Master's Gaze *See* GAZE OF THE MASTER.

Master techniques Two techniques for SOUL TRAVEL given in the ECK SPIRITUAL LIVING COURSES—the DAKAYA TECHNIQUE and the SUANG-TU TECHNIQUE.

They are used by the ECK MASTERS and can be used by ECK CHELAS as well.

Mastership ECK Mastership is the goal for every male and female in ECK. The individual must determine to live and act as the ECK MASTERS do, giving love and service to life in every way imaginable.

Five Keys to ECK Mastership

1. Give thanks for every gift, however small.
2. Be the best you can.
3. Do the best you can.
4. Love the gift of life.
5. Know that ECK is love.

Each of us must someday become the Sound and LIGHT, for in them alone is found the way to God.

See also COWORKER(S) WITH GOD; COWORKER(S) WITH THE MAHANTA.

Matax Roraka *MAH-taks roh-RAH-kah* Succeeded VAJRA MANJUSHRI as the MAHANTA, the LIVING ECK MASTER after having once been one of his greatest doubters.

For a list of ECK MASTERS, see page 341.

material universe The world of energy, matter, space, and time; the ever changing; that of momentary existence; illusion, MAYA.

See also LOWER WORLDS.

Maulani *mah-oo-LAH-nee* One who has received the NINTH INITIATION.

maya *MAH-yah* Many define the world as illusion, or maya, but the ECK CHELA should not think that the world is deprived of all reality—only that it is not what it appears. Its reality is relative. Maya is the way the unenlightened man perceives reality—as limited to matter, energy, space, and time. It is the viewpoint of the MIND or HUMAN CONSCIOUSNESS.

The MAHANTA leads chelas out of the snares of maya into higher STATES OF CONSCIOUSNESS. With this ENLIGHTENMENT comes the awakened viewpoint of SOUL, which extends beyond the LOWER WORLDS into the infinite reality of the SPIRITUAL WORLDS.

See also UNIVERSAL MIND.

Maybury's Two Laws These two laws were originally presented by economist and political analyst Richard Maybury: (1) Do all you have agreed to do, and (2) do not encroach on other persons or their property.

These laws provide a useful code of conduct for ethical living—telling right from wrong—in this world of cause and effect.

May the blessings be *See* BARAKA BASHAD.

Mearp region *meh-AHRP* This is where the SOUL RECORDS of the MAHDIS are kept, within the SOUL PLANE.

The Soul records of those who have had the SIXTH INITIATION are kept in the ANUGA REGION. The ECK-NIDA REGION is where the Soul records of those who have received the SEVENTH INITIATION through TWELFTH INITIATION are kept.

meditation Traditional meditation is a method used by some spiritual paths to seek connection with God; it is a passive state in which the practitioner tries to draw GOD-REALIZATION into himself to attain oneness with God. It is an attempt to use the FEMININE PRINCIPLE to accomplish that which is neither feminine nor masculine.

In ECKANKAR, CONTEMPLATION—a lighter, more active form of meditation—is practiced to reach SELF-REALIZATION and God-Realization.

See also PRAYER; SPIRITUAL EXERCISES OF ECK.

Melnibora *mehl-NEE-boh-rah* The mighty empire of the HYPERBOREANS, the second ROOT RACE; ruled by the fierce VARKAS kings for a hundred centuries.

memory body *See* CAUSAL BODY.

Mental body One of the BODIES OF SOUL (the others are the PHYSICAL BODY, ASTRAL BODY, CAUSAL BODY, and ETHERIC BODY). The Mental body is the protective sheath SOUL uses for experience and expression on the MENTAL PLANE. Also called the Mental Sharir.

See also **The God Worlds Chart** on page 340; MIND; SOUL BODY.

Mental Plane The Fourth PLANE (counting upward) of the LOWER WORLDS. It is the seat of the UNIVERSAL MIND Power and the source of philosophy, ethics, moral teachings, and aesthetics.

Distinctions of the Mental Plane

AUM (pronounced *AHM* or *ah-UHM*) is a word, or CHANT, that one can sing in CONTEMPLATION to

attune oneself to the VIBRATIONS of the Mental Plane or SOUL TRAVEL to a GOLDEN WISDOM TEMPLE or other places there.

An inner experience on this plane may include seeing blue light or hearing the sound of running water.

The HALL OF BRAHMANDA is a Golden Wisdom Temple on this plane; here SATO KURAJ, an ECK MASTER, serves as GUARDIAN of the SHARIYAT-KI-SUGMAD.

The city of MER KAILASH is on the Mental Plane; within this city is the Golden Wisdom Temple of NAMAYATAN; here TOWART MANAGI, the KOJI CHANDA, serves as guardian of the Shariyat-Ki-SUGMAD.

Other ECK Masters working on this plane are JANOS MONETA, TEJAHUA, and WU TENNA (spiritual head of a Golden Wisdom Temple).

The Mental Plane is sometimes called the Maha Kal Lok or Par Brahm Lok; its ruler is OMKAR.

See also **The God Worlds Chart** on page 340.

Mental Sharir *See* MENTAL BODY.

Mental worlds A general term that includes the CAUSAL PLANE, MENTAL PLANE, and ETHERIC PLANE.

Mer *MEHR* One of three mountain peaks on the MENTAL PLANE; the other two are SUMER and KAILASH.

Mer Kailash *MEHR KIE-lahsh* The city on the MENTAL PLANE where the SHARIYAT-KI-SUGMAD is kept in the GOLDEN WISDOM TEMPLE.

Mesi Gokaritz *MEH-see goh-KAHR-eets* The MAHANTA, the LIVING ECK MASTER in the early days of Greece. He is the TSONG SIKHSA, the GUARDIAN of the SHARIYAT-KI-SUGMAD at the ANAKAMUDI TEMPLE on the ALAYA LOK, the Seventh PLANE.

For a list of ECK MASTERS, see page 341.

microcosm *See* MACROCOSM AND MICROCOSM.

middle path Three forces affect humankind: the positive, the negative, and the all-important neutral force.

The neutral or middle way is the ECK path. It is neither positive nor negative, neither masculine (forcing) nor feminine (passive). It is the balanced, well-adjusted outlook—neither being for nor against.

One need not indulge in excesses of any kind to gain spiritually. An ECKIST learns how to walk the middle path and so become a conscious COWORKER WITH GOD twenty-four hours a day.

> Good, sincere humor keeps you on the middle path.

Milarepa *mi-lah-REH-pah* An ECK MASTER, one of the highest in the ancient brotherhood. He has the ability to uplift the CHELA directly through the HEART CENTER.

Description

Milarepa wears a knee-length maroon robe and carries a short walking stick. His face is round, and his eyes are dark, twinkling buttons. He is completely bald and looks like a sweet, mild-tempered Buddha.

The aura around him is permeated with the fragrant aroma of roses and the brightest light. There is the sound of a conch shell being blown in the distance when you view him. His appearance is one of the greatest blessings that we can have.

Biographical Sketch

Like all ECK Masters, Milarepa had a life of undue hardship. Through it all he kept his sense of humor. He is pleasant, buoyant, and good-natured.

Milarepa was an eleventh-century Tibetan saint and poet whose life story is widely known.

The wealthy family Milarepa was born into was reduced to poverty when his father died and the family fortune was stolen. Seeking revenge, his mother sent him to a magician for training in the black arts, which Milarepa used to destroy his enemies. In doing so, he accumulated a great karmic debt.

In time, the ECK led him to MARPA, an ECK Master who put him through severe trials.

Marpa instructed Milarepa to hand-build a house of stone. Upon its completion, Marpa found fault with the building and ordered Milarepa to tear it

down and rebuild it. This occurred repeatedly.

Though bruised and battered in body, mind, and spirit, Milarepa's devotion never wavered. Marpa noted his love for the secret teachings.

Eventually, Milarepa was able to work off all his KARMA in that lifetime and set out on the road that would lead him to ECK MASTERSHIP. To accomplish this, he contemplated in secluded caves for years.

Among the supernatural skills he developed was levitation: periodically he found it convenient to fly from one place to another in the rugged Tibetan countryside. He also learned to travel in his dreams and to free himself from his PHYSICAL BODY through SOUL TRAVEL, allowing him to move among the worlds and PLANES of CREATION.

For a list of ECK Masters, see page 341.

mind The mind's chief function is to serve as an instrument for SOUL to make all Its contact with the psychic and material worlds. There is only one mind acting on different PLANES.

The mind is also the channel through which the negative force, or KAL NIRANJAN, attempts to control Soul and keep It in the LOWER WORLDS through the FIVE PASSIONS OF THE MIND.

Four Faculties of the Mind

- **Chitta**, which takes cognizance of form, beauty, color, rhythm, harmony, and perspective, receiving its impressions mainly through the eyes.

- **Manas**, which has the power to receive feeling, taste, smell, and hearing.
- **Buddhi**, the intellect proper, chief instrument of thought, DISCRIMINATION, decision, and judgment.
- **Ahankar**, the faculty of separating self and self-interest from all else; the I-ness, the faculty which executes orders; when exaggerated, it becomes VANITY.

See also ALIVA MIND; KARAN MIND; PINDA MIND; SUKHSHAM MIND.

mineral state The mineral kingdom. The state in which CONSCIOUSNESS (SOUL) sleeps imprisoned in the rocklike substance of minerals.

This is one of the STATES OF CONSCIOUSNESS Soul experiences via REINCARNATION before It reaches the state of HUMAN CONSCIOUSNESS.

See also REALIZATION, LEVEL(S) OF.

minimasters Refers to those who claim, either overtly or subtly, to be a spiritual leader, guide, or figurehead in ECKANKAR in order to gain a personal following and influence others.

The LORDS OF KARMA never hurry justice. As long as those individuals stay within their present STATES OF CONSCIOUSNESS, their lives will go on as before. But should they ever want to go on toward GOD-REALIZATION, then the old debts created by their VANITY are recalled for payment. That is when they enter the college of hard knocks.

Typically they won't see that the cause for all their trouble is themselves.

Mksha *MUHK-shah* An ancient ECK sage and LIVING ECK MASTER who appeared on earth some 35,000 years ago to teach the people of the Indus Valley the fundamental laws which govern the physical universe.

He also traveled to the Americas in the SOUL BODY, at a time when natives there were using spears to hunt the giant sloth, the woolly mammoth, and the giant beaver.

See also PHYSICAL UNIVERSE, LAWS OF THE.

For a list of ECK Masters, see page 341.

moha *MOH-hah* *See* ATTACHMENT.

Moksha *MOHK-shah* Release from the WHEEL OF AWAGAWAN, birth, death, and rebirth in the LOWER WORLDS; liberation from this wheel through the MAHANTA.

See also HOUSE OF MOKSHA; SPIRITUAL FREEDOM.

Moksha, House of *MOHK-shah* *See* HOUSE OF MOKSHA.

Mokshove *mohk-SHOHV* The eighth MONTH OF THE ECK-VIDYA, corresponding to August. The days of light. The month of the diamond.

The journey of Mokshove brings the translation of spiritual knowledge into great truths by SOUL.

See also ECK-VIDYA WHEEL.

Mongoloid race The sixth ROOT RACE, the yellow race which will come after the current ARYAN RACE. REGNARD will be the ECK MASTER of the time.

month(s) of the ECK-Vidya These twelve periods of the ECK-VIDYA WHEEL correspond to months of the year and signify major experiences SOUL goes through in Its many incarnations.

The names and major experiences are as follows:

1. ASTIK (January), the step where Soul's primary search is for courage for all future incarnations
2. UTURAT (February), the period which brings Soul great concern for love, companionship, and wealth
3. GARVATA (March), the stage during which Soul is restless and has a great sense of urgency
4. EBKIA (April), the journey where Soul's primary search is for peace
5. RALOT (May), the phase where there is a need for the outward manifestation of Soul's inner search
6. SAHAK (June), the era where Soul seeks a resting-place where It can work out Its destiny in peace and quiet
7. KAMITOC (July), the stage where freedom comes through knowledge
8. MOKSHOVE (August), the step which brings the translation of spiritual knowledge into great truths by Soul

9. **Dzyani** (September), the journey of high success, power, achievement, and splendor
10. **Parinama** (October), a quiet period in the journey of Soul, where It strives for the common good—not for glory, but for honor
11. **Hortar** (November), the era where Soul begins to see liberation
12. **Niyamg** (December), the phase where loose ends of Soul's incarnations are gathered up

Moon Worlds Along with the Lightning Worlds and Sun Worlds, these are subplanes which lie between the Physical Plane and the true Astral Plane.

Moraji Desal *moh-RAH-jee deh-SAHL* The Living ECK Master who came after Gopal Das. This was around 1792–50 BC, when Hammurabi ruled Babylon and the land of Canaan was part of his empire.

Moraji Desal traveled most of the kingdom by foot, preaching ECK to all who would listen. He also helped write the great Hammurabic code of laws. Yet he was hunted much of the time by the priestcraft, who believed he was preaching a pagan religion.

For a list of ECK Masters, see page 341.

mountain of death *See* Yama, Mountain of.

Mountain of Light The mountain of Sahasra-dal-Kanwal; the powerhouse of the Astral and the Physical, or Pinda, universe; a huge dynamo out of which flows all the power that creates and sustains all the creations below it.

See also ASTRAL PLANE.

Mountain of Yama *See* YAMA, MOUNTAIN OF.

Mountain world *See* SURATI LOK.

Mu *MOO* Another name for LEMURIA.

Mumsaka *muhm-SAH-ka* One of the ten SPIRITUAL CITIES which help this world, located in the Caucasus Mountains of Georgia, north of easternmost Turkey.

The beings here are the protectors of the MIND of man, keeping it on the road to God. They helped spread Buddhism and uplift the Oriental mind.

The other nine spiritual cities are AGAM DES, AKEVIZ, DAMCAR, KIMTAVED, NAMPAK, RAHAKAZ, SAT DHAM, SHAMBALLA, and ZEZIRATH.

music, days of *See* SAHAK.

Music of the Spheres Mentioned by the ECK MASTER PYTHAGORAS and other philosophers, the Music of the Spheres is the Spirit of the Unwritten TRUTH, the HU, the SOUND CURRENT, the ECK Itself.

Other words for It are BANI, Nad, QUALIMA, heavenly music, and the WORD. It is the Sound we listen for in CONTEMPLATION.

At first it is weak, often imperceptible, but variable. However, by continual training, a transformation takes place, and the Music of the Spheres is heard quite distinctly. Its divine and delectable Sound is of a sweetness and serenity unsurpassed by any.

> This Music draws SOUL upward by Its strong power, like a powerful magnet. It purifies all which Soul picked up as dross during Its sojourn on earth. As the awakened CONSCIOUSNESS makes Soul partake of the joys of heaven, It becomes a greater channel for the MAHANTA to use for spreading the message of ECKANKAR.
>
> Thus Soul, severed from MAYA and its illusions, its seeds of desires, its hopes and fears, is liberated and established in the great Reality of ECK.

See also DHUNATMIK.

Muzuart *MOO-zoo-ahrt* The twelfth TWELVE-YEAR CYCLE of the ECK-VIDYA; called the Years of the Trembling Leaf. Also the twelfth year within a twelve-year cycle.

See also ECK-VIDYA WHEEL.

mystery school(s) Historically, groups of initiates gathered under the guiding hand of a master, or teacher of the spiritual truths, who revealed the mysteries of nature and the universe.

Some of the earliest known mystery schools were in ancient Egypt, where GOPAL DAS founded the mystery schools of OSIRIS and Isis. PYTHAGORAS was instructed in the Egyptian rites and later led a mystery school in ancient Greece, adapted for the consciousness of that people. YAUBL SACABI also helped set up the mystery schools in ancient Greece.

Great prophets such as RAMA, KRISHNA, Hermes, Moses, Orpheus, Plato, and JESUS were known to have been students in the various mystery schools.

ECKANKAR is a modern-day mystery school. All religions and philosophies are the offspring of ECK, the fountainhead of all life.

Naacal records *NAH-kahl* These are the first known records of mankind—the writings of the third ROOT RACE, the Lemurians. YUONT-NA, a teacher of ECK and TOTAL AWARENESS, is mentioned in them. They are kept at the KATSUPARI MONASTERY, in Tibet, under the GUARDIANship of the ECK MASTERS.

Nada Bindu *NAH-dah BIN-doo* The SOUND CURRENT. The seed Sound from which all things grow. The ECK, the BANI.

Nalpa Keljina *NAHL-pah kehl-JEE-nah* The LIVING ECK MASTER who lived in Greece during the time of the Trojan War, 1200 BC.

For a list of ECK MASTERS, see page 341.

Nam *NAHM* The word of the INITIATION; the word that issues from the heart of God; what God says or does; the Divine Being in action; the living ECK or the living WORD.

Namayatan *nah-mah-YAH-tahn* GOLDEN WISDOM TEMPLE in the city of MER KAILASH on the MENTAL PLANE.

It is similar in appearance to the Temple of Diana in Ephesus, where ECKANKAR was taught in ancient times. One may hear the sound of running water when near this temple.

The KOJI CHANDA, currently TOWART MANAGI, is GUARDIAN of the SHARIYAT-KI-SUGMAD here.

Nameless Plane *See* ANAMI LOK.

Nampak *NAHM-pahk* Located in Africa near the western border of Uganda. It is one of the ten SPIRITUAL CITIES which are on earth to help the world.

The beings here help with the care of SOULS that leave the body at death, especially those who have no one to help them cross the borders of life and death.

The other nine spiritual cities are AGAM DES, AKEVIZ, DAMCAR, KIMTAVED, MUMSAKA, RAHAKAZ, SAT DHAM, SHAMBALLA, and ZEZIRATH.

neophyte An ASPIRANT; a beginner in the ECK spiritual works.

Neralit *neh-rah-LEET* The tenth TWELVE-YEAR CYCLE of the ECK-VIDYA; called the Years of the Raging Fires. Also the tenth year within a twelve-year cycle.

See also ECK-VIDYA WHEEL.

nibbuta *ni-BOO-tah* The stage of life when the fires of GREED, hate, VANITY, ATTACHMENT, and other passions have been extinguished; beyond all egoistic desires and illusions. This is the first stage of holi-

ness for the ECK CHELA—the beginning of real life for him.

nidanas *nee-DAHN-ahz* The causes that move each individual SOUL to reincarnate; the twelve ECK-VIDYA signs, or cycles of transmigratory existence, each of which contains within it an impulse to action, or a cause that brings Soul back again into this world.

See also MONTHS OF THE ECK-VIDYA; REINCARNATION.

Night of the SUGMAD (Night of God) See DAY AND NIGHT OF THE SUGMAD; FOUR CYCLES OF LIFE; MAHAYUGA.

Nij mind *See* KARAN MIND.

Nine Silent Ones These Silent Ones are a very mysterious brotherhood. Agents of the SUGMAD, their main duty is to gather up and sort out the unchanging laws that enfold every ripple in life.

There is also a larger body of Silent Ones made up of the MAHAVAKYIS and the VOLAPUKS. They run the clockworks of the spirito-material worlds. They come and go like shadows.

nine unknown ECK Masters *See* COUNCIL OF THE NINE.

nine unknown Gods of Eternity The nine unknown Gods of Eternity are the keepers of the Divine Flame of WISDOM. They watch over and guard the golden scripts of the SUGMAD.

The nine unknown Gods gather the sacred knowledge that derives from the unfoldment of spiritual CONSCIOUSNESS on every PLANE throughout all creation.

These Gods let only a few into their temples to learn the deeper knowledge of what the secret truths might hold for them.

The nine unknown Gods are different from the ECK MASTERS who act as the teachers, instructors, and watch-guards for the portions of the SHARIYAT-KI-SUGMAD kept upon each PLANE. The nine unknown Gods transform the living TRUTH of SUGMAD into knowledge. ECK Masters teach the divine knowledge of this truth, which is simply the manifestation of the SUGMAD's love, to seekers who are ready for it.

When this knowledge comes to an open heart, the result is love, wisdom, and SPIRITUAL FREEDOM.

See also COUNCIL OF THE NINE; NINE SILENT ONES; GUARDIAN(S); MAHAVAKYIS; VOLAPUKS.

Ninth Initiation This is the INITIATION of the AGAM LOK, the Ninth Plane. It is given only through the inner channels after an ECK INITIATE has received all the outer initiations. The MAHANTA, the LIVING ECK MASTER will outwardly acknowledge the initiation to the CHELA.

The Ninth Initiate works with the VIBRATIONS governing all the phases of planetary life. He is the Maulani.

He is the vanguard of the human race because he has fully surrendered himself to the ways of ECK. He becomes honest to the point of pain to himself. He only wants to see that each SOUL has the opportunity

to gain salvation through ECK.

The sacred mystery of the ECK lies in the Initiation of the Ninth Circle.

For a list of the ECK initiations, see page 338.

Ninth Plane *See* AGAM LOK.

Niranjan *nee-RAHN-jahn* The negative power in the LOWER WORLDS.

See also KAL NIRANJAN.

Niranjan, Jot *See* JOT NIRANJAN.

Niranjan, Kal *See* KAL NIRANJAN.

Nirat *nee-RAHT* The LIGHT. Also a SPIRITUAL EXERCISE OF ECK wherein one looks for the Light.

See also SURAT.

Nirguna and Saguna *neer-GOO-nah* and *sah-GOO-nah* The SUGMAD, as we know It, has two parts—an inside and an outside. The inside is called Nirguna, which is to say that it has no qualities and nothing can be said or thought about it.

The outside is called Saguna, which is to say that it may be considered as eternal reality, CONSCIOUSNESS, and joy. This is the part that man knows and remembers after experiencing the GOD-REALIZATION state.

Nirguna Ekam *neer-GOO-nah EHK-ahm* An ECK MASTER who is one of the GUARDIANS of the SHARIYAT-KI-SUGMAD at the Temple of PARAM AKSHAR on the SOUL PLANE.

Description

He is like a golden Buddha, a light within himself, so marvelous that often we see nothing but his misty aura. But a closer look shows that he is standing there, ready to take our hand, as we enter the Soul Plane from the MENTAL PLANE, and guide us to SAT NAM, the first manifestation of God, where we find SELF-REALIZATION.

Nirguna Ekam is tall and well formed. He is accompanied by the sounds of birds singing and sometimes the harp. His features are classic, skin almost a golden color; his eyes are like the azure blue of the sky, and his hair is golden-blond.

He is a fountain of WISDOM pouring out to all with whom he comes in contact. His maroon robe is short, knee-length in size, and roped at the waist in the typical fashion of the ECK Master.

For a list of ECK Masters, see page 341.

nirvana *neer-VAH-nah* The desireless state of enlightenment sought by the Buddhist. A STATE OF CONSCIOUSNESS that can be experienced on the MENTAL PLANE.

Nirvikalpa *neer-vee-KAHL-pah* The deepest form of CONTEMPLATION. Here, the contemplator becomes one with his ideal, the ECK. This is the far-reaching state where SOUL becomes indistinguishable from the ECK Itself.

This spiritual STATE OF CONSCIOUSNESS belongs in

the area of the true ECK worlds. It leads to DETACHMENT, which eventually takes the CHELA through the varied INITIATIONs into the Ninth, when he is invited into the Order of the VAIRAGI, the ECK MASTERS.

See also GOD-REALIZATION; NINTH INITIATION; SAMADHI; VAIRAGI(S), ANCIENT ORDER OF THE.

Niyamg *nee-YAHMG* The twelfth MONTH OF THE ECK-VIDYA, corresponding to December. The days of CHARITY. The month of the onyx.

A period where the loose ends of SOUL'S INCARNATIONS are gathered up.

See also ECK-VIDYA WHEEL.

Noninterference, Law of One of the SPIRITUAL LAWS OF LIFE. It is SOUL's responsibility not to interfere in the affairs of another Soul, but to allow others their freedom.

Even the LIVING ECK MASTER does not enter into someone's personal affairs without definite permission. This spiritual law forbids it.

numbers, doctrine of *See* DOCTRINE OF NUMBERS.

Nuri *NOO-ree* LIGHT, or Light body; ASTRAL BODY.

Nuri Sarup *NOO-ree sah-ROOP* *See* ASTRAL BODY; RADIANT BODY.

Ocean of Love and Mercy The home, or heart, of God. The dwelling place of the SUGMAD (God), the reality of all realities, a place of joy and delight.

It projects Itself in the form of waves emerging out of a fountain. Since It contains all the qualities of the SUGMAD, It can only appear on the lower PLANES, including the physical, as a form of CONSCIOUSNESS.

All SOULS are created in the Ocean of Love and Mercy and are destined to return there and become COWORKERS WITH GOD.

See also AKAHA; **The God Worlds Chart** on page 340.

om *See* AUM.

Omkar *OHM-kahr* The ruler of the MENTAL PLANE. The power of the negative on the Mental Plane, or the region of the UNIVERSAL MIND.

See also **The God Worlds Chart** on page 340.

omnipotence Being all-powerful. This is an attribute, or quality, of the SUGMAD, the ECK, and the MAHANTA.

It is also a natural quality of SOUL when, via SPIRITUAL UNFOLDMENT, It becomes the ECK Itself.

omnipresence Being present everywhere, in all things. This is an attribute, or quality, of the SUGMAD, the ECK, and the MAHANTA. It is also a natural quality of SOUL when, via SPIRITUAL UNFOLDMENT, It becomes the ECK Itself.

omniscience Being all-knowing; having TOTAL AWARENESS. This is an attribute, or quality, of the SUGMAD, the ECK, and the MAHANTA. It is also a natural quality of SOUL when, via SPIRITUAL UNFOLDMENT, It becomes the ECK Itself.

Opposites, Law of *See* POLARITY, LAW OF.

Oracle of Delphi ECK MASTERS PAUL TWITCHELL and HAROLD KLEMP have both visited the site of the Oracle of Delphi, in Greece, which still speaks to those who have the ears to hear.

See also ORACLE OF TIRMER.

Oracle of Tirmer *teer-MEER* A craggy, unexplored site, sometimes called the Valley of Tirmer, in the VALLEY OF SHANGTA in Tibet, where the VOICE OF AKIVASHA is located.

The PASSING OF THE ROD OF ECK POWER from the LIVING ECK MASTER to his successor occurs here at midnight leading up to October 22.

Order of the MAHANTAS *See* MAHANTAS, ORDER OF THE.

Order of the VAIRAGI *See* VAIRAGI(S), ANCIENT ORDER OF THE.

Ori Diogo *OH-ree dee-OH-goh* The LIVING ECK MASTER during the time of Julius Caesar. He foretold the death of Caesar. Few knew Ori Diogo, but he helped shape much of the world in those days for spiritual advancement.

He chose his work on the ASTRAL PLANE, where he is in charge of healing for those who come across after death from some accident, disease, or other affliction.

For a list of ECK MASTERS, see page 341.

Orpheus *OHR-fee-uhs* A musician who was a student in the ancient MYSTERY SCHOOLS. The Orphic mystery school came out of his teachings and sacred poems.

Ousia *OO-see-ah* The spiritual essence that flows out of the Godhead; the ECK.

See also ECK.

Outer Master *See* INNER AND OUTER MASTER.

pad *PAHD* PLANE or place. Similar to LOK.

Padma Gaya *PAHD-mah GAH-yah* The LIVING ECK MASTER at Nineveh when it was destroyed by the Babylonians in 612 BC. He was present at the building of the Hanging Gardens by Nebuchadnezzar as well as the destruction of King Solomon's Temple.

For a list of ECK MASTERS, see page 341.

Padma Samba *PAHD-mah SAHM-bah* The title of the ECK MASTER who is the GUARDIAN of the SHARIYAT-KI-SUGMAD, the holy book of ECK in the SATA VISIC PALACE, the GOLDEN WISDOM TEMPLE on the ANAMI LOK, the Tenth Plane of the GOD WORLDS OF ECK.

For a list of noted guardians, see **A Road Map for Spiritual Travelers** on page 343.

pantheism A belief that God is in everything and everything is God; the worship of all gods.

Parabrahm *pah-rah-BRAHM* Another name for the ETHERIC PLANE. This is a very thin world above the BRAHM LOK, or MENTAL PLANE—between the Mental and SOUL PLANES. Parabrahm is also the title of the ruler of this PLANE.

Param Akshar *PAH-rahm AHK-shahr* The GOLDEN WISDOM TEMPLE, the House of Imperishable Knowledge, on the SOUL PLANE, the Atma Lok.

Par Brahm *PAHR BRAHM* Another name for the KAL NIRANJAN, Lord of the MENTAL PLANE, whose duties are to make all seekers of God believe this is the top of the worlds, the final resting-place.

Par Brahm Lok Another term for the MENTAL PLANE.

See also LOK; PAR BRAHM.

Parinama *pah-ree-NAH-mah* The tenth MONTH OF THE ECK-VIDYA, corresponding to October. The days of beauty. The month of the jasper.

The quiet period in the journey of SOUL, where It strives for the common good; not for glory, but for honor.

See also ECK-VIDYA WHEEL.

passing of the Rod of ECK Power The age-old INITIATION, given by the SUGMAD alone, which transfers spiritual authority from the departing LIVING ECK MASTER to the new one. The outgoing MAHANTA, the Living ECK Master names his successor—a Twelfth Initiate or higher—and the ROD OF ECK POWER is passed to him.

October 22

This rite, overseen by YAUBL SACABI, traditionally occurs at midnight leading up to October 22, at the ORACLE OF TIRMER, in the VALLEY OF SHANGTA, near the KATSUPARI MONASTERY.

All the ECK MASTERS gather in the Valley of Shangta to see the departing Master pass the Rod of ECK Power to his successor, and to greet him.

Nearby gather ECK INITIATES of every level who have a special need to be there.

Prior to the ceremony, the spiritual hierarchy, reflecting the will of the SUGMAD, has made the decision as to who is the most qualified in the ORDER OF THE VAIRAGI to become the next Living ECK Master. All the ECK Masters have had a close interest in the candidate's spiritual education, though the current Living ECK Master handles the final phase of training.

The new Living ECK Master, upon acceptance of his mission, is given recognition in the Order of the VAIRAGI as the key vehicle for the PRIMORDIAL MAHANTA, the sublime ECK in expression at the highest level. His instructions now come directly from the Source of Life Itself. Henceforth the will of the SUGMAD determines his actions on a grand scale.

The passing of the Rod of ECK Power is the marriage of the MACROCOSM AND MICROCOSM in him.

Role of the Torchbearer

Should the outgoing Living ECK Master depart the physical field of action prior to the passing of the Rod of ECK Power, his named successor takes on all the physical duties of spiritual leadership in ECKANKAR.

The Torchbearer of ECKANKAR, REBAZAR TARZS, carries the spiritual power until October 22 when the Rod of ECK Power is passed.

Modern Era

The passing of the Rod of ECK Power has been repeated since before recorded history, ensuring that the world is never without a Living ECK Master.

In the modern era, the rite took place in 1965, 1971, and 1981. The most recent occurrence was in October 1981, when SRI HAROLD KLEMP, a Fourteenth Initiate, accepted the Rod of ECK Power.

The change in spiritual leadership is always a step forward for the CONSCIOUSNESS of the worlds.

See also FIVE SPIRITUAL LEADERS OF MODERN-DAY ECKANKAR; VAIRAGI(S), ANCIENT ORDER OF THE.

passions of the mind *See* FIVE PASSIONS OF THE MIND.

past lives Past-life recall is a prominent feature of ECKANKAR. People are often startled to learn that they carry the past with them on their shirtsleeves.

Whenever we have strong loves or hates, it means we have drawn the past into the present by agreement.

The past is old emotions collected and gathered around us like keepsakes. They appear to us as family members, friends, and enemies. Our past thoughts and actions even shape our physical appearance, as well as our character and temperament.

The cause of everything that occurs in our life is chronicled on the CAUSAL PLANE, and we are a reflection of that journal.

All the lives you have ever lived were for the polishing of SOUL. Regardless of your station or circumstances, you are now at a higher spiritual level than in any previous lifetime.

The Causal Plane is where you find the seed of all KARMA created in the past and learn about the past lives that influence you today.

A Technique to Try

There are various ways to rediscover your past lives. This learning can take place in the DREAM STATE or via the SPIRITUAL EXERCISES OF ECK.

One technique is to chant the word *MANA*, the word for the Causal Plane, in CONTEMPLATION. Ask for the MAHANTA's help to see a past life that would be beneficial for you to be aware of at this time.

See also AKASHIC RECORDS; ECK-VIDYA; REINCARNATION; SOUL RECORDS; WHEEL OF THE EIGHTY-FOUR.

path of Soul The path of SOUL is simply to contemplate the life, love, and beauty of the ECK, affirming ourselves as already giving expression to It. We are each a channel, in thought, feeling, and action, however insignificant our expression of It may appear in the present.

This path is very narrow and humble in its beginning, but it grows ever wider and mounts higher, for it is the continually expanding expression of the action of Divine Spirit, which is infinite and knows no limit.

Therefore, when man asks God, "How can I become a channel for thy great work?" the answer is simple:

Think, feel, and act. That is all there is to it, when combined with beauty, love, and WISDOM.

Path of Spiritual Freedom, the *See* ECKANKAR.

Path of Total Awareness *See* ECKANKAR.

patience *See* FOUR DISCIPLINES OF ECK.

Paulji *PAHL-jee* A respectful name of affection for PAUL TWITCHELL.

See also PEDDAR ZASKQ.

Paul Twitchell

The ECK MASTER who founded modern-day ECKANKAR. His spiritual name is PEDDAR ZASKQ, and he is sometimes affectionately known as PAULJI.

Born in Kentucky in the early part of the twentieth century, Paul explored a

variety of professions in his early life—writer, promoter, military man. Yet his destiny was guided by an ancient line of spiritual teachers known as the VAIRAGI Adepts. Notable among them were SUDAR SINGH and REBAZAR TARZS.

A spirited nonconformist, Paul called himself a CLIFF HANGER, an individual who lives in a high state of SPIRITUAL FREEDOM and self-responsibility. Yet years came and went before his life-changing experience of GOD-REALIZATION in 1957. In October 1965, he became the MAHANTA, the LIVING ECK MASTER.

Paul's Mission

The high teachings of ECK had been scattered to the four corners of the world. Various writers had pieces of the true teachings but often attached strings—such as requiring students to become vegetarian or to spend many hours a day in MEDITATION if they wanted to be true followers on the path to God. This was wrong for our day and age.

Paul Twitchell's mission was to gather the scattered fragments of truth and restore them via the body of teachings now known as ECKANKAR. Paul ventured into a wide range of spiritual traditions under different teachers.

In keeping with his mission, Paul showed himself to be the master compiler. He gathered up the golden teachings strewn around the world and released them from the cultural trappings and social aims which limited their spiritual radiance. He reoriented these fragments to show the direct path home to God.

By the time of his passing in 1971, Paul had established ECKANKAR as a world teaching and set the stage for CONSCIOUSNES FIVE.

Inner-Plane Libraries

The fountainhead from which the ECK writings spring is the Ancient Gospel, the SHARIYAT-KI-SUGMAD, compiled by the NINE SILENT ONES, whose main duty it is to gather up and sort out the unchanging laws that enfold every ripple in life.

On the inner PLANES are libraries connected to the GOLDEN WISDOM TEMPLES. The library alongside the main Temple on the ASTRAL PLANE is an enormous place of many roomy departments, much like the US Library of Congress, providing a comprehensive source of books and materials.

Good researchers—such as Julian Johnson, Paul Brunton, Carl Jung, and others—have come in and selected the paragraphs that suited their audience. Few knew the source of their inspiration.

But there was one who did. Paul's mission was to clarify, reveal, translate, and illuminate the sacred ECK teachings for all.

And the great work continues on. Every article or Wisdom Note by the MAHANTA, the Living ECK Master is taken from the Shariyat-Ki-SUGMAD on the inner planes. The writings of SRI HAROLD KLEMP,

including over 130 books, continue to expand the body of spiritual wealth on earth.

See also FIVE SPIRITUAL LEADERS OF MODERN-DAY ECKANKAR; VAIRAGI(S), ANCIENT ORDER OF THE.

For a list of ECK Masters, see page 341.

Peddar Zaskq *PEH-dahr ZASK* The true spiritual name for PAUL TWITCHELL, the MAHANTA, the LIVING ECK MASTER from 1965 to 1971.

See also PAULJI; FIVE SPIRITUAL LEADERS OF MODERN-DAY ECKANKAR.

For a list of ECK MASTERS, see page 341.

Phidias LIVING ECK MASTER during the Golden Age of Greece. He was responsible for the building of the Parthenon and was more involved with the sculptures, including a renowned statue of Athena.

For a list of ECK MASTERS, see page 341.

Physical body One of the BODIES OF SOUL (the others are the ASTRAL BODY, CAUSAL BODY, MENTAL BODY, and ETHERIC BODY). The Physical body is the protective sheath SOUL uses for experience and expression on the PHYSICAL PLANE. This body is sometimes called the Pinda Sarup.

See also **The God Worlds Chart** on page 340; SOUL BODY; TEMPLE OF GOD.

Physical Plane The First PLANE, part of the LOWER WORLDS. The physical universe. The densest of the material worlds.

Distinctions of the Physical Plane

ALAYI (pronounced *ah-LAH-yee*) is a spiritually charged word that you can use to travel inwardly to GOLDEN WISDOM TEMPLES or SPIRITUAL CITIES here in this world.

The sound of thunder is associated with the Physical Plane, as is green, the color of nature.

A Golden Wisdom Temple on this plane, which people can visit in the PHYSICAL BODY, is the TEMPLE OF ECK in Chanhassen, Minnesota; the LIVING ECK MASTER is GUARDIAN here.

The four other Golden Wisdom Temples on this plane are SUPRAPHYSICAL: the FAQITI MONASTERY, where BANJANI is guardian of the SHARIYAT-KI-SUGMAD; GARE-HIRA, where YAUBL SACABI is guardian of the Shariyat; the HOUSE OF MOKSHA, on Venus, where RAMI NURI is guardian of the Shariyat; and the KATSUPARI MONASTERY, where FUBBI QUANTZ is guardian.

The Physical Plane is sometimes called Pinda; its ruler is ELAM.

See also **The God Worlds Chart** on page 340.

physical universe, laws of the Some thirty thousand years ago in the Indus Valley, the ECK sage MKSHA taught fundamental laws that govern this physical universe through Spirit.

For more about these laws, see **Seven Laws of the Physical Universe** on page 344.

See also SPIRITUAL LAWS OF LIFE.

Pinda *PIN-dah* The PHYSICAL PLANE or universe.

Pinda Lok Another term for the PHYSICAL PLANE.

See also LOK.

Pinda mind *PIN-dah* The MIND operating on the PHYSICAL PLANE. Also called the Pindi mind.

See also ALIVA MIND; KARAN MIND; SUKHSHAM MIND.

Pinda Sarup *PIN-dah sah-ROOP* *See* PHYSICAL BODY.

pink slip The INITIATION slip or form—the invitation the LIVING ECK MASTER sends a CHELA for outer initiations.

plane(s) The spiritual planes, or GOD WORLDS, are the levels of existence (or heavens) through which SOUL must travel on Its way back to the OCEAN OF LOVE AND MERCY, the Godhead. There are an infinite number which blend and shift from one state to another.

These planes are dimensions which are both within us and without. This is known as the microcosm and the macrocosm, the individual and the universal worlds.

Each plane is separated from the others by its own set of laws, and few inhabitants can see beyond their own world. People in any region have a limited range of vision, making it impossible to see a plane beyond or above the one they have adapted to. For this reason, we cannot, for example, see the ASTRAL PLANE with the physical eyes.

See also **The God Worlds Chart** on page 340; LOK;

LOWER WORLDS; MACROCOSM AND MICROCOSM; SPIRITUAL WORLDS.

Plenty, Law of One of the SPIRITUAL LAWS OF LIFE. We live according to the Law of Plenty when we go about life with love and thanksgiving. The viewpoint that there's enough for everybody—more than enough if people know how to find the blessings of God.

plus element *See* PROGRESSIVE CONTINUATION, LAW OF; RECIPROCITY, LAW OF.

Polarians The first ROOT RACE, which lived in Polara, the Garden of Eden; the Adamic race. Adom was the first man and Ede, the first woman. The beginning of the races of man upon earth.

Polarity, Law of The Law of Polarity, or Law of Opposites, states that within all the LOWER WORLDS, nothing exists except in relation to its opposite. Each state, quality, or condition within this universe is supported, animated, and maintained by its opposite.

However, within the worlds of true Spirit, there are no opposites. LIGHT is Light, without shadow or darkness, and there is no opposite to the SOUND CURRENT of ECK.

This is one of the SPIRITUAL LAWS OF LIFE; the third law of the physical universe (see **Seven Laws of the Physical Universe** on page 344).

See also **The God Worlds Chart** on page 340.

Prajapati *prah-jah-PAH-tee* The ECK MASTER who has a special mission in caring for animals.

For a list of ECK Masters, see page 341.

prana *PRAH-nah* The SANSKRIT word for the divine power; the Oriental term for that which the physical scientists call energy. It is only a manifestation of the audible SOUND CURRENT stepped down to meet material conditions. Breath, vital air; the plastic ether.

Prapatti Marg *prah-PAH-tee MAHRG* One of the SEVEN MARGS. Way of liberation by complete surrender and devotion to God via the Master.

prarabdh karma *prah-RAHB-duh KAHR-mah* FATE KARMA; one of the four types of KARMA.

The other types are DAILY KARMA, PRIMAL KARMA, and RESERVE KARMA.

pratyahara *praht-yah-HAH-rah* The fourth of four degrees of DISCRIMINATION, attained only when SOUL passes into the spiritual realm, beyond all MIND and matter. It is the condition in which Soul is able to divert the attention away from all senses and objects of the senses, toward divine knowledge. The practice of complete withdrawal of CONSCIOUSNESS from the environment.

prayer In ECKANKAR, HU is the most beautiful prayer. It is an ancient name for God; and in singing It or holding It in your mind during times of need, It becomes a prayer of the highest sort.

True prayer is nondirected; it acknowledges the wisdom and all-seeing power of God. Also, it is having the grace to accept God's will as it appears,

though it may differ from our own idea of what should be.

There's nothing wrong with telling God something or asking for something, but afterward be quiet and listen. True prayer is opening your heart to God or the Holy Spirit and listening.

Prayer, MEDITATION, and CONTEMPLATION are all ways people communicate with God, or with the Holy Spirit.

See also HU; SPIRITUAL EXERCISES OF ECK.

presence of the Master The INNER MASTER is like the air you breathe; he is everywhere. As the ECK, he is with all his CHELAS at the same time.

It makes little difference whether the person has read only one ECK book, has just become an ECK INITIATE or has passed through all the INITIATIONS; the MAHANTA, the LIVING ECK MASTER is with that individual constantly.

Whether or not you can see the inner form of the Master, you can hold an inner conversation with him, trusting that the Master is speaking to you from the INNER WORLDS.

The presence of the Master is called the Kundun, and practicing the Kundun is part of TOTAL RELIANCE ON THE INNER MASTER.

Another way to practice the presence is to do all deeds in the name of the MAHANTA, the Living ECK Master and let each task hold all your love. Practicing the presence of the Master is the spiritual technique of putting your attention on the MAHANTA and knowing he is with you.

present moment Be aware of the value of the present moment.

At the heart of the ECK life lies the conviction that the ECK is the way as well as the goal. Therefore, whether the way is long or short, and whatever blind corners it has, every moment is as important as the goal.

It is only because to live in the MAHANTA that to die is to gain.

In practical terms this means that every moment is known to be of infinite value, not because of what precedes or follows it, but because it is the moment of communication with God, in which eternity is a present reality as one holds and possesses the whole fullness of life in one moment, here and now, the past, present, and future.

primal karma One of the four types of KARMA. Seed karma established to begin SOUL's journey in the LOWER WORLDS.

See also KARMA, LAW OF.

primal matter force *See* AKASHA.

primal Sound The ECK; creative energy; the divine Voice, out of which all other sounds flow.

See also SOUND CURRENT; VADAN.

primal Word That which gives the life substance to all things; the SOUND CURRENT; the ECK.

primary impulse of Spirit Spirit's primary impulse is to express TRUTH, the love and beauty It feels Itself to be.

primordial MAHANTA *See* THREE ASPECTS OF THE SUGMAD.

principles, feminine and masculine Two aspects of SOUL's nature in the LOWER WORLDS. In the course of Its many INCARNATIONS, Soul takes on male and female bodies, yet every Soul in the lower worlds expresses both the feminine and masculine principles.

Soul Itself has no gender; It is both masculine and feminine in the worlds of God. When one reaches the SOUL PLANE and attains SELF-REALIZATION, the masculine and feminine principles are balanced within that individual.

The feminine principle is receptive in nature. It organizes the social structure of life and holds these elements together. It is the passive counterpart to the active masculine principle.

The masculine principle is positive, active, and progressive in nature. It plans, correlates, and gives impetus to systems of social, religious, and philosophical thought. It discovers and works out the principles of God.

principles of consciousness, seven *See* INVISIBLE LAWS.

Priscus *PREES-kuhs* The LIVING ECK MASTER who followed KETU JARAUL. He was in England at the time of its conquest by William of Normandy, and at the gathering in France in 1095 where Peter the Hermit preached support for the First Crusade. Priscus accompanied this First Crusade and died in the Holy Lands.

For a list of ECK MASTERS, see page 341.

Prithvi Lok *PREETH-vee LOHK* The Earth world, where the SPIRITUAL CITY of AGAM DES is located.

See also ASURATI LOK; LOK; SURATI LOK.

Progressive Continuation, Law of One of the SPIRITUAL LAWS OF LIFE. This is SOUL's instinctive drive toward higher states of being. Also referred to as the plus element. Future conditions grow out of present conditions.

Each created form of life longs for the perfection of the SUGMAD. Spirit, in Itself, is the principle of increase. There is always one more step; there is always one more heaven. Always one more STATE OF CONSCIOUSNESS above the last.

The world of ECK is too vast for words, too vast for feeling, and too vast for imagination.

See also RECIPROCITY, LAW OF.

prophecy Can refer to either foretelling (predicting the future) or telling forth (the inspired utterance of a prophet). It is just one aspect of spiritual awareness on the path of ECKANKAR. The ECK MASTERS use and teach the ECK-VIDYA, ancient science of prophecy, to divine the future and review past events when necessary.

See also PROPHET.

prophet The MAHANTA, the LIVING ECK MASTER is the ECK prophet. He gives divine utterance from the SUGMAD. He is the channel for the Voice of the SUGMAD.

Nothing comes from the MIND, but directly from the heart of the Almighty.

psychic phenomena Supernatural occurrences in the LOWER WORLDS. Among them are things from the ASTRAL PLANE such as palmistry, ESP, mediumship, automatic writing, and ghosts.

Involvement with psychic phenomena can become a KAL trap, a snare of MAYA, slowing SOUL's SPIRITUAL UNFOLDMENT.

The MAHANTA, the LIVING ECK MASTER leads ECK CHELAS beyond psychic phenomena to the SOUL PLANE and SPIRITUAL FREEDOM.

psychic realization The practice of SOUL's control over MIND and matter. Though this is just a stage of realization (or a series of stages) within the LOWER WORLDS, many mistake it for full ENLIGHTENMENT.

See also REALIZATION, LEVEL(S) OF.

psychic space The AURA. More broadly, granting to others the right to be themselves, and by this granting, to be free oneself. The freedom of SOUL to move about as It wishes, have choice, and make decisions.

psychic worlds Another term for the LOWER WORLDS.

purification SOUL has been sent to the LOWER WORLDS for spiritual purification. It is the purpose of your life.

Earth is a schoolroom. We're here to have every possible experience over our many lifetimes. Purification is gained through an exacting process of KARMA and REIN-

CARNATION which readies Soul for the path of ECK.

The journey home to God begins here on earth, which has been called the ash can of the universe. But that just means that earth is nearly too perfect a place to get spiritual purification.

All the negativity of life will get worse before it gets better. More and more inexperienced Souls are coming here, and they are like children who don't know right from wrong. Some people, the immature Souls, always need to beat up on each other to learn that pain hurts. But these people who desire power and control over others have little in common with people of love and COMPASSION.

The role of spiritually mature Souls in this world is to lift themselves above the melee with the SPIRITUAL EXERCISES OF ECK and the art of SOUL TRAVEL. Then use the spiritual love and WISDOM gained from experience with the LIGHT AND SOUND of God to make this a better place—in spite of the odds.

Every experience with the Light and Sound of God purifies Soul.

See also CAVE OF FIRE; CAVE OF PURIFICATION; KARMA; PURIFY OR POLLUTE; PURITY.

purify or pollute Every thought, word, and deed either purifies or pollutes the body. We are working with STATES OF CONSCIOUSNESS which influence the world around and within us.

What you put into the world comes back to you. It will strengthen, entering your world like an echo sooner or later. This echo has a strong influence upon you.

The influence can be for either beneficial things or harmful things. The choice is yours.

An Edge for Health

If you need an edge for health or for peace of mind, look to what you are putting out and what you are allowing in. What is your form of music, or news? What ways are you letting the external world into your internal world?

Again, every thought, word, or deed either purifies or pollutes the body. A simple but powerful truth.

See also KARMA; PURIFICATION; PURITY; SPIRITUAL HEALING; VIBRATIONS, LAW OF.

purity Purity is the truth of SOUL dwelling in God. It calls for the highest in man.

If you look for the good in those around you, you bring out the good within them. Never wish for others what you do not want for yourself. By seeing the good in your neighbor, you are bringing out the good in yourself.

Three practices are key to spiritual purity:

First, chant the sacred names of God; hold them constantly in your heart.

Second, do everything in the name of God, the SUGMAD.

And last, love God with all your passion, and serve your fellow man with divine affection.

You will see the eyes of the MAHANTA shining in every living being.

See also PURIFICATION; PURIFY OR POLLUTE.

purpose of Soul SOUL's purpose of life on earth is to go through every experience, to one day become a COWORKER WITH GOD, and to have our talents used in a way we enjoy.

Purusha *poo-ROO-shah* The presiding and predominating lord on a given PLANE; the source of creative energy responsible for the creation of the next lower plane.

See also AGAM PURUSHA; ALAKH PURUSHA; ALAYA PURUSHA; ANAMI PURUSHA; HUKIKAT PURUSHA; SAT PURUSHA; **The God Worlds Chart** on page 340.

Pythagoras *pi-THAG-ehr-uhs* An ECK MASTER in the sixth century BC. Besides being an Adept in the VAIRAGI ORDER, he was well known as a Greek philosopher and head of a MYSTERY SCHOOL.

PEDDAR ZASKQ (PAUL TWITCHELL, in a previous incarnation) studied under Pythagoras, who was concerned mainly with two points in the teaching of truth: (1) he emphasized love, WISDOM, and CHARITY, and (2) he taught that the kingdom of heaven is within man. A notable statement of Pythagoras was, "Ascending into the radiant Ether, midst the Immortals, thou shalt be thyself a God."

Despite the distortions of time and circumstances, the thread of the ECK teachings given by Pythagoras in ancient Greece is still discernible today.

For a list of ECK Masters, see page 341.

Qualima *kwah-LEE-mah* Absolute TRUTH; the divine melody, the name, the WORD, the ECK, the MUSIC OF THE SPHERES. Sometimes called Nad.

Quetzalcoatl *keht-sahl-koh-AH-tuhl* An ECK MASTER who left ATLANTIS prior to its final destruction and established the mysteries of ECK in what is now Mexico around 1055 BC.

Quetzalcoatl was also one of the spiritual teachers of PEDDAR ZASKQ.

To archaeology and history, Quetzalcoatl is the name of a Mesoamerican god and is among several saviors, from around the world, who were crucified.

For a list of ECK Masters, see page 341.

Quintan Life manifesting in the perfect body of the SUGMAD via the MAHANTA. The WORD made flesh. The vehicles used by the MAHANTA, which are the PHYSICAL, ASTRAL, CAUSAL, MENTAL, and SOUL BODIES, which function as the instruments of God upon each PLANE, including the true SPIRITUAL WORLDS. Also called the living Quintan or quinbodies.

Rabinowitz An ECK MASTER who gave SRI HAROLD KLEMP encouragement on his road to ECK MASTERSHIP.

For a list of ECK Masters, see page 341.

Rabjung *rahb-YUHNG* The sixty-year cycle of the ECK-VIDYA system is known as the Rabjung.

Sixty is an important number in the ECK-Vidya. It signifies the heart of the SUGMAD, the dwelling place of the unknown deity.

It is here that the MAHANTA, the LIVING ECK MASTER is born and comes forth upon the earth as the GODMAN. The number twelve, multiplied five times, brings into life the greatest of all AVATARs, who uplifts mankind with his presence in the world.

See also LHOKHOR; TWELVE-YEAR CYCLE(S).

radiant body The Nuri Sarup, the Light body of the MAHANTA, the LIVING ECK MASTER which gleams like a thousand stars in the night and appears on the inner to those who follow his teachings. The term *radiant body* also sometimes refers to the Atma Sarup, or SOUL BODY.

Raging Fires, Years of the *See* NERALIT.

Rahakaz *rah-hah-KAHZ* One of the ten SPIRITUAL CITIES on earth. Located at Land's End in Cornwall, England, it is the legendary Camelot and home of the Order of the Golden Dawn.

This SUPRAPHYSICAL city is a center for the magical forces of this planet.

The other nine spiritual cities are AGAM DES, AKEVIZ, DAMCAR, KIMTAVED, MUMSAKA, NAMPAK, SAT DHAM, SHAMBALLA, and ZEZIRATH.

Ralot *rah-LOHT* The fifth MONTH OF THE ECK-VIDYA, corresponding to May. The days of truth. The month of the sapphire. In this journey of SOUL there is a need for the outward manifestation of Soul's inner search.

See also ECK-VIDYA WHEEL.

Rama *RAH-mah* Rama was one of the first initiates in the ANCIENT ORDER OF THE VAIRAGI. He served as the MAHANTA, the LIVING ECK MASTER in a period after the fall of ATLANTIS, when the ARYANS, the fifth ROOT RACE, became dominant.

The Journey of Rama

He started out in the dense forests of northern Europe and brought the HU and the teachings of the LIGHT AND SOUND to the primitive people there.

Rama then went on to Tibet, where he was lifted out of his body and taken to the GOLDEN WISDOM TEMPLE in the SPIRITUAL CITY of AGAM DES. There, an ancient ECK MASTER revealed the portion of the

SHARIYAT-KI-SUGMAD in safekeeping in that inaccessible temple (accessible only by invitation, and then only via SOUL TRAVEL).

From Tibet, Rama went to teach ECK in KHARA KHOTA, capital of the UIGHUR EMPIRE. The priestcraft there, bent on retaining control, drove him out of that country. Rama returned to Tibet and founded the KATSUPARI MONASTERY.

Next, he traveled through Persia and established what would later become the MAGI Order, leaving the seeds of ECK among his followers, some of whom were ancestors of ZOROASTER.

Continuing his journey, Rama went to India. Here he planted the ECK teachings, in seed form, from which evolved the Hindu religion and its many offshoots.

For a list of ECK Masters, see page 341.

Ramamurta *RAH-mah-MOOR-tah* An ECK MASTER during the time of Minos I, ruler of Crete.

For a list of ECK Masters, see page 341.

Rami Nuri *RAH-mee NOO-ree*

Rami Nuri served as the MAHANTA, the LIVING ECK MASTER. He is now the GUARDIAN of the SHARIYAT-KI-SUGMAD at the HOUSE OF MOKSHA, a GOLDEN WISDOM TEMPLE in the SUPRAPHYSICAL city of RETZ, on the planet Venus.

Description

He is a rather tall man with dark features and has a very short beard which is as white as his hair. His eyes are dark and flashing. The letter *M* appears on his forehead.

A Jewel of Wisdom from Rami Nuri:

"He who drinks of the stream of ECK can never thirst, but in him is a well of water springing up into life everlasting.

"He who drinks of it will never again search the world looking for food for the inner man. It is there, always within him, the great flowing ECK.

"It is the SUGMAD shining through him, lighting the world to all who have the eyes to see!"

For a list of ECK MASTERS, see page 341.

Ramkar *rahm-KAHR* The lord of the Third PLANE, the CAUSAL PLANE. Also called the Maha Kal Brahm.

See also **The God Worlds Chart** on page 340.

Ra Mu *rah MOO* The emperor of Mu, or LEMURIA, the Empire of the Sun, who was the representative of the Supreme Deity for the Lemurians but was not worshipped by them.

realization of Truth There are three things necessary to the realization, or recognition, of TRUTH:

Knowing Spirit as Love

1. An awareness that God, or Spirit, is good, unchangeable, and eternal, and that It is the sum total of all the good that has ever been, or is, or will be.
2. An awareness that you (SOUL) exist because It exists in you, and that without It you could not exist.
3. An ardent desire to unite with It so It can express Itself through you to others.

We must come to know Spirit as love before we can even be able to love others—for love is the way to realization.

See also CONSCIOUSNESS; REALIZATION, LEVEL(S) OF; RECIPROCITY, LAW OF.

realization, level(s) of Conscious awareness expands from the human and psychic levels to beyond GOD-REALIZATION.

Levels of Realization

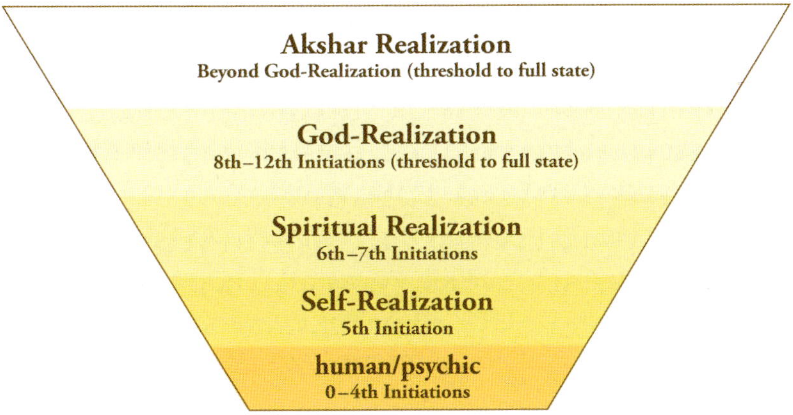

Level	Initiations
Akshar Realization	Beyond God-Realization (threshold to full state)
God-Realization	8th–12th Initiations (threshold to full state)
Spiritual Realization	6th–7th Initiations
Self-Realization	5th Initiation
human/psychic	0–4th Initiations

This is reflected in the levels of ECK INITIATION.

See also AKSHAR REALIZATION; CONSCIOUSNESS; COSMIC CONSCIOUSNESS; HUMAN CONSCIOUSNESS; PSYCHIC REALIZATION; SELF-REALIZATION; SPIRITUAL REALIZATION.

For a list of the ECK initiations, see page 338.

Real Self, the The SOUL.

Rebazar Tarzs *REE-bah-zahr TAHRZ*

Rebazar Tarzs, a Tibetan, served as the MAHANTA, the LIVING ECK MASTER when Tibet was the spiritual center of the world. The teachings were then conveyed only in secret.

Having immortalized his body, he is said to be over five hundred years old. He maintains a mud-and-brick hut in the HINDU KUSH Mountains, high on a cliff over a roaring blue river. Rebazar has been the spiritual teacher of many other ECK MASTERS.

Description

Rebazar is about six feet in height and wears a full beard that is as thick as black wool and neatly trimmed. He has large, square hands, testimony to the rugged outdoor life he enjoys. He is often attired in a maroon robe, tied at the waist.

His eyes are like two dark pools in a bottomless sea—they seem to see all, know all. They are eyes of compassion and mercy, all-seeing eyes that serve both as a mirror of Soul and a microscope to the universe.

To look into them is to become lost in the LIGHT AND SOUND of God, the ECK. The liquid of God pours from them like a sweet nectar to fill the emptiness of the heart.

Torchbearer

The staff he carries symbolizes the ROD OF ECK POWER. As Torchbearer of ECKANKAR, he has the special duty of stepping in to carry the spiritual power should the Living ECK Master leave the physical field of action before the Rod of ECK Power is passed to his successor.

This happened upon SUDAR SINGH's TRANSLATION (probably in the 1940s or 1950s), after which Rebazar Tarzs stood in until 1965, when he passed the Rod of ECK Power to PEDDAR ZASKQ (PAUL TWITCHELL).

Many seekers and CHELAS benefit from Rebazar's WISDOM, COMPASSION, and companionship as he helps the present Living ECK Master in the works of ECKANKAR. Rebazar has given his whole life to helping others find the perfection of God.

For a list of ECK Masters, see page 341.

rechemicalization The burning off of KARMA is the state of rechemicalization. It is the process man must go through while living on this earth.

Only when he can walk the middle path of ECK can he leave the WHEEL OF THE EIGHTY-FOUR and find the gates of heaven.

ECK CHELAS do this with the help of the LIVING ECK MASTER.

See also PURIFICATION.

Reciprocity, Law of One of the SPIRITUAL LAWS OF LIFE. God created SOUL so It (God, the SUGMAD) could know Itself more fully. Soul exists because God loves It.

Each is a unique atom of God and has the potential and mission to manifest a distinct expression of DIVINE LOVE. Invested with the gift of unlimited creativity, Soul is eternally unfolding into greater realization and Coworkership with the LIGHT AND SOUND of God.

> As the individual wakes up to the oneness with Spirit, Spirit wakes up to the same thing. It becomes conscious of Itself through the CONSCIOUSNESS of the individual.

INDIVIDUALITY is the necessary complement of the Spirit. Until actualized and distributed by Souls, the ECK, the GOD CURRENT, is undifferentiated.

Compelled by Its love for the SUGMAD, Soul never ceases in Its CONTEMPLATIONs and thereby unfolds into infinitely greater expressions of Spirit. It becomes a law of love unto Itself, and nothing can contain Its love.

No Soul can ever know the SUGMAD fully. Only Its relationship to It. And the SUGMAD knows no halting.

See also COWORKER(S) WITH GOD; COWORKER(S) WITH THE MAHANTA.

Records of the Kros *KROHS* These are the ancient

transcripts of the history of this earth planet and what will become of it. This history and prophecy is kept in the KATSUPARI MONASTERY in the BUIKA MAGNA mountain range.

Also, the second section of the SHARIYAT-KI-SUGMAD, displayed in the Temple of GARE-HIRA, is called "The Records of the Kros." This is also the title of a chapter in *The Shariyat-Ki-SUGMAD*, Book Two.

Regional ECK Spiritual Aide (RESA) A RESA is a specially trained ECK SPIRITUAL AIDE appointed by the LIVING ECK MASTER to serve as his key administrative representative and head of the ECK SATSANG SOCIETY in a designated region. RESAs report to the ECKANKAR SPIRITUAL CENTER.

In this high leadership role, the RESA acts as a watcher, listener, and guardian in matters related to the message of ECK.

See also the **ECKANKAR Organizational Chart** on page 64.

Regnard *REHG-nahrd* An ECK MASTER of the future who will be the LIVING ECK MASTER during the time the MONGOLOID RACE will be in power.

For a list of ECK Masters, see page 341.

reincarnation Rebirth, the process of SOUL entering a new body each time It enters this world.

Reincarnation also refers to the whole journey of Soul in the LOWER WORLDS, the karmic coming and going, via many births and deaths, on the WHEEL OF THE EIGHTY-FOUR. We are reincarnated on various

PLANES and planets until we meet the SAT GURU and progress through the ECK INITIATIONS on our way to complete SPIRITUAL FREEDOM on the SOUL PLANE.

The SECOND INITIATION in ECKANKAR frees one from the need to reincarnate on the PHYSICAL PLANE.

See also AKASHIC RECORDS; KARMA; PAST LIVES; REMODELING OF SOUL; SOUL RECORDS; TRANSLATION.

religion(s) God has made a path for every STATE OF CONSCIOUSNESS. There is a religion, a belief, or a perspective for every person on earth.

It is against spiritual law to interfere in the religious freedom of others.

One may take many paths before coming to the teachings of ECK. Religions are offshoots of ECK, the original source of all life, and, along with faiths and philosophies, make up the necessary steps to reach the path of ECK.

remodeling of Soul In the course of REINCARNATION, SOULs have between-life experiences and lessons to prepare for the next life.

Should a Soul be completely negative, causing harm to many others, that Soul is put into isolation for a time to reflect. If the guides for that particular Soul then see that there is no hope for this Soul to progress, they remodel the Soul by moving the atoms around.

Once a Soul is created, It is never destroyed, but Its atoms may be rearranged.

This is not done as punishment. It is done to regenerate this Soul and allow It to have the experi-

ences necessary to someday become a servant of God, a COWORKER WITH GOD.

RESA *See* REGIONAL ECK SPIRITUAL AIDE.

reserve karma One of the four types of KARMA. A surplus of credits and debits from PAST LIVES. Past-life karma sometimes issued to a SOUL in Its present incarnation.

See also KARMA, LAW OF; REINCARNATION.

Resonance, Law of One of the SPIRITUAL LAWS OF LIFE. Each INITIATION opens the gate to certain regions of the corresponding PLANE and new levels of CONSCIOUSNESS.

Returns, Law of *See* KARMA, LAW OF.

Retz *REHTS* The SUPRAPHYSICAL capital of the planet Venus, where a section of the SHARIYAT-KI-SUGMAD is kept in the HOUSE OF MOKSHA, a GOLDEN WISDOM TEMPLE.

Reversed Effort, Law of One of the SPIRITUAL LAWS OF LIFE. The harder you try to avoid something, the more it will be attracted to you. The harder you struggle to achieve some goal, the more difficulty you will have to overcome—difficulty caused, at least in part, by the strain of your effort.

The solution is to relax, take it easy, and try again. We should never try to force results.

See also KARMALESS ACTION.

riddle of God God is what each SOUL believes It is. Everyone is right in their belief about God. Yet God is vastly more than the human MIND can encompass.

Belief in God must reveal itself in the life of a believer, or it is not a true belief.

"The Riddle of God" is a key chapter in the ECK book *Stranger by the River.*

rite, ritual *See* ECK CELEBRATIONS OF LIFE; INITIATION(S); PASSING OF THE ROD OF ECK POWER.

rite of passage *See* ECK RITE OF PASSAGE.

River of God An image of the ECK as a river which pervades all the universes. The great spiritual current flowing out from the throne of God.

See also ECK.

River of Light The great circular wave of LIGHT which flows in a continual stream from God; the great spiritual current flowing to all the worlds upon worlds.

See also ECK.

Rod of ECK Power The Rod of ECK Power is the spiritual scepter of the LIVING ECK MASTER.

It is not an object that can be seen or handled, but rather the power of ECK that comes through the Living ECK Master in order to sustain the creations of God.

It is a concentration of Sound and LIGHT, the power of the WORD bestowed by the SUGMAD, that works through the Living ECK Master and is inseparable from him.

> With the Rod of ECK Power comes the all-seeing and all-knowing vision and power of the MAHANTA CONSCIOUSNESS. As long as the Living ECK Master holds the Rod of ECK Power, he is the chief agent of the SUGMAD in all Its worlds.

Only the Living ECK Master holds the Rod of ECK Power, but it is the channel of power that comes straight from the OCEAN OF LOVE AND MERCY down into all the worlds.

The ECK MASTERS have arranged their spiritual aims with that of the SUGMAD. Therefore, power from the Rod of ECK Power is at their disposal too.

See also ECK SPIRITUAL NEW YEAR; PASSING OF THE ROD OF ECK POWER.

root race(s) The various races which have occupied and successively dominated the earth or will do so in the future.

In order up to the present, they are the POLARIANS, the HYPERBOREANS, the Lemurians, the Atlanteans, and the ARYANS.

The root races which will be in power in the future include the MONGOLOID RACE, the ZOHAR, the ULEMANS, the SHATIKAYAS, the ARRIANS, the KAISHVITS, the HERACLIANS, the CLEMAINS, and the FRETICRETS.

See also ATLANTIS; LEMURIA.

Rumi *ROO-MEE* Jalal ad-Din ar-Rumi was a sage

and extraordinary poet of thirteenth-century Persia and one of earth's great teachers. He was a disciple of the ECK MASTER SHAMUS-I-TABRIZ and author of the *MASNAVI*. Rumi's poetry exemplifies the bond of love between the CHELA and the Master.

Sach Khand *SAHCH KAHND* The Atma Lok; the Fifth PLANE, or SOUL PLANE; the true home of SOUL; the grand headquarters of all CREATION, and the region of immortality; changeless, perfect, and deathless; untouched by dissolution or reconstruction; the world where the ECK saints live.

Also refers to the SPIRITUAL WORLDS, the pure positive GOD WORLDS in general.

See also **The God Worlds Chart** on page 340.

sacred numbers According to the ECK-VIDYA, numbers are symbols of divine realities; the key to the ancient views on life and the evolution of the human race, spiritually as well as physically.

An overview of the sacred numbers and their meaning can be found in *The ECK-Vidya, Ancient Science of Prophecy*.

See also LHOKHOR; RABJUNG.

Saguna *sah-GOO-nah* *See* NIRGUNA AND SAGUNA.

Saguna Brahm *sah-GOO-nah BRAHM* Ruler of the

Saguna Lok, the upper division of the MIND plane, or ETHERIC PLANE, who has jurisdiction over all entities and beings living on this PLANE.

See also SOHANG, LORD.

Saguna Lok *sah-GOO-nah LOHK* *See* ETHERIC PLANE; LOK.

Saguna Sati *sah-GOO-nah SAH-tee* *See* DIRECT PROJECTION.

Sahak *SAH-hahk* The sixth MONTH OF THE ECK-VIDYA, corresponding to June. The month of the moonstone. The days of music.

In this journey SOUL seeks a resting-place where It can work out Its destiny in peace and quiet.

See also ECK-VIDYA WHEEL.

Sahasra-dal-Kanwal *sah-HAHS-rah-dahl-KAHN-wahl* Means thousand-petaled lotus. Name of the capital city of the ASTRAL PLANE, sometimes called the City of Lights.

Also the MOUNTAIN OF LIGHT at the top of the Astral.

The CROWN CHAKRA is also sometimes referred to as the Sahasra-dal-Kanwal.

Sakapori, Temple of *sah-kah-POHR-ee* The GOLDEN WISDOM TEMPLE on the BRAHMANDA LOK, the Third, or CAUSAL, PLANE, in the city of HONU. SHAMUS-I-TABRIZ is the GUARDIAN of the SHARIYAT-KI-SUGMAD in this temple.

Description

The temple is a square building made of heavy, grey-green, stonelike material, with a peaked roof. The walls and roof are sprinkled with amber that gleams so brightly in the light that the temple looks like a fairy castle.

There is a pair of massive iron doors that swing open on the lightest touch and lead into a long, wide nave with auditorium seating on each side for the CHELAS who come to this wondrous temple of WISDOM.

The Master stands and speaks from the far end of the nave. Behind him is the fifth section of the Shariyat-Ki-SUGMAD, which is encased in a wide, but short, glass fiberlike casing. It is on a stand where a soft light shines upon its open pages.

salamanders *See* ELEMENTALS.

Salokiam *sah-loh-kee-AHM* The first of the FOUR STATES OF THE HIGH INITIATE. The other three are Samipiam, Sayodiyam, and Souaroupiam.

samadhana *sah-mah-DAH-nah* A state of joy beyond all doubts.

Samadhi *sah-MAH-dee* A form of CONTEMPLATION and ENLIGHTENMENT. This is the coming into an understanding of all the forces in the LOWER WORLDS.

Samadhi becomes a spiritual tool for the ECK CHELA beginning with the FIRST INITIATION. The supreme goal of Samadhi is SELF-REALIZATION.

See also NIRVIKALPA.

Samipiam *sah-mee-pee-AHM* The second of the FOUR STATES OF THE HIGH INITIATE. The other three are Salokiam, Sayodiyam, and Souaroupiam.

samsara *sahm-SAH-rah* WHEEL OF THE EIGHTY-FOUR. SOUL's journey through the LOWER WORLDS.

sanskaras *sahn-SKAH-rahz* Karmic impressions gathered in the CAUSAL BODY during earthly lives; the impressions of all former lives.

See also KARMA; PAST LIVES; REINCARNATION.

Sanskrit Ancient language of India. The Vedas and other religious texts were written in Sanskrit, and some Sanskrit terms are used in the writings of ECKANKAR.

santosha *sahn-TOH-shah* Another word for the spiritual virtue of CONTENTMENT.

See FIVE VIRTUES.

Sardar Lhunpo *SAHR-dahr LOON-poh* The LIVING ECK MASTER in Rome during the early years of the Republic. His work is now on the CAUSAL PLANE.

For a list of ECK MASTERS, see page 341.

Sar-Kurteva *SAHR-kuhr-TEH-vah* A city in ancient ATLANTIS.

See also DECATES.

sarup *sah-ROOP* Another term for body, as in Atma Sarup (SOUL BODY).

See also SHARIR.

sastras *SAHS-trahz* Scriptures or teachings. Chapter 2 of *THE SHARIYAT-KI-SUGMAD*, Book One, is "The ECK Sastras."

sat *SAHT* Means true, as in SAT NAM (true name).

Sata Visic Palace *SAH-tah VEE-seek* The GOLDEN WISDOM TEMPLE on the ANAMI LOK, the Tenth PLANE, where a section of the SHARIYAT-KI-SUGMAD is kept.

Sat Desha *SAHT DEH-shah* Also Sat Desh. Means true country. The pure SPIRITUAL WORLDS of God; the world of being; the ANAMI LOK, the grand region of all CREATION and of immortality.

Sat Dham *SAHT DAHM* One of the ten SPIRITUAL CITIES on earth. Sat Dham is located in the Pyrenees Mountains of northern Spain.

It is the home of the Brown Robe Monks, who are concerned with the healing principles and physical phenomena.

The other nine spiritual cities are AGAM DES, AKEVIZ, DAMCAR, KIMTAVED, MUMSAKA, NAMPAK, RAHAKAZ, SHAMBALLA, and ZEZIRATH.

Sat Guru *SAHT GOO-roo* The MAHANTA, the LIVING ECK MASTER. The son of God; one who is responsible directly to the supreme Deity; the chief spiritual authority who speaks for God on every PLANE through all the universes from the lowest negative to the highest spiritual one; the LIGHT GIVER; the superior teacher of spiritual works.

Sat Kanwal-Anda Lok *SAHT KAHN-wahl-AHN-dah*

LOHK Another name for the ASTRAL PLANE.

See also LOK.

Sat Lok *SAHT LOHK* The Fifth PLANE, or SOUL PLANE; the first step of SOUL into the worlds of God.

See also LOK; SAT.

Sat Nam *SAHT NAHM* Sat Nam (or Sat Purusha) is an individualized manifestation of the SUGMAD and the ruler of the Atma Lok, the SOUL PLANE.

Sat Nam created each region of the LOWER WORLDS. *Sat Nam* means true name.

This Divine Being is the power, the LIGHT, the great master current flowing down and out into all CREATION below the Soul Plane to create, govern, and sustain all regions. This power is the audible SOUND CURRENT, the Life Stream which permeates all the cosmic worlds like a gigantic stream of water.

Though in reality neither male nor female, Sat Nam has the form of a male—an immense, golden-bronze, muscular being with a shaved head. His body is a shining essence in the sea of spiritual LIGHT AND SOUND, and his smile is that blessing which reaches into all the worlds below.

Sato Kuraj *SAH-toh KOO-raj* An ECK MASTER who is the GUARDIAN of the SHARIYAT-KI-SUGMAD, in the HALL OF BRAHMANDA, on the MENTAL PLANE.

Description

He is a small, lithe being with quick gestures and a benign expression that melts all hearts.The

letter *A* appears on his forehead in the area of the SPIRITUAL EYE.

He is surrounded by a soft, blue light which looks like the blue of the sky on a summer day. His presence is accompanied by the sound of running water. His face is very narrow, his eyes are dark, and his close-cropped hair is black.

He wears the maroon robe of the VAIRAGI ADEPTS, wrapped very neatly, much like the traditional Japanese kimono.

For a list of ECK Masters, see page 341.

satori *sah-TOH-ree* To transcend the flesh and become reawakened in the spirit.

Sat Purusha *SAHT poo-ROO-shah* Another name for SAT NAM.

See also PURUSHA; SAT.

Satsang *SAHT-sahng* Satsang is union with that which is pure and imperishable. *Sat* means true or unchangeable; *sang* means union.

The Many Forms of Satsang

- Being in the company of the LIVING ECK MASTER or one of the higher devotees
- CONTEMPLATION and making contact with the SOUND CURRENT
- Studying the works of ECK

- Spiritual gatherings of study or service in the name of the MAHANTA
- The union of one with the Living ECK Master

As a collective body the Satsang brings HARMONY, peace, and happiness to the individual, and to all entities within the universes of God.

The Satsang acts as a channel for the ECK and is part of the TRINITY OF ECKANKAR.

When one is in Satsang, he becomes closer to the MAHANTA in spirit, and they can communicate secretly. The relationship between the two is of a love greater than words can express; it is the highest of any love.

See also ECK SATSANG CLASS(ES).

Satsang class *See* ECK SATSANG CLASS(ES).

Satsang Society *See* ECK SATSANG SOCIETY.

Satya Yuga *SAHT-yah YOO-gah* The Golden Age.

See also FOUR CYCLES OF LIFE; MAHAYUGA; YUGA(S).

savior gods The MAHANTA CONSCIOUSNESS manifesting physically to different races at different periods of human history in the form to which they were most accustomed and by the name familiar to them.

Sayodiyam *sah-yoh-dee-YAHM* The fourth of the FOUR STATES OF THE HIGH INITIATE. The other three are Salokiam, Samipiam, and Souaroupiam.

Seat of Power On October 22, 1990, the TEMPLE OF ECK in Chanhassen, Minnesota, was dedicated as ECKANKAR's Seat of Power, its spiritual center on earth. A seat of power is an organization's connection with the world, from which its thought forms, energies, and power flow.

Second Grand Division *See* GRAND DIVISIONS, FIRST AND SECOND.

Second Initiation The Second INITIATION comes after two years of formal study of the ECK SPIRITUAL LIVING COURSES. It is the only initiation which can be requested.

A Key Initiation

This key initiation is the linking up of SOUL, by the MAHANTA, to the returning wave of the SOUND CURRENT, which frees Soul from the need to ever again reincarnate on the PHYSICAL PLANE.

The Second Initiation is the point where the INNER MASTER begins to give the SECRET DOCTRINE in earnest. The CHELA'S KARMA is taken over by the MAHANTA, the LIVING ECK MASTER and given back to him to work off in an orderly manner, sometimes through the DREAM STATE.

The Second Initiate receives a SECRET WORD which greatly assists his SPIRITUAL UNFOLDMENT. This word is a tuning fork—a master key to one's spiritual progress. The initiate begins to rise beyond his mechanical reactions and enjoys more spaciousness and freedom in his approach to life.

The Outer Ceremony

The Second Initiation is both an inner and an outer ceremony.

The Master sends the candidate an invitation—an initiation slip for him to present to an ECK INITIATOR. The ceremony takes place in a private, quiet location and lasts about an hour.

This is a sacred spiritual event of simplicity, grace, and beauty.

During the ceremony the Initiator gives the chela a personal secret word. It fits his VIBRATIONS and opens his SPIRITUAL EYE.

There is also a short spiritual exercise.

The Inner Ceremony

On the inner PLANES the MAHANTA comes to the chela in a sparkling body of light, connects him with the LIGHT AND SOUND of God, and firmly plants his feet on the road home to God.

The MAHANTA and chela may sit down together on the banks of the RIVER OF GOD and discuss the magnificent ECK.

Although the chela may or may not be aware of all that goes on during the initiation, he certainly enters a greater state of the Light and Sound of God.

In time, the chela will remember all that is necessary for his continued unfoldment.

A Dedication to the Holy Spirit

The chela is dedicating his spiritual life to the Holy Spirit, the divine ECK, under the guidance of the MAHANTA, the Living ECK Master.

In return, the MAHANTA helps him see the spiritual opportunities hidden in every event and circumstance of his life.

Through dreams, insights, and spiritual revelations, the MAHANTA awakens the initiate to a new and higher purpose in his spiritual life—the secret of true living.

The Second Initiation corresponds to the ASTRAL PLANE.

This is the essential start on the path to SELF-REALIZATION, which comes at the FIFTH INITIATION.

For a list of the ECK initiations, see page 338.

Second Plane *See* ASTRAL PLANE.

second root race *See* HYPERBOREANS; ROOT RACES.

secret doctrine The secret doctrine is the portion of the SHARIYAT-KI-SUGMAD that the MAHANTA passes to the CHELA by means of the SPIRITUAL EXERCISES OF ECK.

SRI HAROLD KLEMP's spiritual name, Z, or WAH Z, means the secret doctrine.

See also LOVE, LAW OF.

secret side of ECK In time, an ECKIST learns of the secret side of ECK. Nothing is ever the same as before. Everything changes all the time. The Holy Spirit touches every living creature, all the time.

How You Can Begin to See the Secret Side of ECK

1. Know that the ECK is behind everything.
2. Learn to do one small deed for someone else each day, without any expectation of reward.
3. Love God with all your heart.

Do this, and the ECK will show you Its secrets. You will then find love and become the master of your fate.

See also ESOTERIC; INNER TEACHINGS; MASTERSHIP; SECRET DOCTRINE.

secrets to spiritual living *See* TWELVE SECRETS TO SPIRITUAL LIVING.

secret teachings *See* DREAM TEACHINGS; INNER TEACHINGS; SECRET DOCTRINE.

secret word The individual word given to the CHELA at the time of INITIATION. As an expression of the holy ECK, your personal word is a master key to the kingdom of heaven.

It opens the channel between you and the Master so he can give you the INNER TEACHINGS.

> The MAHANTA animates and quickens the ECK MANTRA, making it a mass of radiant energy. He injects his own CONSCIOUSNESS and its subjective LIGHT into the chela receiving the initiation.
>
> The chela then feels the shock of spiritual consciousness. It is an unspeakable feeling of blessedness which comes upon him.

When the individual secret word is used, all the accumulated forces of Soul's INCARNATIONS are aroused in the initiate. This produces the conditions and power for which the word is intended. The uninitiated may utter any specific word or mantra as often as he likes, but it will not produce anything for him.

For more on the use of the secret word, see the MANTRA entry on page 174.

See also ZIKAR.

seed body *See* CAUSAL BODY.

seed karma Another term for primal KARMA.

Seeing, Knowing, and Being When SOUL enters into the SOUL PLANE and beholds Itself as pure Spirit, It gains the state of Seeing, Knowing, and Being.

This is direct perception, beyond SOUL TRAVEL, and is a key attribute of SELF-REALIZATION, the ECKSHAR consciousness.

Self, Law of the One of the SPIRITUAL LAWS OF LIFE. Each must understand and act to solve the mystery of their LITTLE SELF before they can solve the mystery of God.

self-discipline One of the FOUR FUNDAMENTALS OF ECK. The control of the self; control of the emotional feelings and the imaginative forces.

The CHELA must be aware of the subtle things that occur in his MIND and heart. In this way, he can focus on what brings him the most spiritual benefit in every aspect of life. He gains self-direction and SPIRITUAL FREEDOM.

See also FOUR DISCIPLINES OF ECK.

Self-Discovery Another term for SELF-REALIZATION.

self-indulgence *See* LUST.

Self-Realization This is the ECKSHAR, the STATE OF CONSCIOUSNESS which comes when one receives the FIFTH INITIATION and thus becomes a HIGHER INITIATE (Mahdis) and gains Jivan Mukti, SPIRITUAL FREEDOM, in this lifetime.

This occurs on the SOUL PLANE, where SOUL recognizes Itself as pure Spirit. It is released from the limits and bonds of the HUMAN CONSCIOUSNESS and is fully a COWORKER WITH THE MAHANTA, able to move forward toward the goal of GOD-REALIZATION and becoming a COWORKER WITH GOD.

See also **The God Worlds Chart** on page 340; REALIZATION, LEVEL(S) OF; SEEING, KNOWING, AND BEING.

self-renunciation The way to success in GOD CONSCIOUSNESS lies in giving up the feeling of need, letting go your hold, resigning the care of your destiny to God, and being genuinely indifferent to what becomes of all.

You will not only gain a perfect inner relief, but often the particular things you sincerely thought you were renouncing.

This is salvation through self-renunciation. The dying to be truly reborn.

To get to it, a critical point must be passed, a corner turned within. Something must give way. A native hardness must break down and liquefy.

This event is frequently sudden and natural, and it leaves one with the impression that he has received the blessings of God.

See also DETACHMENT; SELF-SURRENDER.

self-surrender The spiritual practice of releasing ATTACHMENT and trusting the Master's love in all things.

It is the process of first doing everything we can do to resolve a situation ourselves. We then release the issue to Divine Spirit to handle in whatever way is for the spiritual good of all. We release our attachment to the outcome in a state of acceptance.

Surrender to the Master, who is the instrument of the ECK, is the great pleasure of life. This spiritual surrender is not to be confused with its worldly connotation; it relates only to the inner self.

The ECK INITIATE learns that by self-surrender he does not resist life, but goes along with it in an active manner.

See also DETACHMENT; SELF-RENUNCIATION.

Seltea *SEHL-tee-ah* The eighth TWELVE-YEAR CYCLE of the ECK-VIDYA; called the Years of the Bountiful Earth. Also the eighth year within a twelve-year cycle.

See also ECK-VIDYA WHEEL.

Sepher *SEHP-hehr* The ECK MASTER who will be responsible for the spiritual welfare of the ZOHAR, the seventh ROOT RACE.

For a list of ECK Masters, see page 341.

Seres *SEER-eez* A mighty host of beings from the ASTRAL PLANE who explored the LOWER WORLDS, leaving traces on earth. The fathering tribe of the Lemurians and Atlanteans, they had superior knowledge and occult powers.

See also ATLANTIS; LEMURIA.

service margs The four orders within the body of ECK INITIATEs which each initiate may become a part of to give service to the MAHANTA, the LIVING ECK MASTER and ECK Itself.

The service margs are the ARAHATA MARG, the BHAKTI MARG, the GIANI MARG, and the VAHANA MARG.

See also SEVEN MARGS.

seva *see-VAH* A service of love. A spiritual word that can be sung or chanted to inspire greater love and service to all life.

seven laws of the physical universe *See* PHYSICAL UNIVERSE, LAWS OF THE.

seven margs The seven margs, or paths to God, in ECKANKAR are

- the **ARAHATA MARG**, the teaching order;
- the **BHAKTI MARG**, the loving service order;
- the **ECK MARG**, secret path of the holy Sound Current;

- the **GIANI MARG**, study at the Golden Wisdom Temples;
- the **KARMA MARG**, similar to the Bhakti Marg, but of a more personal path of service to God;
- the **PRAPATTI MARG**, way of liberation via the Master; and
- the **VAHANA MARG**, the order of missionaries.

Four of the seven (Arahata, Bhakti, Giani, and Vahana) are SERVICE MARGS. The seven margs blend into one another, and there is a full harmony between them—like waves in the ocean.

seven principles of consciousness *See* INVISIBLE LAWS.

Seventh Initiation This is the INITIATION of the ALAYA LOK, the Seventh PLANE, and is both an inner and outer ceremony.

The Seventh Initiate enters the path of pure love. He has become entirely the ECK in principle and spirit. He speaks and acts mainly in the name and service of the MAHANTA, the LIVING ECK MASTER, for that has become the Seventh Initiate's purpose in the world.

The initiate has learned that by SELF-SURRENDER he does not resist life, but goes along with it in an active manner. He is like the willow bough which is weighed down by the winter snow and does not resist but bends spontaneously under the weight so the snow falls off.

The Seventh Initiate is the lover of life, called the Shab or sometimes the Bhakti.

For a list of the ECK initiations, see page 338.

Seventh Plane *See* ALAYA LOK.

Shab *SHAHB* One who has reached the SEVENTH INITIATION. Also called the BHAKTI.

Shabda *SHAHB-dah* The Voice of the SUGMAD as the vibration of the SUGMAD Itself; the SOUND CURRENT; the ECK.

Shabda Dhun *SHAHB-dah DOON* The Voice of the SUGMAD, the HEAVENLY MUSIC, the Divine Spirit that gives life to all.

See also DHUNATMIK; ECK.

Shabda-MAHANTA *SHAHB-dah-mah-HAHN-tah* One of the two modes of CONTEMPLATION—communication on the inner with the MAHANTA CONSCIOUSNESS.

See also SHABDA-SUGMAD.

Shabda-SUGMAD *SHAHB-dah-SOOG-mahd* One of the two modes of CONTEMPLATION—communication on the inner with the SUGMAD.

See also SHABDA-MAHANTA.

Shamballa *shahm-BAH-lah* One of the ten SPIRITUAL CITIES which help this world, located in the Himalayan mountains between India and Tibet. It is the home of the White Brotherhood, who keep vigil on the physical aspects of world evolution along paths of peace

and righteousness.

The other nine spiritual cities are AGAM DES, AKEVIZ, DAMCAR, KIMTAVED, MUMSAKA, NAMPAK, RAHAKAZ, SAT DHAM, and ZEZIRATH.

Shamus-i-Tabriz *SHAH-muhs-ee-tah-BREEZ,* also Shams-i-Tabrizi (*SHAMS-ee-tah-BREEZ-ee*)

An ECK MASTER who once served as the MAHANTA, the LIVING ECK MASTER. He is now the GUARDIAN of the SHARIYAT-KI-SUGMAD at the Temple of SAKAPORI on the CAUSAL PLANE.

Description

Shamus was born in AD 1184 and, in the next century, was a Sufi master who taught his followers SOUL TRAVEL. A prize student of Shamus was RUMI, the famed Persian poet and sage who was also a follower of ECK.

The scent of jasmine is frequently associated with Shamus. He is a broad, heavyset man of medium height and appears to be about forty. His brown beard is short and full.

When he is not wearing a turban, one notices his long, thick, dark-brown, wavy hair, which looks almost black. His flashing eyes are also a dark brown. Sometimes he appears to seekers in a floppy, wide-brimmed hat and a maroon robe draped casually over his left shoulder. His deep, resonant voice is like honey.

For a list of ECK Masters, see page 341.

Shandava *shahn-DAH-vah* An ECK MASTER who dwells on the SOUL PLANE.

For a list of ECK Masters, see page 341.

Shangta, Valley of *See* VALLEY OF SHANGTA.

Shanti *SHAHN-tee* A spiritually charged word attuned to the ALAKH LOK, the Sixth PLANE. You can chant *Shanti* in CONTEMPLATION to visit GOLDEN WISDOM TEMPLES, meet ECK MASTERS, and have other experiences on this plane. *Shanti* means peace.

For an overview of the planes and their charged words, see **The God Worlds Chart** on page 340.

sharir Another term for body, as in Buddhi Sharir (ETHERIC BODY).

See also SARUP.

Shariyat *SHAH-ree-aht* The SHARIYAT-KI-SUGMAD or the LIVING SHARIYAT.

Shariyat, The Year of the The third of the SPIRITUAL YEARS OF ECK.

For a description, see **The Spiritual Years of ECK** on page 354.

Shariyat-Ki-SUGMAD The Shariyat-Ki-SUGMAD, which means WAY OF THE ETERNAL, is the holy book of ECKANKAR. The Shariyat takes up and discusses every phase of life in both the worlds of matter and the highest planes.

There are twelve volumes. Sections of the Shariyat are kept in each GOLDEN WISDOM TEMPLE, beginning on Earth and continuing on each spiritual PLANE

upward into the very heart of the Kingdom of God.

At each Temple, a particular ECK MASTER serves as GUARDIAN and preceptor of the sacred writings in his charge.

Accessing the Shariyat

These ancient scriptures can be spoken and written in the LOWER WORLDS, but in the higher worlds it is only the heavenly white music.

Two volumes of the Shariyat have been transcribed from the inner planes and are available in print as *The Shariyat-Ki-SUGMAD, Books One & Two*.

Only a small part of the whole Shariyat can be, or ever has been, put into the printed word. Most of it comes straight into the individual during the SPIRITUAL EXERCISES OF ECK as the LIVING WORD, the LIGHT AND SOUND of ECK.

CHELAS can also study these great scriptures in the DREAM STATE or via SOUL TRAVEL. The guidance of the MAHANTA, the INNER MASTER, is key to any true understanding of the Shariyat-Ki-SUGMAD.

The LIVING ECK MASTER turns the chela over to the ECK Master in charge of the Shariyat-Ki-SUGMAD on the chela's plane of INITIATION to be given the golden wisdoms.

History and Contents

The Shariyat-Ki-SUGMAD is said to have been known in antediluvian times, and before that on the continents known as LEMURIA and ATLANTIS.

On Earth, only the KATSUPARI MONASTERY, in

northern Tibet, and the Temple of GARE-HIRA, in AGAM DES, have these writings in their keeping. At the FAQITI MONASTERY, an introduction to the Shariyat is taught by ECK Master BANJANI.

Other sections of the Shariyat are located on other planets and on other planes beyond this world.

Each of the twelve books of the Shariyat contains twelve to fifteen chapters, each of about thirty thousand words. Much of it is made up of cantos, or what we call verse in dialogue form.

Not all the writing is made up of cantos or free verse. Often it is straight narrative, or legends and stories. Sometimes it is allegories or fables. But altogether it is the whole truth, concise in all its parts, and tells everyone what life really consists of and how to live it.

The Word of God

The Shariyat-Ki-SUGMAD contains the WISDOM and ecstatic knowledge of the SPIRITUAL WORLDS beyond the regions of time and space. To read and study this inspired book will give you insight into the scriptures found in the Temples of Golden Wisdom from which these teachings emanate.

The essence of God knowledge is laid down here. Those who follow ECK are involved in these writings of golden wisdom. The Shariyat-Ki-SUGMAD is their bible, their everlasting gospel.

There has probably never been a greater gift from

ECKANKAR to the world. One will find within the pages of the Shariyat an answer to every question man has ever devised to ask of any greater ones. All that which is truth is here now, within its pages.

See also guardian(s); LIVING SHARIYAT; NINE UNKNOWN GODS OF ETERNITY; SECRET DOCTRINE; SHARIYAT TECHNIQUE.

Shariyat technique One of the key SPIRITUAL EXERCISES OF ECK. Some who have had difficulties with the imaginative techniques for SOUL TRAVEL will find success with this method.

To learn how to do this exercise, see **Three Key Spiritual Exercises of ECK** on page 347.

Shatikayas *shah-tee-KAY-yahz* A fierce, warlike tribe whose ancestors were the warrior tribes of old India. They will come out of the Shatikaya continent which will form during the upheaval when parts of the present world will sink and land masses break up around the year AD 2500.

See also ROOT RACES.

Shiv Sena *SHEEV SEH-nah* An ECK MASTER who works on the SOUL PLANE under SAT NAM.

Shiv Sena, a Hindu, was MORAJI DESAL's successor as LIVING ECK MASTER and predecessor to YAUBL SACABI. During his term as Living ECK Master, Shiv Sena inspired Moses to lead the Israelites out of Egypt.

For a list of ECK Masters, see page 341.

Shraddha *SHRAHD-dah* One who has reached the SIXTH INITIATION.

siddhis *SEED-deez* Psychic powers, spiritual powers, supernormal powers, PROPHECY, healing, etc.

Silence, Law of One of the SPIRITUAL LAWS OF LIFE. Also called kamit. An essential discipline in ECKANKAR; it means keeping silent about most communications between you and the INNER MASTER—about the INNER TEACHINGS, personal affairs with ECK, and the SECRET WORD given in the INITIATIONS.

It requires DISCRIMINATION and includes honoring confidentiality and respecting the privacy of others.

Silent Ones *See* MAHAVAKYIS; NINE SILENT ONES; VOLAPUK.

Silent Ones, Nine *See* NINE SILENT ONES.

silver age *See* FOUR CYCLES OF LIFE; MAHAYUGA; YUGA(S).

silver cord The communication link which is attached to each of the bodies which SOUL takes on; the line which holds the material bodies to the various PLANES: PHYSICAL, ASTRAL, CAUSAL, and MENTAL.

Simha *SEEM-hah* The Simha is the Lady of ECK and the nurturing principle in the ECK works. Little is known about Simha, because that is her preference.

The Compassion of Simha

She is considered to be the mother of all ECK MASTERS born in the world of matter. While she is

not their actual mother, of course, her compassion and understanding is of great support to candidates for ECK MASTERSHIP. An ECK Master herself, she is there to help those in the early stages of training to become ECK Masters.

She also comes to encourage the young. Simha inspires them when times get very hard and the problems of daily life make them doubt their goal of GOD-REALIZATION. In that, she fulfills the spiritual role of a mother.

She regards the cults of feminism and other aberrations like male dominance as the effects of emotional waves that cover the skies of human doings like clouds. She knows that those under the spell of such psychic waves are simply showing the response of adolescent spiritual beings.

By way of example, then, she is the very essence of HUMILITY.

A number of ECK INITIATES have had the grace of her spiritual instruction in the DREAM STATE.

Should you ever be in great pain of body or heart, this tall and thin figure may come to bring cheer and comfort. You will be soothed by her warm, compassionate smile and understanding eyes.

For a list of ECK Masters, see page 341.

sinchit karma *SEEN-cheet KAHR-mah* RESERVE KARMA, one of the four types of KARMA.

The other types are DAILY KARMA, FATE KARMA, and PRIMAL KARMA.

single eye, the *See* EYE OF GOD.

Sixth Initiation The INITIATION of the ALAKH LOK, the Sixth PLANE, is both an inner and outer ceremony.

At the Sixth Initiation, the CHELA can work consciously with the ECK MASTERS with intelligence and awareness of what is taking place.

His knowledge of the universes of God is ever expanding. He has become the wholly spiritual man, which he has struggled all these many lifetimes to become.

The initiate's COMPASSION and HUMILITY increases, making him a refined channel for the Master. The Sixth Initiate is the Shraddha.

For a list of the ECK initiations, see page 338.

Sixth Plane *See* ALAKH LOK.

sixty-year cycle *See* RABJUNG.

skandhas *SKAHN-dahz* Ideas, wishes, dreams, and CONSCIOUSNESS of the lower self which create ATTACHMENTs to the physical realm.

social consciousness *See* HUMAN CONSCIOUSNESS.

Socrates An ECK MASTER and well-known Greek philosopher of the fifth century BC.

Sohang, Lord *SOH-hahng* The Lord of the ETHERIC PLANE, the land of Bhanwar Gupha. The great power current flows through him into this region and downward. The name means "I am that!" Also known as SAGUNA BRAHM.

See also **The God Worlds Chart** on page 340.

Sokagampo *soh-kah-GAHM-poh* The title of the GUARDIAN of the SHARIYAT-KI-SUGMAD, at the TAMANATA KOP GOLDEN WISDOM TEMPLE on the ALAKH LOK, the Sixth PLANE. TOMO GESHIG is currently the Sokagampo.

For a list of noted guardians, see **A Road Map for Spiritual Travelers** on page 343.

Souaroupiam *swah-roo-pee-YAHM* The third of the FOUR STATES OF THE HIGH INITIATE. The other three are Salokiam, Samipiam, and Sayodiyam.

Soul Soul is the True Self—who and what we actually are; the individual manifestation of the ECK. Each Soul is an eternal, unique atom of God.

Soul exists because God loves It. We are of the essence of God, and therefore, no matter how imperfect our knowledge of God is, we are still holy.

Soul is immortal, and Its future is the future of a thing whose growth and splendor has no limits. The SUGMAD (God) creates Souls so that, through their experiences, It can know Itself in a greater way. The SUGMAD imparts to Soul the creative element of Itself, the God-spark of IMAGINATION.

Soul has FREE WILL, imagination, and the ability to postulate and create. Soul can see, know, and perceive all things.

Soul is the creative center of Its own world as It unfolds into the higher realms of God and becomes

> a COWORKER WITH GOD. WISDOM, power, love, and freedom are states of Soul.

The divine power of ECK can only work, in the LOWER WORLDS, through the individual. The function of the individual is to differentiate and distribute the creative power. Man's place in the cosmic order is that of a distributor of divine power, subject to the inherent law of the power he distributes.

Soul is always in eternity. It is always in the present NOW. Soul is the medium between the outer world of the CHELA and the heavenly worlds within himself.

Other words for Soul are *Atma* and *Tuza*.

See also PATH OF SOUL; PURPOSE OF SOUL; RECIPROCITY, LAW OF; SELF-REALIZATION.

Soul body The body in which SOUL dwells on the ATMA LOK. An extremely sensitive body which, in Its natural state, is a perfect vessel of the Divine Being. Also called the Atma Sarup, or Atma Sharir.

See also BODIES OF SOUL.

Soul, dark night of *See* DARK NIGHT OF SOUL.

Soul, Law of The Law of Soul states that SOUL is the manifested individual beingness of the ECK Spirit (Holy Spirit). It has FREE WILL, opinions, intelligence, imagination, and immortality.

This is one of the SPIRITUAL LAWS OF LIFE; the second law of the physical universe (see **Seven Laws of**

the Physical Universe on page 344).

soul mates A popular belief, sometimes called the time-twins theory, which is not part of ECKANKAR but is discussed in the book *The ECK-Vidya, Ancient Science of Prophecy*.

Soul is never in need of another Soul to complete Itself; rather, each individual Soul, when it becomes Self-Realized, experiences the blending of masculine and feminine forces within.

See also PRINCIPLES, FEMININE AND MASCULINE; SELF-REALIZATION.

Soul, path of *See* PATH OF SOUL.

Soul Plane The Fifth PLANE (counting upward), the first of the pure, positive SPIRITUAL WORLDS; the dividing plane between the LOWER WORLDS and the true spiritual worlds.

It is the plane of SELF-REALIZATION, or SOUL recognition; it is the first step of Soul into the worlds of God, the kingdom of heaven where we gain freedom and INDIVIDUALITY which is self-recognized and allows Soul to enter into that state called GOD-REALIZATION.

Distinctions of the Soul Plane

SUGMAD—spelled out letter by letter—is the word, or CHANT, that one can sing in CONTEMPLATION to attune oneself to the VIBRATIONS of the Soul Plane or travel inwardly to a GOLDEN WISDOM TEMPLE or other places there.

An inner experience on this plane may include

hearing the sound of a single note of the flute.

The main Golden Wisdom Temple on this plane is PARAM AKSHAR; here TINDOR SAKI, the JAGAT GIRI, serves as GUARDIAN of the SHARIYAT-KI-SUGMAD. Other ECK MASTERS working on this plane are NIRGUNA EKAM, SHANDAVA, SHIV SENA, and TURA YUNG. The spiritual community of HONARDI is on this plane.

The Soul Plane is also called the Atma Lok or SACH KHAND; its ruler is SAT NAM.

See also **The God Worlds Chart** on page 340.

Soul Realization Another term for SELF-REALIZATION; also sometimes refers to SPIRITUAL UNFOLDMENT in general.

See also REALIZATION, LEVEL(S) OF.

Soul records The Soul records are a complete accounting of a SOUL'S INCARNATIONS in the LOWER WORLDS. They are found in various places on the SOUL PLANE.

Soul records of those who have attained the FIFTH INITIATION are kept in the MEARP REGION of the Soul Plane. The records of those with the SIXTH INITIATION are kept in the ANUGA REGION. The records of those with the SEVENTH INITIATION through the TWELFTH INITIATION are kept in the ECK-NIDA REGION. The records of those who have attained the THIRTEENTH INITIATION (the MAHANTA Maharai) or FOURTEENTH INITIATION (the MAHANTA) are kept in the abode of the SAT NAM.

Only the MAHANTA, the LIVING ECK MASTER has the training to read any of these records for others, although a few CHELAS do undergo the training to learn to read their own.

Anyone who undertakes the needed disciplines can make a personal study of the methods employed by the ECK MASTERS in order to see his own Soul records.

See also AKASHIC RECORDS; ECK-VIDYA; PAST LIVES; REINCARNATION.

Soul Travel Soul Travel is getting in touch with your higher nature, which is SOUL. As Soul, you have the ability to transcend the PHYSICAL BODY and travel into the spiritual worlds of God.

This is essentially the expansion of CONSCIOUSNESS. It can take place in the DREAM STATE or via the SPIRITUAL EXERCISES OF ECK, or even in the natural course of your daily life.

Soul Travel, which is taught only by the LIVING ECK MASTER, makes you aware of God's plans. Via Soul Travel you can prove to yourself the existence of God and life after death, and you can discover the purpose of your life.

The Experience of Soul Travel

Soul Travel is both an art and a science. In its purest form, Soul Travel is simply Soul leaving behind Its awareness of the HUMAN CONSCIOUSNESS and moving into a higher one closer to God.

Sometimes it is a subtle shifting of consciousness from everyday problems to a commanding overview of how those same problems fit into the divine plan of Soul's evolution to a higher state of PURITY. Soul Travel ranges far and wide.

Some people experience Soul Travel as a shift of consciousness. All of a sudden, something happens in their lives where they become aware that they understand something they haven't before. It comes in like a soft, golden kiss of God. Then, they just *know*.

Soul Travel can also be a dramatic experience where people are lifted out of the body and have conscious experience in the other worlds.

It depends on what you, as Soul, are ready for and what's necessary for your SPIRITUAL UNFOLDMENT.

The Purpose of Soul Travel

Soul Travel deals with the expansion of spiritual awareness. People have to, at some time, become aware of who and what they are. This knowledge can come through dreams or revelations of PAST LIVES and possibilities for the future.

Soul Travel transcends the limits of astral or MIND travel and rote PRAYER, elevating one into profound spiritual realms. Whenever Soul reaches the far orbits of the inner PLANES through Soul Travel, the human

> heart opens to God's all-consuming love.
>
> This is what life is all about.

See also SEEING, KNOWING, AND BEING.

Sound Current The Audible Life Stream; the ECK (Holy Spirit), the WORD of God, the Spirit of the Unwritten TRUTH.

The Sound Current is that divine essence, the Voice of the SUGMAD, which sustains all life and can be seen and heard, outwardly and inwardly, by the faculties of SOUL. It is the sound of spiritual atoms moving in space.

> The Audible Life Stream is the Divine Being expressing Itself like a wave flowing out from the heart of God. It is the creative current, the purifying element which carries Soul home to God.

Listening for the Sound Current is a key element of the SPIRITUAL EXERCISES OF ECK.

See also BANI; DHUNATMIK; ECK; HEAVENLY MUSIC; LIGHT AND SOUND; MUSIC OF THE SPHERES; NADA BINDU.

Sound of Soul *See* HU.

Sound of Soul event An ECKANKAR event to introduce the HU CHANT and share in spiritual conversation.

Spirit, Law of One of the SPIRITUAL LAWS OF LIFE. Life is only Spirit, and being Spirit, It has nothing; it has only intelligence with the peculiar ability to perceive, penetrate, and survive, and to have causation, specialization, creativeness, beauty, love, and ethics. This law has also been called the Law of MKSHA.

spirito-material worlds The LOWER WORLDS—the five PLANES of matter, energy, time, and space which lie below the SOUL PLANE.

spiritual cities The ten cities which are on earth to help this world: AGAM DES, AKEVIZ, DAMCAR, KIMTAVED, MUMSAKA, NAMPAK, RAHAKAZ, SAT DHAM, SHAMBALLA, and ZEZIRATH. These spiritual cities are SUPRAPHYSICAL; they can be visited by invitation only, and then only in the SOUL BODY. Yet many, including ECK CHELAS, do go there in the DREAM STATE or via SOUL TRAVEL.

Agam Des is the chief spiritual city; the others are outposts for Agam Des.

Map of Ten Spiritual Cities on Earth

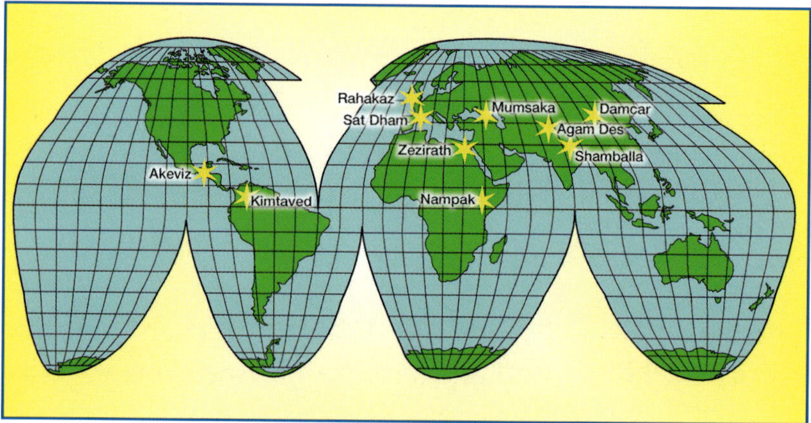

Spiritual Evolution, Law of One of the SPIRITUAL LAWS OF LIFE. The Law of Spiritual Evolution presup-

poses inequality in all things and beings and their continued effort for SPIRITUAL UNFOLDMENT.

We are led by the SPIRITUAL HIERARCHY from the lowest state of spiritual evolution to the highest. We are led gradually through the different religions and various moral precepts until we gain enough strength to come to an awareness of the overarching spiritual laws of life.

See also PROGRESSIVE CONTINUATION, LAW OF; STATE(S) OF CONSCIOUSNESS.

Spiritual Exercises of ECK The spiritual exercises are the essential method for gaining SPIRITUAL UNFOLDMENT and ENLIGHTENMENT on the path of ECKANKAR. This is one of the FOUR FUNDAMENTALS OF ECK.

A spiritual exercise is the daily practice of aligning with the SOUND CURRENT for direct, personal spiritual experience. The chela practices creative techniques, using CONTEMPLATION and the singing of sacred words, to bring the higher awareness of SOUL into daily life.

These spiritual exercises keep the HEART CENTER, the SPIRITUAL EYE, and the CROWN CHAKRA open and facilitate SOUL TRAVEL. They are a sacred form of SATSANG.

Spiritual Transformation

When you start to do the Spiritual Exercises of ECK, the LIGHT AND SOUND of the Holy Spirit begin to enter you through an invisible communication line, and changes come about in your personality.

You become a more independent, thoughtful, self-motivated individual because you are taking the first steps toward self-mastery.

You will find that your connection with the INNER MASTER and the ECK grows stronger with the practice of these exercises. Day by day, you will realize more clearly the love of the MAHANTA for each SOUL in the worlds of God.

In time you will understand that you no longer walk alone, for the Inner Master serves as your constant guide and companion.

Try New Things

The spiritual exercises should be approached with a sense of excitement and anticipation. Experiment with them. Try new things. You're in your own God Worlds.

It's like a vein of gold running through a mountain. You're on it for a while, then the vein runs out and you have to scout around and find another one.

If you practice the spiritual exercises on a regular schedule, like a meal, you'll get the inner nourishment you seek. Try setting a specific time and place for this daily appointment with the Holy Spirit.

See **Three Key Spiritual Exercises of ECK** on page 347. Many more Spiritual Exercises of ECK can be found in the ECK SPIRITUAL LIVING COURSES and ECK books.

See also MANTRA; ZIKAR.

Spiritual Eye The Spiritual Eye serves as a window

between our physical world and the worlds of God beyond. Also called the Tisra Til, or the Third Eye, it is the seat of SOUL in the human body.

Its physical counterpart is the pineal gland, which is located directly between and behind the eyebrows, almost at the center of the brain. The ECK MASTERS call this the Tenth Door.

It is the way station that Soul uses to boost Itself into the unutterably magnificent PLANES OF LIGHT AND SOUND that defy description.

spiritual freedom ECKANKAR is the Path of Spiritual Freedom. Along with WISDOM and power, freedom is one of the THREE ATTRIBUTES OF GOD.

Spiritual freedom is growing into a state of godliness, becoming more aware of the presence of God. It brings liberation from KARMA and REINCARNATION and the ability to come and go at will in the GOD WORLDS. This is the perfect freedom to make decisions out of one's own STATE OF CONSCIOUSNESS.

Three things are needed for spiritual freedom:

1. the LIVING ECK MASTER,
2. the SOUND CURRENT, and
3. Jivan Mukti, spiritual liberation here and now, which comes at the FIFTH INITIATION.

Spiritual Growth, Law of One of the SPIRITUAL LAWS OF LIFE. TRUTH has to be continually rediscovered, reformed, and transformed; the same truth has

to be experienced in ever-new forms.

spiritual healing The only true healing in all the worlds of God is spiritual healing.

To heal your body is a noble undertaking, for it is an active expression in your life of the ECK, the LIVING WORD. The ECK MASTERS recognize that healthy bodies aid the concentration necessary to reach GOD-REALIZATION.

Divine Spirit often heals through the field of medicine and guides you to the doctor who is right for your condition. Yet the ways of healing by Divine Spirit are truly endless.

Healings may be physical, emotional, mental, and spiritual.

All the help that comes to us is from the Holy Spirit, whether it comes in a dream or through the help of a friend or a doctor. The trick is the DISCRIMINATION you need: to tell what's good for you and what's not good for you.

This comes by listening to your heart.

Tips for Spiritual Healing

Health is HARMONY. To maintain harmony, one must guard the three entrances—the mouth, the ears, and the eyes. Be aware of what enters the mouth and what comes out of it. Watch closely what your ears hear and how you process this information. Observe carefully what your eyes see and how that affects your emotions.

Health is SELF-DISCIPLINE. The ECK MASTERS who

have been granted LONGEVITY work at it all the time. They work to maintain harmony in their being.

The way to stay in harmony with the ECK is to continually practice the SPIRITUAL EXERCISES OF ECK, in one way or another, so that in the end, you become the HU Itself.

See also AYUR VEDHA; KAYA KALP; PURIFY OR POLLUTE; SPIRITUAL HEALING, A YEAR OF.

Spiritual Healing, A Year of The second of the SPIRITUAL YEARS OF ECK.

For a description, see **The Spiritual Years of ECK** on page 354.

spiritual hierarchy The SUGMAD formed the spiritual hierarchy to administrate the creation and maintenance of all the universes.

The hierarchy began with the SUGMAD, followed by the ECK and the MAHANTA, the LIVING ECK MASTER, then the Adepts of the Order of the VAIRAGI, the Lords of each PLANE within the SPIRITUAL WORLDS, and the GUARDIANS of the SHARIYAT-KI-SUGMAD.

Over the lower worlds SUGMAD placed the KAL NIRANJAN, Lord of the negative worlds. Then came the LORDS OF KARMA, the ANGELS, planetary spirits, and ELEMENTALS. Then came man and all creatures subordinate to him: mammals, reptiles, fish, plants, and stones.

Every CHELA who accepts a role of service in ECKANKAR is a member of the spiritual hierarchy. As

> a chela of the MAHANTA, you are working within the spiritual hierarchy every moment of your day.

See also VAIRAGI(S), ANCIENT ORDER OF THE.

spiritual laws of life The laws of the universes which are found in the SHARIYAT-KI-SUGMAD, the holy scriptures of ECK.

These laws spell out the vast cosmic order which manifests throughout every part of the worlds of the SUGMAD. These are the great laws of life, which exist in and by themselves without relation to any other laws and are never changing or varying.

For a list of spiritual laws of life, see page 346.

spiritual liberation *See* SPIRITUAL FREEDOM.

spiritual living *See* SPIRITUAL LIVING COURSES; TWELVE SECRETS TO SPIRITUAL LIVING.

Spiritual Living Courses The ECKANKAR Spiritual Living Courses prepare the CHELA for the ECK INITIATIONS. They are a key benefit of enrollment in ECKANKAR. These are sets of twelve monthly lessons by SRI HAROLD KLEMP and PAUL TWITCHELL. Each lesson includes a new spiritual technique, an audio recording, and other study aids.

They are written with a secret, internal rhythm

that gradually unfolds the consciousness in a very precise and orderly manner.

The courses are studied individually and can also be reviewed in ECK SATSANG CLASSES.

The 17 Years of Spiritual Living Courses

The Easy Way Discourses

The ECK Dream 1 Discourses

The ECK Dream 2 Discourses

For Second Initiates and above:

Letters of Light & Sound 1

Letters of Light & Sound 2

Soul Travel 1—The Illuminated Way

Soul Travel 2

The Secret Way

The Precepts of ECKANKAR

The ECK Satsang Discourses, First Series

The ECK Satsang Discourses, Second Series

The ECK Satsang Discourses, Third Series

The ECK Satsang Discourses, Fourth Series

The Master 1 Discourses

The Master 2 Discourses

The Master 3 Discourses

The Master 4 Discourses

spiritual new year *See* ECK SPIRITUAL NEW YEAR.

spiritual realization *See* SPIRITUAL UNFOLDMENT.

Spiritual Realization A level of realization which comes after SELF-REALIZATION and before GOD-REALIZATION.

Sometimes called Realization of Spirit, it is a high level of SPIRITUAL UNFOLDMENT where a COWORKER WITH THE MAHANTA is refined in character and starts moving into far greater responsibilities, learning a bit of what it means to be a COWORKER WITH God.

See also REALIZATION, LEVEL(S) OF.

Spiritual Traveler The MAHANTA, the LIVING ECK MASTER.

spiritual travelers The ECK MASTERs, the Adepts of the Ancient Order of the VAIRAGI.

See also VAIRAGI(S), ANCIENT ORDER OF THE.

spiritual unfoldment The step-by-step unfolding by SOUL of awareness of Itself and Its relationship with Spirit and the SUGMAD. The path to becoming a CO-WORKER WITH GOD. This is the purpose of ECKANKAR.

See also REALIZATION, LEVEL(S) OF; UNFOLDMENT, LAW OF.

spiritual worlds In contrast to the LOWER WORLDS, the spiritual worlds are the pure positive GOD WORLDS beyond matter, energy, space, and time.

These PLANES, or worlds, from the SOUL PLANE (the Fifth Plane, or Atma Lok) up to the SUGMAD, are the ALAKH LOK, the ALAYA LOK, the HUKIKAT LOK, the AGAM LOK, the ANAMI LOK, the SUGMAD WORLD, and the SUGMAD, the OCEAN OF LOVE AND MERCY.

More generally, the term *spiritual worlds* often refers to all planes beyond the physical. In the broadest sense, all worlds (including the PHYSICAL PLANE) are spiritual, since they are all part of the God Worlds of ECK.

See also **The God Worlds Chart** on page 340.

spiritual years of ECK, the In ECKANKAR, each year carries a spiritual theme and embodies a secret to spiritual living. The twelve themes, starting with The Year of Light and Sound in 2001, perpetually run in order, as shown on the chart below. Each spiritual year begins on the ECK SPIRITUAL NEW YEAR, October 22.

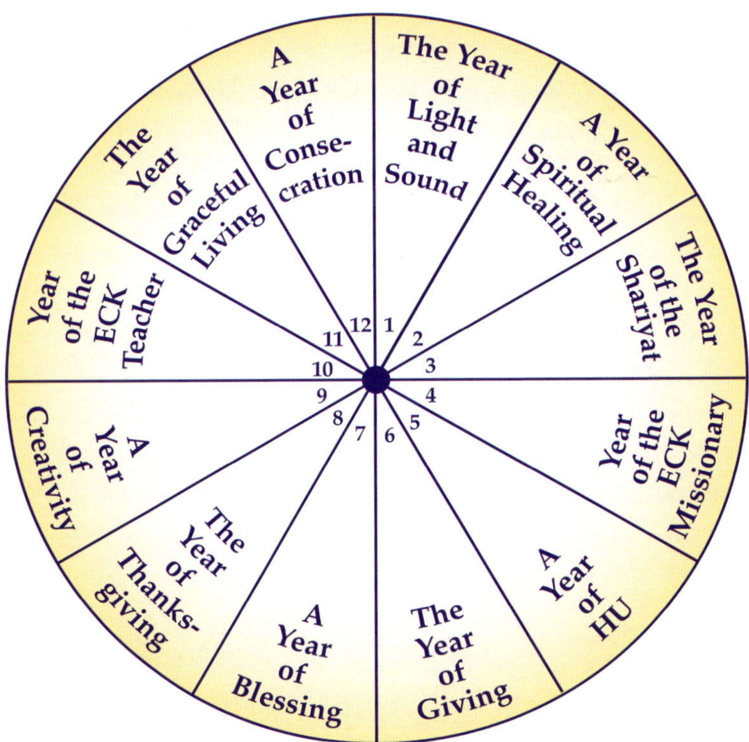

The Spiritual Years of ECK, Beginning in 2001

It was in 1985 that SRI HAROLD KLEMP first brought out the spiritual years and their themes. (For the years and themes from 1985 to 2000, see page 358.) In 1997, Sri Harold created the perpetual cycle of years shown here, noting that it would begin in 2001.

For a description of each spiritual year, see page 354.

Sri *SREE* A title of spiritual respect, similar to reverend or pastor, used for those who have attained the Kingdom of God. In ECKANKAR, it is reserved for the MAHANTA, the LIVING ECK MASTER.

Stabilization, Era of *See* ERA OF STABILIZATION.

States of Being, Law of *See* ATTITUDES, LAW OF.

state(s) of consciousness The levels of awareness that SOUL experiences on Its journey home to God.

These range from the MINERAL STATE up through the HUMAN CONSCIOUSNESS and eventually to SELF-REALIZATION, GOD-REALIZATION, and beyond.

> Your state of consciousness is the level of acceptance you have to changes in conditions and the amount of love you can accept from God.

See also CHANGE, LAW OF; REALIZATION, LEVEL(S) OF.

Strange Storms, Years of the *See* KURITEE.

Strength, Law of One of the SPIRITUAL LAWS OF LIFE. Only the spiritually strong enter the kingdom of heaven.

Suang-tu technique *soo-wang-TOO* The second of the MASTER TECHNIQUES; the first is the DAKAYA TECHNIQUE. Used by the ECK MASTERS of the Order of the VAIRAGI for SOUL TRAVEL and can be used by CHELAS as well.

subconscious *See* ETHERIC BODY.

subtle body *See* ASTRAL BODY.

Sudar Singh *SOO-dahr SING* The LIVING ECK MASTER who lived in Allahabad, India, and taught PEDDAR ZASKQ (PAUL TWITCHELL).

Life of Sudar Singh

Sudar Singh was born into a well-to-do family in the middle part of the nineteenth century. In his youth, he turned his back on his inheritance, dressed in rags, and set off in search of truth. A sadhu told him to make his way to Agra and find REBAZAR TARZS.

Sudar Singh visited one of Rebazar's students, who was also a government official, and questioned the student for several days. Meanwhile, the ECK MASTER was there the whole time, disguised as a servant and observing the seeker closely. However, Sudar Singh concluded there was nothing in the teachings of ECKANKAR for him. Very sadly, he left.

A year later, around 1885, after exploring other religions, he had nearly lost hope. Wandering in the foothills of the Himalayas, he wondered if there was anything left to live for.

One day, hungry and tired, he fell into a light sleep, then awoke suddenly. There stood Rebazar Tarzs, offering a pitcher of milk for nourishment. This time Sudar Singh recognized the Master, and from that point on he began earnestly to make his own steps on the path to God.

Sudar Singh was an elusive ECK Master, and little is known of his life. He had an ashram in Allahabad in the 1930s. He is also known to have spread the message of ECK in Europe and other places. One of his students says the Master later left India and fled to Canada because of a political uprising.

Sudar lived past his nineties and probably died around 1955. Rebazar Tarzs then took over the leadership of ECKANKAR until 1965, when Paul Twitchell became the MAHANTA, the Living ECK Master.

For a list of ECK Masters, see page 341.

SUGMAD *SOOG-mahd* The supreme God. The formless, all-embracing, impersonal, infinite, the OCEAN OF LOVE AND MERCY.

From It flows all life, all TRUTH, all reality; all WISDOM, love, and power. It is beyond any conception of the human MIND.

It is neither male nor female, old nor new, great nor small, shaped nor shapeless. Having no opposite, It is what opposites have in common.

It takes many forms in order that Its purposes may be carried out in all creations, but none of them express Its totality; what there is and all there is, so that no name

can really be given It except the poetic name of God.

It has an inside called NIRGUNA, which is to say It has no qualities and nothing can be said or thought about It, and an outside called SAGUNA, which is to say that It may be considered as eternal reality, CONSCIOUSNESS, and joy.

Each created form of life, by its own nature, longs for the perfection of the SUGMAD.

Before becoming the MAHANTA, the LIVING ECK MASTER, SRI HAROLD KLEMP had a profound experience in a high, golden world of the SUGMAD. This fragment of a poem came through as a blessing:

The SUGMAD

Heart of my Heart,
Soul of my Soul,
This is the Golden Moment.
O Ancient of Days,
How can I but love Thee?

See also SPIRITUAL HIERARCHY; THREE ASPECTS OF THE SUGMAD; **The God Worlds Chart** on page 340.

SUGMAD (word or chant) *SOOG-mahd* A spiritually charged word attuned to the SOUL PLANE, the Fifth PLANE. You can chant *SUGMAD* in CONTEMPLATION to visit GOLDEN WISDOM TEMPLES, meet ECK MASTERS, and have other experiences on this plane.

For an overview of the planes and their charged words, see **The God Worlds Chart** on page 340.

SUGMAD world The beginning of the abode of the SUGMAD; the PLANE above the ANAMI LOK. Only those who have become ECK MASTERS reach this world.

See also **The God Worlds Chart** on page 340.

Sukhsham mind *SOOK-shahm* The MIND operating on the ASTRAL PLANE.

See also ALIVA MIND; KARAN MIND; PINDA MIND.

Sultan-ul-Azkar *SOOL-tahn-ool-AZ-kahr* Another name for the ECK.

See also SHABDA DHUN.

Sumer *SOO-mehr* One of three peaks seen from the city of MER KAILASH on the MENTAL PLANE. The other two are KAILASH and MER.

Sun Worlds Along with the LIGHTNING WORLDS and MOON WORLDS, these are subplanes which lie between the PHYSICAL PLANE and the true ASTRAL PLANE.

Supaku *soo-pah-KOO* The LIVING ECK MASTER during one of the high periods of the civilization of ATLANTIS. He helped to compile a number of the herbs, roots, seeds, flowers, and plants which were researched in the government health laboratories.

For a list of ECK MASTERS, see page 341.

supraphysical Supraphysical cities and Temples exist on the PHYSICAL PLANE. Because of their high VIBRATIONS which place them at the uttermost edge of physical matter, they are visible only to those with the spiritual eyes to see.

There are four supraphysical GOLDEN WISDOM TEMPLES on the Physical Plane: the FAQITI MONASTERY, GARE-HIRA, the HOUSE OF MOKSHA, and the KATSUPARI MONASTERY. These temples are accessible only by invitation and then only via SOUL TRAVEL.

See also SPIRITUAL CITIES.

Supreme Being *See* SUGMAD.

supreme form of activity SOUL's receptiveness to the majesty of pure TRUTH.

According to *THE SHARIYAT-KI-SUGMAD*, Book Two, "To see the perfect truth of ECK, as It is, demands and compels the subjugation of Soul.

"This is the Everlasting Gospel, which, in Its majesty and uniqueness of pure truth, necessitates a suspension of the personal activity of thought. One ceases to assert his thought against It. He is passive before It; but in that passivity, which requires the utmost opening of his receptiveness, is the supreme form of activity."

Surat *soo-RAHT* Another name for SOUL. Also a SPIRITUAL EXERCISE of ECK wherein one listens for the SOUND CURRENT.

Surati Lok *soo-RAH-tee LOHK* The Mountain World; home of the KATSUPARI MONASTERY in northern Tibet. ECK CHELAS study in this GOLDEN WISDOM TEMPLE under the ECK MASTER FUBBI QUANTZ.

See also ASURATI LOK; LOK; PRITHVI LOK.

Surat Shabda *soo-RAHT SHAHB-dah* One of the

many names for the Divine Spirit, the HEAVENLY MUSIC, the VADAN, the LOGOS, the WORD, the ECK.

Surat technique *soo-RAHT* One of the SOUL TRAVEL techniques of ECKANKAR wherein one listens for the SOUND CURRENT.

surrender *See* SELF-SURRENDER.

Survival, Law of One of the SPIRITUAL LAWS OF LIFE. Each must take care of himself by earning his own way in society; SOUL must keep growing.

Suto T'sing *SOO-toh TSING* A Chinese ECK MASTER who lived for 267 years in the same body.

For a list of ECK Masters, see page 341.

svaha *SVAH-hah* The interval between any two points in time that we choose to be important.

It can refer to what happens between the flash of lightning and the sound of thunder that follows, or between the time we find ECK and the time we reach the goal of GOD-REALIZATION.

sylphs *See* ELEMENTALS.

Tamanata Kop *tah-mah-NAH-tah KOHP* The GOLDEN WISDOM TEMPLE on the Sixth PLANE, the ALAKH LOK. TOMO GESHIG, the SOKAGAMPO, is the ECK MASTER in charge of the SHARIYAT-KI-SUGMAD here.

Tamaqui *tah-MAH-kee* A minor ECK MASTER in Germany during the latter part of the nineteenth century.

For a list of ECK Masters, see page 341.

Tarika Takom *tah-REE-kah tah-KOHM* An ECK MASTER who once served in what is today northern Africa.

For a list of ECK Masters, see page 341.

Tat *TAHT* The supreme Deity worshipped by the Atlanteans.

See also ATLANTIS.

Tat Tsoks *TAHT tsohks* The cruel king-priests who ruled ATLANTIS with an iron hand.

teaching Arahata An ARAHATA (Second Initiate or above in ECKANKAR) who has been trained to teach ECK SATSANG CLASSES and helps each person find their own relationship with Divine Spirit.

Tejahua *teh-jah-HOO-ah* An ECK MASTER on the MENTAL PLANE.

For a list of ECK Masters, see page 341.

Tejas *TEH-jahs* The radiant principle; the glory of the ECK.

You can have the experience of God in many different ways. The people who have these experiences often try to put them into words. Many times the closest they can come is in the form of poetry.

An ECKIST wrote three good poems about his experiences. The first one is about the Tejas, the glory of the ECK. Even though the second and third are written as two separate poems, they actually are part of the first one.

This poem illustrates very well how we carry the LIGHT of ECK into the world in ways that we often don't understand.

Tejas

Gazing out across the great expanse of mountains and trees,
An inner hush calms the sounds of the wilderness.
I stand here by the babbling stream, as its waves leap into space,

And crash noisily to their destiny beneath the falls.
The plight of many Souls, it seems.
This is your place, O Lord,
And my heart leaps to Thee in your presence.
And with the reassuring onement,
My yearning grows to return to Thee.
For here is Thy breath of freedom, as seized in rapture of this moment.
For to be of these heights and survey Thy lands is truly but a great blessing.
And yet to know is greater still.
Surrounded by many, yet here I stand alone,
And silent is the contemplation that is drawn from Thy omnipresence.
The driving winds rush upon the cliff face,
Sweeping spray from the falls, upward to fleck upon my face,
As refreshing now as the winds of heaven to Soul that sustained a special place.

All Giving

A quintessence; a placid moment of still time,
Captured not here nor there, but everywhere.
You share this moment, and in your giving I feel Love.

But what is the fine thing I have done to deserve this great gift?

The question rings, and Love is the only answer.

The Answer

What creations unmanifest must I bring to life?

What breath today must I put to bring forth the Light?

The strangest thing then happened as someone passed my way:

I smiled a smile of gladness, and saw it carried on its way.

Temple of Akash *See* KAZI DAWTZ.

Temple of ECK The Temple of ECK in Chanhassen, Minnesota, serves as both a worldwide GOLDEN WISDOM TEMPLE and a community church. This Temple is ECKANKAR'S SEAT OF POWER and spiritual home on earth.

It provides a direct line of spiritual energy from the higher worlds into the PHYSICAL PLANE.

This is the central vortex from which the MAHANTA, the LIVING ECK MASTER (who is also the GUARDIAN of this Temple) gives the ECK message to the world.

A special place, the Temple stands as an outer symbol for the holy temple of God within every heart.

History

In 1970, PAUL TWITCHELL had a vision of the Temple of ECK, but the dream was not realized during his time. In 1980, SRI HAROLD KLEMP had his own vision of the Temple and saw that it would be in Minnesota.

After a site was found, work on the Temple began in 1988. Two years later it was completed, and Sri Harold presided over the dedication on October 22, 1990.

Visitors to the Temple often comment upon a very definite, loving presence there, for it reflects and rings with the subtle LIGHT AND SOUND of God. Many visitors from around the world recognize they're in a unique, holy place. They return again and again to renew their spiritual lives.

The Temple of ECK is a place for all people who love God, a starting place for SOUL's dream of reaching God.

See also ECKANKAR SPIRITUAL CAMPUS; ECK CENTER(S); ECK TEMPLE(S).

Temple of ECK ziggurat symbol

This symbol reflects the distinctive golden ziggurat roof of the TEMPLE OF ECK in Chanhassen, Minnesota, ECKANKAR's spiritual home on earth.

The nine steps of the ziggurat represent the first nine INITIATIONS of ECK, taking the CHELA into the

first stages of GOD-REALIZATION where one becomes a COWORKER WITH GOD.

temple of God Every SOUL manifesting in a body in the LOWER WORLDS has the Spirit dwelling within and is a temple of God.

While we live in the human body, it is a temple of God, to be kept clean and used here on earth in the most useful and uplifting ways possible.

See also BODIES OF SOUL.

Temple of Sakapori *See* SAKAPORI, TEMPLE OF.

Temple of the Aluk *See* JARTZ CHONG.

Temples of Golden Wisdom *See* GOLDEN WISDOM TEMPLE(S).

ten spiritual cities on earth *See* SPIRITUAL CITIES.

Tenth Door The SPIRITUAL EYE.

Tenth Initiation This is the INITIATION of the Tenth PLANE, the ANAMI LOK, and is given only through the inner channels.

At the Tenth Initiation the CHELA becomes the Adepiseka, one who has entered the divine WISDOM POOL. This is the true WISDOM, not that which is found in the LOWER WORLDS. It is a wisdom beyond human capacity and only when one enters into the Tenth Circle does he have any concept of this.

The spiritual fire growing within him finds that the ECK is the only part of life worth living.

For a list of the ECK initiations, see page 338.

Tenth Plane *See* ANAMI LOK.

Thanksgiving, The Year of The eighth of the SPIRITUAL YEARS OF ECK.

For a description, see **The Spiritual Years of ECK** on page 354.

Thigala *thee-GAH-lah* The first TWELVE-YEAR CYCLE of the ECK-VIDYA; called the Years of the Fierce Winds. Also the first year within a twelve-year cycle.

See also ECK-VIDYA WHEEL.

Third Eye The SPIRITUAL EYE.

Third Initiation At the Third INITIATION the CHELA receives a new SECRET WORD which assists him with the resolution of PAST LIVES, allowing him to live more fully in the present. This is working from the CAUSAL PLANE where there is much to be gained.

The Third Initiate is the Ahrat (sometimes called the Kurnai), a superior SOUL, the worthy one.

This is both an inner and outer ceremony.

The initiate is also concerned with the creative cycle of threes—the positive, the negative, and the neutral (ECK). He discovers that perpetual change is the essence of manifestation.

As a Third Initiate, the chela has become a greater channel for the ECK in his world.

For a list of the ECK initiations, see page 338.

Third Plane *See* CAUSAL PLANE.

third root race *See* LEMURIA; ROOT RACES.

Thirteenth Initiation The Thirteenth Circle of INITIATION in ECKANKAR, the MAHANTA Maharai, the LIVING ECK MASTER working in the MAHANTA CONSCIOUSNESS.

For a list of the ECK initiations, see page 338.

thirty-two facets of ECKANKAR Phases of SPIRITUAL UNFOLDMENT which the ECK CHELA must go through in some lifetime as part of the journey home to God. The thirty-two facets are given in the ECK SPIRITUAL LIVING COURSES.

thousand-petaled lotus *See* CROWN CHAKRA; SAHASRA-DAL-KANWAL.

three aspects of the SUGMAD Also known as the three bodies of the MAHANTA.

The first is the absolute, eternal, *primordial MAHANTA*, called the clear Voice of God, which dwells in the OCEAN OF LOVE AND MERCY.

> The new LIVING ECK MASTER, upon acceptance of his mission, is given recognition by the Ancient Order of the VAIRAGI as the key vehicle for the primordial MAHANTA.

This part has no personality but is only the sublime ECK in expression at the highest level.

The second body of the MAHANTA is the *body of glory, the ECK*, the cosmic Spirit, the SOUND CURRENT—that which is all life, giving existence to all things.

The third body of the MAHANTA is the body of manifestation, the transformation, the *historical MAHANTA*, the Living ECK Master in every age, who is the Eternal One, the bodily manifestation of the SUGMAD.

See also VAIRAGI(S), ANCIENT ORDER OF THE.

three attributes of God-Realization WISDOM, power, and freedom. SOUL acquires these attributes upon reaching GOD-REALIZATION.

three basic principles of ECK First, SOUL is eternal; It has no beginning or end.

Second, whosoever travels the high path of ECK dwells in the spiritual PLANES.

Third, Soul always lives in the present; It has no past and no future.

By the realization of these three principles, the CHELA becomes a transparency for the divine impulse. He comes into a greater awareness of the divine plan in this world and his part in it.

three bodies of the MAHANTA *See* THREE ASPECTS OF THE SUGMAD.

Time for Reaching Out, A (2005–17) See **Twelve-Year Cycles of the Master's Spiritual Mission** on page 352.

Time Track The past, present, and future track upon which each individual life is lived while in the LOWER WORLDS.

See also ECK-VIDYA; REINCARNATION; WHEEL OF THE EIGHTY-FOUR.

Tindor Saki *TIN-dohr SAH-kee* A renowned ECK MASTER on the Fifth, or SOUL, PLANE, who was instrumental in bringing ECK out into the open.

As GUARDIAN of the SHARIYAT-KI-SUGMAD at the Temple of PARAM AKSHAR, his title is the JAGAT GIRI.

For a list of ECK Masters, see page 341.

Tirich Mir *TEER-eech MEER* An imposing mountain peak in the HINDU KUSH Mountains, near where the ECK MASTER REBAZAR TARZS has his abode.

Tirmer *teer-MEER* One of the earlier ECK MASTERS. He was martyred under Shipue, supposedly the first king of Tibet, several hundred centuries BC. The ORACLE OF TIRMER is named after him.

For a list of ECK Masters, see page 341.

Tirmer, Oracle of *teer-MEER* *See* ORACLE OF TIRMER.

Tisra Til *TIZ-rah TIL* The SPIRITUAL EYE.

Tissot Leins *tees-SOHT leh-EENS* The LIVING ECK MASTER during the late seventeenth century in France when the Protestants were being persecuted. He was responsible for the migration of the Huguenots and those of other faiths to America.

For a list of ECK MASTERS, see page 341.

Tiwaja *tee-WAH-jah* The GAZE OF THE MASTER.

tolerance *See* FORGIVENESS AND TOLERANCE.

Tomo Geshig *TOH-moh GEH-shig* The ECK MASTER on the Sixth PLANE, the ALAKH LOK, who appears in the form of a halo of light.

He studied under GOPAL DAS in Egypt five thousand years ago and was the teacher of LAI TSI, the ECK Master on the ETHERIC PLANE.

As GUARDIAN of the SHARIYAT-KI-SUGMAD at the TAMANATA KOP GOLDEN WISDOM TEMPLE, his title is the SOKAGAMPO. He once served as the MAHANTA, the LIVING ECK MASTER.

For a list of ECK Masters, see page 341.

Torchbearer of ECKANKAR *See* REBAZAR TARZS.

total awareness The movement of the inner CONSCIOUSNESS, SOUL, beyond time and space, to where all is omniscient, omnipresent, and omnipotent. The state of SPIRITUAL FREEDOM, our goal in ECKANKAR.

Total awareness, an attribute of the ECK MASTERS, means seeing things as a whole. This becomes a feature of the ECKIST's attitude, for now he faces every problem in life, finding solutions without having to depend on anyone else.

When you enter the Eighth PLANE, the HUKIKAT LOK, you come to the highest state SOUL can generally reach—total awareness. NIRVIKALPA can take you beyond, into the Ninth Plane (the AGAM LOK), where you will be invited to join the Order of the VAIRAGI ADEPTS; into the Tenth Plane (the ANAMI LOK), where you come to the divine WISDOM POOL; and into the Eleventh Plane, where you become the KEVALSHAR. Here the full realization of God occurs.

See also GOD-REALIZATION; REALIZATION, LEVEL(S) OF.

total reliance on the Inner Master One of the FOUR FUNDAMENTALS OF ECK.

> The INNER MASTER is the highest form of all love, the inner form of the LIVING ECK MASTER.
>
> Every moment the MAHANTA is with the CHELA, protecting and guiding him even when it may appear the chela is alone and floundering.

The chela must trust the MAHANTA's love in all things.

Towart Managi *TOH-wahrt mah-NAH-gee*

The ECK MASTER in charge of the SHARIYAT-KI-SUGMAD in the NAMAYATAN GOLDEN WISDOM TEMPLE in the city of MER KAILASH on the MENTAL PLANE. As GUARDIAN his title is the KOJI CHANDA.

He was the MAHANTA, the LIVING ECK MASTER in Abyssinia, an ancient kingdom in what is now Ethiopia. The foremost black ECK Master known in the ECK writings, he is slight of stature, with delicate features, closely cropped hair, and a short white beard.

For a list of ECK Masters, see page 341.

traditions of ECK The traditions of ECK are patterns that shape the ECK culture, which includes the knowledge found in the SHARIYAT-KI-SUGMAD, ECK art, and all the things that ECKISTS do together in the spiritual community.

The person who lives and breathes the ECK culture becomes a dynamic channel for Spirit in his daily life.

Some specific traditions of ECKANKAR are BEAUTIFY

DAY, ECKANKAR FOUNDER'S DAY, HARJI DINNERS, and the ECK SPIRITUAL NEW YEAR (celebrated at an annual ECK seminar).

translation Another term for death—leaving the PHYSICAL BODY permanently and moving into a higher world, or PLANE.

SOUL carries Its body of knowledge from one lifetime to the next. This is similar to translating something from one language into another, such as French into English: the content is the same, and only the words change.

The death of the physical body here on earth is not the death of the personality. The personality lives on as the Astral, Causal, and Mental bodies of the individual until Soul is reincarnated.

This is why so many times after a parent or a loved one dies, people have dream experiences with that person.

At the time of translation, those Souls under the guidance of the LIVING ECK MASTER are taken to whatever region of the INNER WORLDS they have earned. Others, not under the Living ECK Master, are taken before YAMA, who administers KARMA according to their deeds.

Process of Translation

In most cases, as we make the transition into the heavenly worlds, we are totally unconcerned about it. As bright as the sunlight appears to our eyes, this physical world is a dark, small, mean place com-

> pared to the other worlds. You will see settings similar to those on earth, but larger and with a lot more light.
>
> There will be a lightness and spaciousness about the body that you wear there. Soul is once again wearing a body, but It is on a higher plane. It is so natural that generally you don't give it a second thought.
>
> And you are always greeted by someone you know and love.

For people who love TRUTH and God, it's a smooth change.

See also REINCARNATION.

translator *See* DREAM CENSOR.

Trembling Leaf, Years of the *See* MUZUART.

Tretya Yuga *TREHT-yah YOO-gah* The Silver Age.

See also FOUR CYCLES OF LIFE; MAHAYUGA; YUGA(S).

Trikuti *tree-KOO-tee* The Brahm Lok; the MENTAL PLANE; home of the UNIVERSAL MIND.

Triloki *tree-LOH-kee* Another name for the LOWER WORLDS—the PINDA, ANDA, and BRAHMANDA regions between the negative pole of CREATION and the SOUL PLANE.

trinity of ECK The SUGMAD, the ECK, and the MAHANTA.

trinity of ECKANKAR The SAT GURU, the MAHANTA,

the LIVING ECK MASTER; the ECK SATSANG, or his company of followers; and the ECK, or the true name, which is the BANI, or the SOUND CURRENT.

trinity of liberation The LIVING ECK MASTER, the INITIATION, and the SOUND CURRENT.

troglodytes *TRAHG-leh-diets* A primitive red race of ATLANTIS who were able to survive the destruction. Among their descendants today are the Polynesians and American Indians.

true contemplation of the ECK works One of the FOUR FUNDAMENTALS OF ECK.

The attention is focused upon some definite spiritual principle, thought, or idea, or upon the LIVING ECK MASTER.

The CHELA strives to gain inspiration from everything he sees or hears in the ECK works and looks for inner meaning behind the written words, revealed to him by the INNER MASTER.

true prayer *See* PRAYER.

True Self *See* SOUL.

Truth The essence, Spirit, SOUL, and life of everything that exists or appears to exist, itself unchangeable and immortal; the essence of essences, Spirit of spirits, Soul of Souls, omniscient, omnipotent, formless, boundless, unapproachable, unchangeable; the source and beginning of life, an unlimited ocean of love and WISDOM; the ECK.

> The highest truth is not written in any book; it's written in your heart.

As Soul, you have the God knowledge within you. The Master's main job is to awaken the knowledge and the love for the divine things that are already in your heart.

truth, days of *See* RALOT.

Tsong Sikhsa *TSOHNG SEEK-sah* The title of the GUARDIAN of the holy book of ECKANKAR, the SHARIYAT-KI-SUGMAD, at the ANAKAMUDI GOLDEN WISDOM TEMPLE on the Seventh PLANE, the ALAYA LOK. MESI GOKARITZ is currently the guardian.

For a list of noted guardians, see **A Road Map for Spiritual Travelers** on page 343.

Tulsi Das *TUHL-see DAHS* One of the pioneers of the FAR COUNTRY, who was a seventeenth-century Hindu mystic poet and follower of ECK.

Tura Yung *TOO-rah YOONG* The ECK MASTER who is the spiritual head of the GOLDEN WISDOM TEMPLE on the SOUL PLANE, the Fifth PLANE.

For a list of ECK Masters, see page 341.

Turiya Pad *TOOR-ee-yah PAHD* Another name for the ASTRAL PLANE.

See also PAD.

Tuza *TOO-zah* *See* SOUL.

Twelfth Initiation This is the INITIATION of the

Twelfth Circle, where it is learned that the ECK is not energy of itself but It controls and directs energy in all the worlds of God.

The ECK INITIATE must be free at all times to follow the MAHANTA, the LIVING ECK MASTER. The Twelfth Initiate is the Maharaji, a leader in the spiritual community of ECK.

He will be approached by those ECK MASTERS who are the body of the brotherhood of the ANCIENT ORDER OF THE VAIRAGI for membership with this august body.

The duties and responsibilities of these God-Realized beings are beyond human comprehension. It is the destiny of all who love the SUGMAD, heart and SOUL, to eventually reach these splendid heights.

For a list of the ECK initiations, see page 338.

twelve secrets to spiritual living Each spiritual-year theme given by the Master (see SPIRITUAL YEARS OF ECK, THE) embodies a secret to spiritual living.

See **The Spiritual Years of ECK** on page 354.

twelve-year cycle(s) The 12-year (duodenary) cycle, called the LHOKHOR, is a great cycle of the ECK-VIDYA. Greater cycles include a factor multiplied by it, such as the 60-year cycle, the RABJUNG. Lesser cycles include the 3- and 4-year cycles.

> The 12-year cycle provides a key turning point in the life of a person.
>
> Each 12-year cycle can mark a time of spiritual

upliftment, if a person keeps his face toward God. It's a time to balance the rate of vibrations.

The number twelve is expressed in the world in the person of the MAHANTA, the LIVING ECK MASTER. Each great cycle of twelve is a new period of starting over again, developed only through the LIGHT of the MAHANTA, the Living ECK Master, who is the embodiment and expression of the twelve.

The twelve cycles of twelve in the ECK-Vidya are THIGALA, GINTHE, DORETI, YIGERTA, FARANK, KURITEE, LENURIG, SELTEA, ERUTUA, NERALIT, HIAFI, and MUZUART.

See also ECK-VIDYA WHEEL; SPIRITUAL YEARS OF ECK, THE; **Twelve-Year Cycles of the Master's Spiritual Mission** (p. 352).

twelve-year cycles of the Master's spiritual mission *See* **Twelve-Year Cycles of the Master's Spiritual Mission** on page 352.

Twitchell, Paul *See* PAUL TWITCHELL.

two faces of the Master *See* INNER AND OUTER MASTER.

Uighur Empire *WEE-guhr* The empire of the fifth ROOT RACE, the ARYANS, in the Gobi Desert of central Asia. A highly developed civilization which was the center of the world in its day and had as its capital city KHARA KHOTA. It had previously been a province of LEMURIA.

Ulemans *OO-leh-mahnz* A race which presently occupies the planet Jupiter and will descend upon Earth and other planets throughout the solar system to occupy them with absolute ruling power. A future ROOT RACE.

undines *See* ELEMENTALS.

Unfoldment, Law of One of the SPIRITUAL LAWS OF LIFE. SOUL is inevitably bound to become a COWORKER WITH GOD. It means going through all the steps that lead to this, learning how to give and receive DIVINE LOVE.

See also SPIRITUAL UNFOLDMENT.

Unity, Law of The ECK is the unity in the midst of diversity and multiplicity. The Law of Unity is thinking in the whole instead of the parts. It is a way of knowing the solution to a problem the instant it presents itself. This law simply means one must be wholly within the ECK (Holy Spirit) in order to enjoy himself as the whole man.

This is one of the SPIRITUAL LAWS OF LIFE; the seventh law of the physical universe (see **Seven Laws of the Physical Universe** on page 344).

See also UNIVERSAL LAW OF GOD.

Universal Compensation, Law of *See* KARMA, LAW OF.

universal law of God Each half of a cycle of a wave from the BANI eternally gives to the other half for regiving; Life forever unfolds into many for the purpose of refolding into the one.

See also RECIPROCITY, LAW OF; UNITY, LAW OF.

Universal Mind A neutral but highly unstable and inconstant force on the MENTAL PLANE that SOUL takes on when operating in the LOWER WORLDS. The lower worlds, the PLANES ruled by the KAL NIRANJAN, are sometimes called the Universal Mind realm.

See also KAL; MIND; OMKAR; TRIKUTI.

upaya *oo-PAH-yah* A device for the spiritual seeker to use to move into the higher states, like a raft or boat to get across a river.

Uri *OO-ree* The city on the ETHERIC PLANE, where

many essential parts of the spiritual essence for the worlds below are put together, and the seeds, or SOULS (unmanifested atoms), are prepared to be sent into the LOWER WORLDS for experiences.

Uturat *OO-too-raht* The second MONTH OF THE ECK-VIDYA, corresponding to February. The days of love. The month of the bloodstone.

This journey brings SOUL great concern for love, companionship, and wealth.

See also ECK-VIDYA WHEEL.

Vadan *VAH-dahn* The primal music of the universe; the music of ECK; the WORD of the SUGMAD; the essence of life.

See also DHUNATMIK; SOUND CURRENT; VARNATMIK.

Vahana *vah-HAH-nah* The Vahana, or ECK missionary, is a CHELA who aids the LIVING ECK MASTER in carrying the message of ECK into the world.

Every ECK INITIATE is a vehicle for the ECK in his daily life as a carrier of the LIGHT AND SOUND.

The mission of a Vahana is to carry the news and benefits to others of God's love for SOUL. The ultimate goal of any ARAHATA or ECK Vahana is to teach a seeker how to connect directly with the Light and Sound of God. To know that Soul exists because God loves It.

The scope of the ECK missionary effort is vast. And it is a team effort, as the entire ECK SPIRITUAL HIERARCHY is working on connecting willing Souls with the MAHANTA so he can lead them home to God. For Vahanas on Earth, the link with this missionary effort is through the ECKANKAR SPIRITUAL CENTER.

Help from the Council of the Nine

If spreading the teachings of ECK is your goal, put attention upon the COUNCIL OF THE NINE, the ECK MASTERS responsible for the distribution of the ECK message in the LOWER WORLDS.

Invite their help; ask them to accompany you to work or ECK meetings. Remember, no ECK Master will interfere, but will wait for you to give an express invitation. So you have to approach them during CONTEMPLATION to request help formulating plans.

Then be aware of these Masters throughout your day. This team of nine is unbeatable.

An Exercise

The FOUR-STEP SPIRITUAL EXERCISE OF ECK uses "ECK Vahana" as a chant; *see* page 347.

Vahana Marg *vah-HAH-nah MAHRG* One of the SEVEN MARGS. The order of the missionary. The ECK INITIATE gives of himself to the ECK as a carrier of the message of ECK into the world and among the masses of mankind. These are the true messengers of the spiritual truths of ECKANKAR.

See also VAHANA.

vairag *vie-RAHG* Another word for the spiritual virtue of DETACHMENT.

Vairag is the chief characteristic of the God-Realized states.

See also FIVE VIRTUES; GOD-REALIZATION; VAIRAGI(S), ANCIENT ORDER OF THE.

VAIRAGI Adepts *vie-RAH-gee* Another name for the ECK MASTERS.

See also VAIRAGI(S), ANCIENT ORDER OF THE.

VAIRAGI(s), Ancient Order of the This is the brotherhood of ECK MASTERS, also called VAIRAGI Adepts or simply the VAIRAGIs (*vairag* means DETACHMENT).

> It is the only pure line of spiritual Adepts and has been unbroken since before the beginning of time. The MAHANTA, the LIVING ECK MASTER is the head of the VAIRAGI Order, and the missions of all ECK Masters are aligned with his.

The existence of this order has been known to mystics and occultists in every age. Yet for centuries, since the beginning of this world, the ECK Masters have kept themselves well hidden from human eyes and ears in order to fulfill their missions.

The MAHANTA, the Living ECK Master, as well as the Order of the VAIRAGI, has been the chief factor in producing all civilizations, including the present modern civilization. Those who have done the most for the human race in the intellectual and spiritual aspects, as well as its material life, have been the ECK Masters of the Ancient Order of the VAIRAGI.

But nothing other than giving the human race spiritual upliftment has ever been the aim of the ECK Masters. Rather all else, other than the spiritual aim, has been the consequence—almost the by-product—of their search for helping man reach perfection through the SPIRITUAL EXERCISES OF ECK.

See also MAHARAJ; SPIRITUAL HIERARCHY. For a list of ECK Masters, see page 341.

VAIRAGI Order *See* VAIRAGI(S), ANCIENT ORDER OF THE.

Vaita Danu *vie-EE-tah DAH-noo* The LIVING ECK MASTER who succeeded PHIDIAS and whose successor was JU CHIAO.

Vaita Danu, a Hindu, was present during Alexander the Great's march into India. He tested Alexander but found him wanting; then, just as an officer was poised to strike Vaita Danu with a sword, the ECK MASTER disappeared into thin air. He lived for more than 150 years because of his great knowledge of the AYUR VEDHA, a system for renewing the body's health.

For a list of ECK Masters, see page 341.

Vajra Manjushri *VAHJ-rah mahn-JOO-shree* The LIVING ECK MASTER who tried to teach ECKANKAR to the Persians around 700 BC, at the time of King Hakhamanish I. The people of those times had sunk deeply into the HUMAN CONSCIOUSNESS, and Manjushri tried to find ways to raise them into the SPIRITUAL WORLDS.

For his trouble, he was arrested, condemned, and executed. Stretched out on a block of wood shaped like the letter *E*, the king's men fired arrows into his body.

His followers buried his body in a cave. But the next morning they found the body missing and fell to arguing over who stole it. Suddenly a voice stopped the quarrel. Vajra Manjushri stood there, clothed in a shimmering white robe, and said, "My sons, why do you fight among one another over a piece of clay?

I have not left you, neither will you nor the world be without me!"

He taught them for twenty-five days and appointed MATAX RORAKA to inherit the mantle of spiritual leadership and serve as the MAHANTA, the Living ECK Master. Then Manjushri ascended into the spiritual worlds. He now teaches on the CAUSAL PLANE.

For a list of ECK Masters, see page 341.

Valley of Shangta *shahng-TAH* The valley near the KATSUPARI MONASTERY in northern Tibet where the ECK MASTERS gather for the passing of the ROD OF ECK POWER from a departing Master to his successor.

See also ORACLE OF TIRMER; VOICE OF AKIVASHA.

vanity Also called ahankara, vanity is one of the FIVE PASSIONS OF THE MIND.

Vanity is self-admiration, the abnormal exaggeration of interest in the LITTLE SELF or the intelligence of the MIND. This manifests as self-righteousness, a lack of humor, bigotry, self-assertion, or an obtrusive show of wealth or power. Likewise, it is marked by bossiness, scolding, faultfinding, liking publicity, making a show of religion, and being noisy about giving to charity.

The antidote for vanity is HUMILITY, one of the FIVE VIRTUES.

Vardrup *VAHR-droop* The LIVING ECK MASTER in the sixteenth century. Originally from Germany, he sailed to the Americas during the Spanish conquest.

He came to give spiritual aid, and he took several

Indian chiefs, as well as many Europeans and Asians, to a high place in the SPIRITUAL WORLDS.

For a list of ECK Masters, see page 341.

Varkas *VAHR-kahz* The fierce kings who were the rulers of the HYPERBOREANS, the second ROOT RACE. Their awful powers were used to conquer their foes and their subjects, while some of them conquered time and lived for centuries.

Varnatmik *vahr-NAHT-mik* That part of the spiritual teachings which can be written and spoken; the Sound which breaks into many sounds in the LOWER WORLDS.

The scriptures of the SHARIYAT-KI-SUGMAD can be spoken and written on the lower PLANES. But in the higher worlds it is only the heavenly white music.

See also DHUNATMIK.

Vedanta One of six schools of Hindu philosophy. Some Vedanta terms are used in ECKANKAR.

vibration(s) Vibrations are wavelengths of Spirit, of the ECK. The whole life of any individual is one great wavelength. Music and electricity are also wavelengths, as is every particle in the LOWER WORLDS. Waves of LIGHT AND SOUND are made up of spiritual atoms.

> When God speaks, everything, as Spirit, vibrates, and Its WORD can be heard by the INNER EAR which has been trained to hear It.

See also ECK; SOUND CURRENT; VIBRATIONS, LAW OF.

Vibrations, Law of The Law of Vibrations governs all the influences upon SOUL and the body in this world, such as wavelengths, outflows from the planets, stars, and heavenly bodies, music, sound, color, and general harmonics. Under this principle falls KARMA, cause and effect, and inflow and outflow.

> Every thought, word, and deed either purifies or pollutes the body.

This law is also called the Law of Harmonics. It is one of the SPIRITUAL LAWS OF LIFE; the fourth law of the physical universe (see **Seven Laws of the Physical Universe** on page 344).

See also KARMA, LAW OF; PURIFY OR POLLUTE; RESONANCE, LAW OF.

Vi-Guru *VIE-goo-roo* The MAHANTA, the highest of all ECK MASTERS. Supreme GURU, or spiritual teacher.

Vipula *VEE-poo-lah* An ECK sage who said, "An external thing will have its effect according to the nature and purity of the CONSCIOUSNESS." Knowing this, an individual boldly relies upon a greater intelligence than his own—that of Divine Spirit. By establishing a personal relation to the ECK, the sphere of the individual becomes enlarged.

virtues, five *See* FIVE VIRTUES.

visualization Using the SPIRITUAL EYE to perceive inner experiences.

See also CREATIVE IMAGINATION; INNER VISION.

viveka *vee-VEH-kah* Another word for the spiritual

virtue of DISCRIMINATION.

See FIVE VIRTUES.

Voice of Akivasha *ah-kee-VAH-shah* The oracle, which was in order until the beginning of the twentieth century, at a craggy, unexplored site called the ORACLE OF TIRMER in the VALLEY OF SHANGTA in northern Tibet. It is here that the ROD OF ECK POWER is passed from the departing LIVING ECK MASTER to his successor on October 22, at midnight; sometimes called the Voice, or Oracle, of Tirmer.

Voice of God *See* ECK.

Voice of Tirmer *See* VOICE OF AKIVASHA.

Volapuk(s) *voh-lah-POOK* A Silent One, an agent of the SUGMAD capable of expression without limits.

The Volapuks are part of a larger body of Silent Ones which include the MAHAVAKYIS; they run the clockworks of the spirito-material worlds and come and go like shadows.

See also NINE SILENT ONES.

Wah Z *WAH zee* A spiritual name of SRI HAROLD KLEMP, the MAHANTA, the LIVING ECK MASTER. *Wah Z* means the SECRET DOCTRINE. For more, see the Z entry on page 331.

See also FIVE SPIRITUAL LEADERS OF MODERN-DAY ECKANKAR.

For a list of ECK MASTERS, see page 341.

waking dream(s) Waking dreams are unusual coincidences or symbols that crop up in your daily life for a spiritual purpose. They are a form of the GOLDEN-TONGUED WISDOM (an aspect of the ECK-VIDYA) and can answer spiritual questions or give outer confirmation of something that was revealed in your INNER WORLDS.

> Whenever something out of the ordinary comes up—a deviation from the humdrum, routine activities that account for most of your life—it is bringing you a spiritual lesson.

It is up to you to take the trouble to try to recognize

what this lesson could be. One way is just to say to the INNER MASTER, "I know you are trying to tell me something. Let me see what it is." Then become still; become the watcher.

Wandering Seas, Years of the *See* LENURIG.

Way of the Eternal This is another name for the SHARIYAT-KI-SUGMAD, the ancient and most holy scriptures of ECKANKAR.

The sections of the Way of the Eternal are placed in GOLDEN WISDOM TEMPLES on the various PLANES under the GUARDIANship of ECK MASTERS. ECK CHELAS travel to these Temples with the MAHANTA, in their SOUL BODIES, to be taught the sacred and secret truths contained in the Way of the Eternal.

See also NINE UNKNOWN GODS OF ETERNITY.

Wayshower *See* MAHANTA.

wealth, days of *See* HORTAR.

wedding ceremony *See* ECK WEDDING CEREMONY.

Wei Wu Wei *WAY woo WAY* To do without doing, to act without action; let God be God in you.

See also KARMALESS ACTION; REVERSED EFFORT, LAW OF.

Wheel of Awagawan *ah-WAH-gah-wahn* Another name for the WHEEL OF THE EIGHTY-FOUR.

Wheel of Life *See* WHEEL OF THE EIGHTY-FOUR.

Wheel of Samsara *See* WHEEL OF THE EIGHTY-FOUR.

Wheel of the Eighty-Four In SOUL's journey of SPIRITUAL UNFOLDMENT, It goes through a long process of REINCARNATION, taking on different forms and experiencing many STATES OF CONSCIOUSNESS. Soul does this in order to conquer the influences outside Itself.

This spiritual journey takes Soul through the twelve paths, or divisions, of the Wheel of the Eighty-Four. This wheel is also called the Bhavachakra, the Wheel of Awagawan, the Wheel of Becoming, the Wheel of Life, or the Wheel of Samsara.

The number eighty-four indicates the almost countless incarnations Soul may experience, for It may have to spend many lifetimes in each of the twelve paths, divisions, or zodiacal signs and repeat this seven times. This journey is sometimes measured in lacs—periods of one hundred thousand years—so it might take eight million, four hundred thousand years.

There is an escape from these endless cycles: meeting with the LIVING ECK MASTER and accepting him.

The Master links Soul to the ECK Stream of Life, via INITIATION. This Soul is then released from the rounds of births and deaths and is free of the Wheel of the Eighty-Four.

This is spiritual liberation in this lifetime.

See also ECK-VIDYA WHEEL; KARMA.

white magic *See* MAGIC.

wisdom That which is revealed when the MIND is stilled and SOUL makes contact with the LIGHT AND

SOUND; knowledge gained directly from looking and knowing in the SPIRITUAL WORLDS.

THREE ATTRIBUTES OF GOD-REALIZATION are SPIRITUAL FREEDOM, power, and wisdom.

wisdom, days of *See* ASTIK.

wisdom order *See* GIANI MARG.

wisdom pool SOUL enters into the divine wisdom pool upon receiving the TENTH INITIATION. This is the true WISDOM, a wisdom beyond human capacity. By now the ECK INITIATE begins to see the wisdom of the THREE BASIC PRINCIPLES OF ECK.

Wisdom Temple(s) *See* GOLDEN WISDOM TEMPLE(S).

word, secret *See* SECRET WORD.

Word, the The eternal Voice; the true BANI; SHABDA; the LIGHT; the real life and true light, the true nectar which is the ECK; that which is within; the name, the ECK, MUSIC OF THE SPHERES, the QUALIMA; absolute TRUTH, the divine melody.

See also DHUNATMIK.

Worlds of ECK Another term for the GOD WORLDS.

worship True worship is any act that brings one closer to God.

Wu Tenna *WOO TEHN-nah* An ECK MASTER who is the spiritual head of a GOLDEN WISDOM TEMPLE on the MENTAL PLANE.

For a list of ECK Masters, see page 341.

Yama *YAH-mah* The King of the Dead, also called the Dharam Raya. The Lord of Karma who judges those who die, or leave the PHYSICAL PLANE, according to their deeds. All uninitiated SOULS must pass through his court.

See also LORDS OF KARMA; TRANSLATION.

Yama, Mountain of The mountain of death. SRI HAROLD KLEMP mentions the Mountain of Yama in his autobiography, in connection with his passage to GOD-REALIZATION.

Yama Dutas *YAH-mah DOO-tahz* The messengers of YAMA, the King of the Dead.

Yaubl Sacabi *YEEOW-buhl sah-KAH-bee*

Yaubl Sacabi served as the MAHANTA, the LIVING ECK MASTER among the ancient Greeks, soon after the arrival of the Mycenaeans, who brought new ideas in art and architecture to Greece between 2000 and 1700 BC. He was the leading figure among the Greek mystery cults.

> Legend has it that Yaubl Sacabi's dream of destiny led to the founding of the spiritual city of AGAM DES. He is now the head of this spiritual city, the home of the Eshwar-Khanewale (GOD-EATERS), and the GUARDIAN of the SHARIYAT-KI-SUGMAD (the sacred book of ECK) there.

Yaubl Sacabi takes great pleasure in teaching others the secret laws of life, which give new meaning to our existence here.

He also oversees the rite of the PASSING OF THE ROD OF ECK POWER to a new Living ECK Master.

Yaubl Sacabi stands to become a central figure in the next era of human destiny.

For a list of ECK MASTERS, see page 341.

Yavata *yah-VAH-tah* The Yavata is an ECK MASTER teaching on the inner PLANES. The odor of sweet musk, the sound of violins, and a white light indicate his presence.

He puts himself into the world of the physical senses in order to help the LIVING ECK MASTER and other ECK Masters whenever there is a crisis in the human race.

He is approximately seven feet tall, with large features that might be called Mongolian. He is a former Tibetan lama who served in this world and went on to the higher worlds to help with the work of ECK.

For a list of ECK Masters, see page 341.

Year of Blessing, A *See* BLESSING, A YEAR OF.

Year of Blessing, The *See* appendix, page 358.

Year of Consecration, A *See* CONSECRATION, A YEAR OF.

Year of Creativity, A *See* CREATIVITY, A YEAR OF.

Year of Giving, The *See* GIVING, THE YEAR OF.

Year of Graceful Living, A *See* appendix, page 358.

Year of Graceful Living, The *See* GRACEFUL LIVING, THE YEAR OF.

Year of HU, A *See* HU, A YEAR OF.

Year of Light and Sound, The *See* LIGHT AND SOUND, THE YEAR OF.

Year of Spiritual Healing, A *See* SPIRITUAL HEALING, A YEAR OF.

Year of Spiritual Healing, The *See* appendix, page 358.

Year of Thanksgiving, A *See* appendix, page 358.

Year of Thanksgiving, The *See* THANKSGIVING, THE YEAR OF.

Year of the Arahata, The *See* appendix, page 358.

Year of the ECK Missionary *See* ECK MISSIONARY, YEAR OF THE.

Year of the ECK Teacher *See* ECK TEACHER, YEAR OF THE.

Year of the HU *See* appendix, page 358.

Year of the Shariyat, The *See* SHARIYAT, THE YEAR OF THE.

Year of the Shariyat, The First *See* appendix, page 358.

Year of the Shariyat, The Second *See* appendix, page 358.

Year of the Vahana *See* appendix, page 358.

Year(s) of the Abundant Fruits *See* ERUTUA.

Year(s) of the Beautiful Flowers *See* YIGERTA.

Year(s) of the Bountiful Earth *See* SELTEA.

Year(s) of the Bright Snows *See* GINTHE.

Year(s) of the Brilliant Sun *See* DORETI.

Year(s) of the Fierce Winds *See* THIGALA.

Year(s) of the Full Moon *See* FARANK.

Year(s) of the Lavish Grains *See* HIAFI.

Year(s) of the Raging Fires *See* NERALIT.

Year(s) of the Strange Storms *See* KURITEE.

Year(s) of the Trembling Leaf *See* MUZUART.

Year(s) of the Wandering Seas *See* LENURIG.

Yigerta *yee-GEHR-tah* The fourth TWELVE-YEAR CYCLE of the ECK-VIDYA; called the Years of the Beautiful Flowers. Also the fourth year within a twelve-year cycle.

See also ECK-VIDYA WHEEL.

yin/yang *yin/yahng* Chinese terms used in describing the Law of Polarity (*see* POLARITY, LAW OF); yin is the feminine, the negative principle; yang is the male, the positive principle.

See also PRINCIPLES, FEMININE AND MASCULINE.

Yreka *yuh-REE-kah* The tunnel between the ETHERIC PLANE and SOUL PLANE; the dark area through which SOUL must travel to reach the Soul Plane and SELF-REALIZATION. No Soul can pass through without the help of the MAHANTA, the LIGHT GIVER.

yuga(s) A yuga is a great cycle of time—one of the four ages, or stages, of cosmic history: the Satya Yuga, or Golden Age; the Tretya Yuga, or Silver Age; the Dwapara Yuga, or Copper (or Bronze) Age; and the Kali Yuga, or Iron Age.

These four ages together comprise a MAHAYUGA (also known as a kalpa or manvantara).

For more, *see* FOUR CYCLES OF LIFE.

Yuont-Na *yownt-NAY* An ECK MASTER who was the leading teacher of ECKANKAR in the region of Uighur, which had been part of the empire of LEMURIA. He is now a teacher of the SHARIYAT-KI-SUGMAD on the ASTRAL PLANE.

Yuont-Na lived and taught in the capital city of KHARA KHOTA. Some of the old NAACAL RECORDS speak of Yuont-Na and his teachings of ECK.

For a list of ECK Masters, see page 341.

Yu Rantga *yoo RAHNT-gah* The LIVING ECK MASTER in China, who lived in the Gobi Desert during the middle and late nineteenth century. He brought back to the Chinese many of their old religious customs and gave spiritual succor to the masses.

He left this world after seventy-two years of service and went to the ASTRAL PLANE to work. His successor was SUDAR SINGH.

For a list of ECK MASTERS, see page 341.

Z *ZEE* This is the spiritual name for SRI HAROLD KLEMP. It is the name of the ages that embodies within it the full love, WISDOM, and power of the ECK in all Its manifestations.

All the waves of the Audible Life Stream (SOUND CURRENT) converge at one point in it.

The name Z, even as the letter of the alphabet, is the bridge that links the ends of the physical universe with the beginnings of the invisible ones. The source from which Z derives continues practically without end into the spiritual PLANES—and this is the ECK, the source of all living things.

See also FIVE SPIRITUAL LEADERS OF MODERN-DAY ECKANKAR; WAH Z.

Zadok *ZAH-dohk* The LIVING ECK MASTER in the country of Judea, north of Jerusalem. He taught JESUS the basic fundamentals of ECK. Out of this knowledge of ECK came what we know today as Christianity.

Zadok also founded a mystical organization which still exists today in the Middle East and accepts the MAHANTA.

Zadok is often seen as a man in a white robe, with a healthy head of black, curly hair and a long beard.

For a list of ECK MASTERS, see page 341.

Zarathustra *See* ZOROASTER.

Zaskq, Peddar *See* PAUL TWITCHELL; PEDDAR ZASKQ.

Zezirath *ZEHZ-eer-ahth* One of the ten SPIRITUAL CITIES which are on earth to help the world. The old spiritual city of Zezirath is near the ruins of Memphis in Egypt.

The beings here were responsible for the pyramids and mystery religions of ancient Egypt and the metaphysical systems of old Greece.

The other nine spiritual cities are AGAM DES, AKEVIZ, DAMCAR, KIMTAVED, MUMSAKA, NAMPAK, RAHAKAZ, SAT DHAM, and SHAMBALLA.

ziggurat *See* TEMPLE OF ECK ZIGGURAT SYMBOL.

zikar *ZIE-kahr* Making contact with the Holy Spirit within by chanting a holy word or one of the holy names of God such as *HU*.

See also CHANT; MANTRA.

ziquin *ZEE-kwin* In the AMDO language, *zi* means above, *quin* means five. Above the five PLANES; the

reading of the ECK-VIDYA from the Fifth, or SOUL, PLANE.

Zoas *ZOH-ahz* *See* FOUR ZOAS.

zodiac *ZOH-dee-ak* The twelve signs of ASTROLOGY which influence the PHYSICAL BODY and character traits of man.

See also MONTH(S) OF THE ECK-VIDYA; WHEEL OF THE EIGHTY-FOUR.

Zohar, the *ZOH-hahr* A future ROOT RACE who will come from a far distant planet to colonize the world after its destruction by a great catastrophe in the twenty-first and twenty-second centuries.

Their colonization attempts will fail, and after several centuries they will withdraw.

See also SEPHER.

Zoroaster *ZOH-roh-as-tehr* The Persian avatar, also called Zarathustra, who taught SOUL TRAVEL almost six hundred years before the coming of Christ and his followers.

Zrephs *ZREHFS* The flowering gardens of the ASTRAL PLANE near the ASTRAL MUSEUM and the GOLDEN WISDOM TEMPLE there.

APPENDICES

Amazing HU

1.

Amazing HU, how sweet the Sound,
That touched a Soul like me!
I once was lost, but now am found,
Was blind, but now I see.

2.

'Twas HU that taught my heart to sing,
And HU my fears relieved;
How precious did HU then appear
The hour I first believed!

3.

Through many dangers, toils, and snares,
I have already come;
'Tis HU has brought me safe thus far,
And HU will lead me home.

4.

The HU has given life to me,
Its Sound my hope secures;
My shield and portion HU will be
As long as life endures.

5.

The earth will someday pass away;
The sun forbear to shine;
But God, who sent me here below,
I'll be forever Thine.

Lyrics adapted by Joan and Harold Klemp from the public-domain song "Amazing Grace" by John Newton (1725–1807).

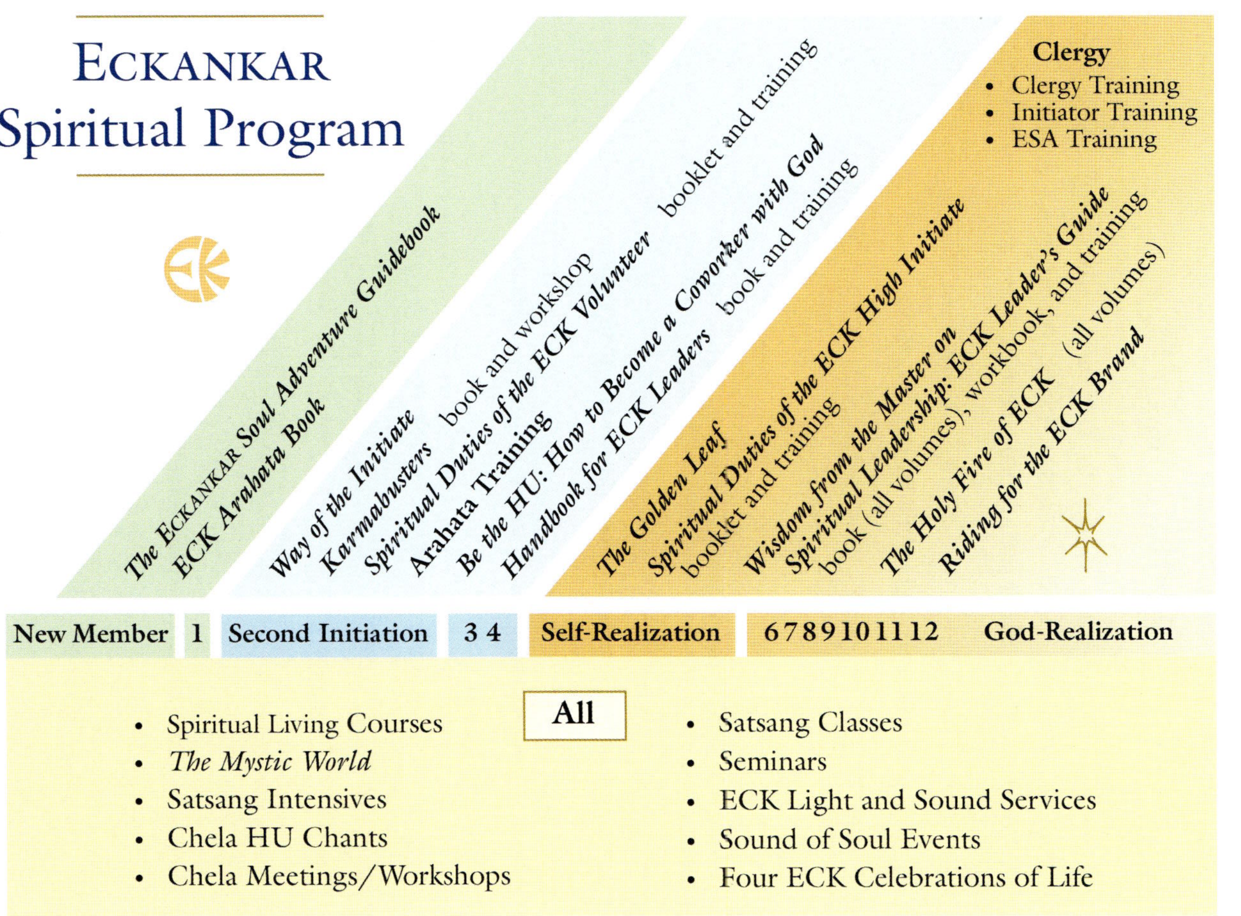
ECKANKAR
Spiritual Program
The ECKANKAR Soul Adventure Guidebook
ECK Arahata Book
Way of the Initiate
Karmabusters book and workshop
Spiritual Duties of the ECK Volunteer booklet and training
Arahata Training
Be the HU: How to Become a Coworker with God
Handbook for ECK Leaders book and training
The Golden Leaf
Spiritual Duties of the ECK High Initiate
booklet and training
Wisdom from the Master on
Spiritual Leadership: ECK Leader's Guide
book (all volumes), workbook, and training
The Holy Fire of ECK (all volumes)
Riding for the ECK Brand
Clergy
• Clergy Training
• Initiator Training
• ESA Training
New Member
1
Second Initiation
3 4
Self-Realization
6 7 8 9 10 11 12
God-Realization
All
• Spiritual Living Courses
• The Mystic World
• Satsang Intensives
• Chela HU Chants
• Chela Meetings/Workshops
• Satsang Classes
• Seminars
• ECK Light and Sound Services
• Sound of Soul Events
• Four ECK Celebrations of Life

Initiations in ECK

For deeper insights on each initiation, see chapter 12, "The Circles of ECK Initiations," in *The Shariyat-Ki-SUGMAD*, Book Two.

1. The Acolyte—Initiate of the First Circle
   See FIRST INITIATION on page 84.
2. The Arahata—Initiate of the Second Circle
   See SECOND INITIATION on page 249.
3. The Ahrat—Initiate of the Third Circle
   See THIRD INITIATION on page 297.
4. The Chiad—Initiate of the Fourth Circle
   See FOURTH INITIATION on page 97.
5. The Mahdis—Initiate of the Fifth Circle
   See FIFTH INITIATION on page 83.
6. The Shraddha—Initiate of the Sixth Circle
   See SIXTH INITIATION on page 266.
7. The Bhakti (also Shab)—Initiate of the Seventh Circle
   See SEVENTH INITIATION on page 257.
8. The GYANEE—Initiate of the Eighth Circle
   See EIGHTH INITIATION on page 76.
9. The MAULANI—Initiate of the Ninth Circle
   See NINTH INITIATION on page 194.
10. The ADEPISEKA—Initiate of the Tenth Circle
    See TENTH INITIATION on page 296.

continued

Initiations in ECK (continued)

11. The KEVALSHAR—Initiate of the Eleventh Circle
See ELEVENTH INITIATION on page 77.
12. The MAHARAJI—Initiate of the Twelfth Circle
See TWELFTH INITIATION on page 306.
13. The MAHANTA MAHARAI—Initiate of the Thirteenth Circle
See THIRTEENTH INITIATION on page 298.
14. The MAHANTA—Initiate of the Fourteenth Circle
See FOURTEENTH INITIATION on page 97.

See also ECKANKAR Spiritual Program (page 337), **The God Worlds Chart** (page 340), and the LEVELS OF REALIZATION chart (page 231).

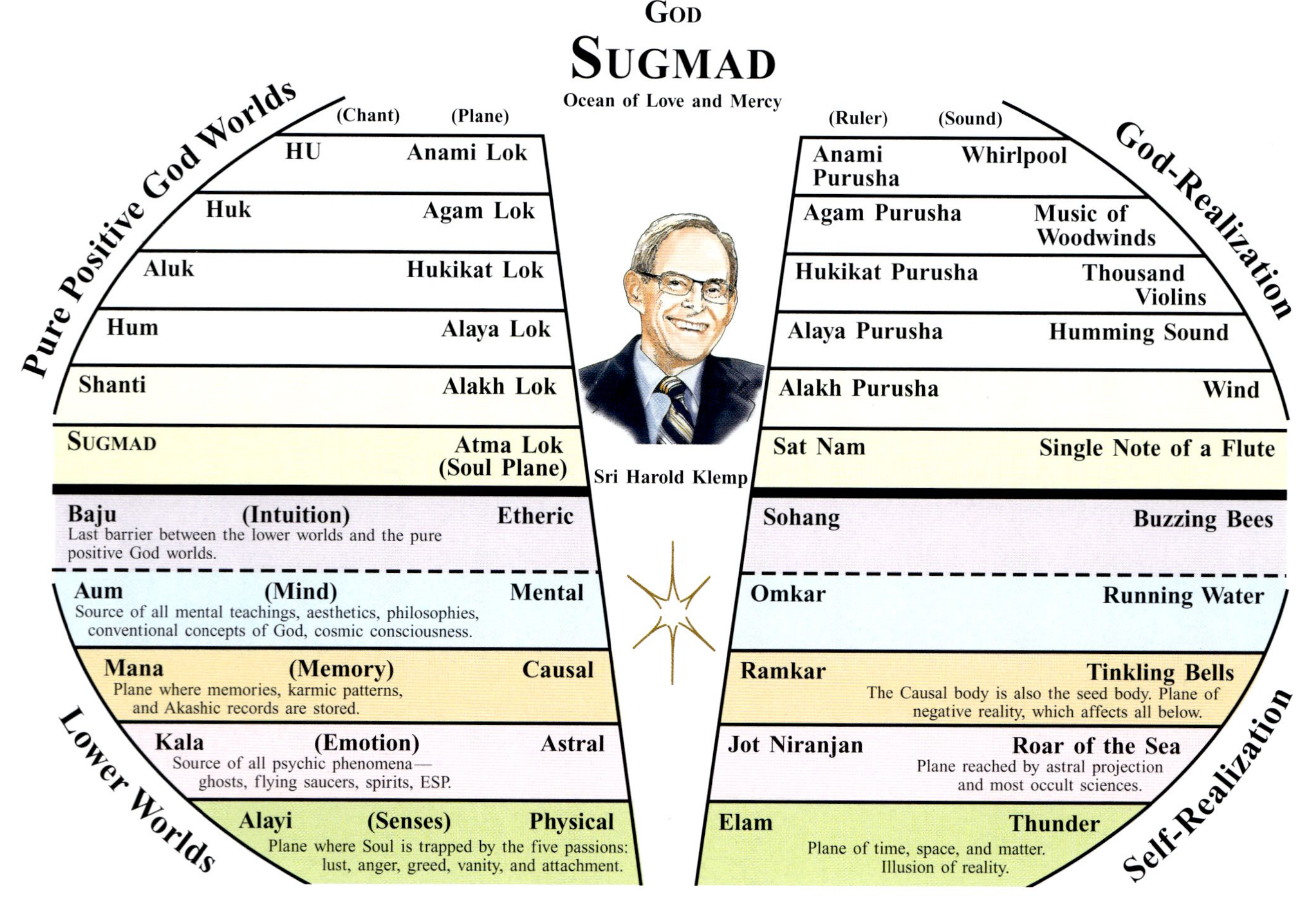

The God Worlds Chart

Names of ECK Masters

An alphabetical list of the ECK MASTERS noted in this book

ADONI
AGNOTTI
AHMAD QAVANI
APOLLONIUS OF TYANA
ASOKI
BABLA MOHENJO
BANJANI
CASTROG
CHU-KO YEN
DAYAKA
DECATES
EPICTETUS
FUBBI QUANTZ
GAKKO
GEUTAN
GOPAL DAS
HABU MEDINET
HARI TITA
HAROLD KLEMP (WAH Z)
HELVIDIUS PRISCUS
HIPOLITO FAYOLLE
ISMET HOUDONI
JAGAT HO
JANOS MONETA
JOYTI BASJI
JU CHIAO
KADMON
KAI-KUAS
KASSAPA
KATA DAKI
KETU JARAUL
KITA SORGI
LAI TSI
LAMOTTA
MALATI
MARPA
MATAX RORAKA
MESI GOKARITZ
MILAREPA
MKSHA
MORAJI DESAL
NALPA KELJINA
NIRGUNA EKAM
ORI DIOGO
PADMA GAYA
PAUL TWITCHELL (PEDDAR ZASKQ)

continued

Names of ECK Masters (continued)

- PHIDIAS
- PRAJAPATI
- PRISCUS
- PYTHAGORAS
- QUETZALCOATL
- RABINOWITZ
- RAMA
- RAMAMURTA
- RAMI NURI
- REBAZAR TARZS
- REGNARD
- SARDAR LHUNPO
- SATO KURAJ
- SEPHER
- SHAMUS-I-TABRIZ
- SHANDAVA
- SHIV SENA
- SIMHA
- SOCRATES
- SUDAR SINGH
- SUPAKU
- SUTO T'SING
- TAMAQUI
- TARIKA TAKOM
- TEJAHUA
- TINDOR SAKI
- TIRMER
- TISSOT LEINS
- TOMO GESHIG
- TOWART MANAGI
- TURA YUNG
- VAITA DANU
- VAJRA MANJUSHRI
- VARDRUP
- WU TENNA
- YAUBL SACABI
- YAVATA
- YUONT-NA
- YU RANTGA
- ZADOK

A Road Map for Spiritual Travelers

This overview of the GOD WORLDS gives key words, names, and phrases which can be chanted in a spiritual exercise to visit a desired PLANE or temple or meet a specific ECK MASTER. All terms in this chart are explained in this book's alphabetical listing.

(*See also* **The God Worlds Chart** on page 340.)

Plane (Lok = Plane)	Chant	Guardian(s) of the Shariyat-Ki-SUGMAD	Main Temple(s)
10 Anami Lok	HU *(HYOO)*	The Padma Samba	Sata Visic Palace
9 Agam Lok	Huk *(HOOK)*	Agnotti (The Mahaya Guru)	Kazi Dawtz (Temple of Akash)
8 Hukikat Lok	Aluk *(ah-LOOK)*	Kadmon (The Asanga Kaya)	Jartz Chong (Temple of the Aluk)
7 Alaya Lok	Hum *(HYOOM)*	Mesi Gokaritz (The Tsong Sikhsa)	Anakamudi Temple
6 Alakh Lok	Shanti *(SHAHN-tee)*	Tomo Geshig (The Sokagampo)	Tamanata Kop
5 Soul Plane (Atma Lok)	SUGMAD *(SOOG-mahd)*	Tindor Saki (The Jagat Giri)	Param Akshar
*Etheric Plane (Saguna Lok)	Baju *(BAH-joo)*	Lai Tsi	Dayaka Temple
4 Mental Plane	Aum *(AHM* or *ah-UHM)*	Towart Managi (The Koji Chanda) Sato Kuraj	Namayatan Temple Hall of Brahmanda
3 Causal Plane	Mana *(ma-NAH)*	Shamus-i-Tabriz	Temple of Sakapori
2 Astral Plane	Kala *(kah-LAH)*	Gopal Das	Askleposis
1 Physical Plane	Alayi *(ah-LAH-yee)*	Banjani Yaubl Sacabi Rami Nuri Fubbi Quantz Sri Harold Klemp (The MAHANTA, the Living ECK Master)	Faqiti Monastery Gare-Hira Temple House of Moksha Katsupari Monastery Temple of ECK

* The Etheric Plane is the top of the Mental Plane and is not numbered separately.

Seven Laws of the Physical Universe

There are fundamental laws that govern this physical universe through Spirit. These were once taught by an ancient sage named MKSHA, who appeared on earth some thirty-five thousand years ago to teach the people of the Indus Valley.

Law of HU

Spirit is the all-penetrating power, the forming power of the universes. The Voice of HU has one great quality, and that is to create effect.

Law of Soul

SOUL is the manifested individual beingness of the ECK Spirit (Holy Spirit). It has FREE WILL, opinions, intelligence, IMAGINATION, and immortality.

Law of Polarity

The Law of Opposites. Within all the LOWER WORLDS, nothing exists except in relation to its opposite. Each state, quality, or condition within this universe is supported, animated, and maintained by its opposite. However, within the worlds of true Spirit, there are no opposites. LIGHT is Light, without shadow or darkness, and there is no opposite to the Sound of ECK.

Law of Vibrations

Governs all the influences upon SOUL and the body in this world, such as wavelengths, outflows from the planets, stars, and heavenly bodies; music; sound; color; and general harmonics. Under this principle falls KARMA, cause and effect, and inflow and outflow. Every thought, word, and deed either purifies or pollutes the body.

Law of Attitudes

The power of IMAGINATION rules over will in the actions in this universe.

Law of Facsimiles

All effects in life are brought about by the thoughts and pictures in the MIND of the individual.

Law of Unity

The ECK is the unity in the midst of diversity and multiplicity. Thinking in the whole instead of the parts. It is a way of knowing the solution to a problem the instant it presents itself. This law simply means one must be wholly within the ECK (Holy Spirit) in order to enjoy himself as the whole man.

Spiritual Laws of Life

Below are the names of the SPIRITUAL LAWS OF LIFE defined in this book.

- ASSUMPTION, LAW OF
- ATTITUDES, LAW OF
- BALANCE, LAW OF
- CHANGE, LAW OF
- CONSCIOUSNESS, LAW OF
- CREATIVITY, LAW OF
- DESTINY, LAW OF
- DHARMA, LAW OF
- ECONOMY, LAW OF
- ETHICS, LAW OF
- FACSIMILES, LAW OF
- GOD, LAW OF
- GRACE, LAW OF
- GRATITUDE, LAW OF
- HU, LAW OF
- INVISIBLE LAWS
- KARMA, LAW OF
- LOVE, LAW OF
- NONINTERFERENCE, LAW OF
- PLENTY, LAW OF
- POLARITY, LAW OF
- PROGRESSIVE CONTINUATION, LAW OF
- RECIPROCITY, LAW OF
- RESONANCE, LAW OF
- REVERSED EFFORT, LAW OF
- SELF, LAW OF THE
- SILENCE, LAW OF
- SOUL, LAW OF
- SPIRIT, LAW OF
- SPIRITUAL EVOLUTION, LAW OF
- SPIRITUAL GROWTH, LAW OF
- STRENGTH, LAW OF
- SURVIVAL, LAW OF
- UNFOLDMENT, LAW OF
- UNITY, LAW OF
- VIBRATIONS, LAW OF

Three Key Spiritual Exercises of ECK

There are countless variations of the SPIRITUAL EXERCISES OF ECK, and new ones can always be devised.

Below are three well-known and widely practiced exercises, explained in some detail. For many more, see the book *The Spiritual Exercises of ECK.*

The appropriate setting for any spiritual exercise is a quiet time and place.

The Four-Step Spiritual Exercise of ECK

This spiritual exercise will help you remember the special purpose you had in mind before coming into this present life.

It can also be an aid in one of the other spiritual interests you may have. Or it can help you understand a passage from one of the ECK books, like *The Shariyat-Ki-SUGMAD*, any of the MAHANTA Transcripts books, or *Stranger by the River*. The four steps are as follows:

1. Sing "HU" three times, slowly and softly. This name for God allows the consecration of the human will to that of ECK, Divine Spirit.
2. Sing "MAHANTA" three times, softly and slowly. This word takes one into the second level of contemplation. "MAHANTA," sung in this order, after "HU," is an invitation to the MAHANTA to be a

guest in the home of your STATE OF CONSCIOUSNESS. It is a very important step in this exercise.

3. Sing your personal, SECRET WORD or "SUGMAD" (if you don't have a personal word) three times. This word will instantly take you into the third level of CONTEMPLATION. The singing of this word, third in the sequence, is your special key to love, WISDOM, and understanding.

4. At the fourth level of contemplation, there is a wide choice of ECK words to sing. Whichever word you choose from the list below, sing it three times too, slowly and softly. This choice of an ECK word or term defines your particular area of interest.

    - **"ECK-VIDYA"**—for an insight into the past, present, or future about an area of concern, like a family, work, health, or spiritual matter, to name a few
    - **"KAYA KALP"**—for specific help with improving one's physical health
    - **"ECK-YNARI"**—for help with understanding the secret knowledge of dreams
    - **"ECK VAHANA"**—for ideas on how to present the teachings of ECK to people who show an interest in them
    - **"ECK ARAHATA"**—for insights into how to be a more effective teacher in the ECK SATSANG CLASSES
    - **"GIANI MARG"**—for ways to learn the secrets of the SPIRITUAL WORLDS so as to pass them

along to others in writings, songs, music, the arts, and other creative outlets

- "BHAKTI"—for guidance on how to open your heart to DIVINE LOVE. This word certainly ranks above all the rest on this list.

If you awaken in the night and wish to resume this exercise, use a shortcut. Simply sing each of the four words one time. That's all it takes to reestablish your connection with the MAHANTA. This shortcut is also handy for naps.

The Fifteen-Times Spiritual Exercise

This technique is based on the principle of focusing on a spiritual goal. You focus by writing that goal down fifteen times every day.

This is more than an affirmation; an affirmation is a discipline of the MIND only. As a form of CONTEMPLATION, this exercise opens the door to the Holy Spirit to help you change your life according to Its will. So whenever you do this exercise, do it with the attitude "Thy will be done." That lifts it from a simple mental affirmation to true contemplation.

Sit down at a table or desk and form your spiritual goal, whatever the INNER MASTER prompts you to ask for. Start with "I" and use the present tense. For example, you might choose to write, "I am healthy, happy, wise, and free." Or you might choose a more specific goal, such as, "I travel in my dreams" or "I know the secret of divine love." It can be anything at all. Choose your words carefully. Keep it short enough that you will write it fifteen times—all at once—every day.

As you write, be creative; let yourself go. If you usually write neatly, you might scribble instead. Or write very big. Maybe write on shopping bags or a chalkboard. Or don't use any punctuation. What you're doing is opening up the windows of your world.

This contemplative writing exercise is an open invitation to the ECK. Watch how Divine Spirit begins to bring these objects of your spiritual desire into your life. As time goes on, you'll see changes beginning. Little things will happen. Events will start to shape themselves to where you have new choices. It's up to you to make the right choice, but doors will begin to open for you.

Be aware. Watch the Voice of God, the Holy Spirit, the living water, pour into your cup. Be a worthy vessel.

The Shariyat Technique

This technique uses *THE SHARIYAT-KI-SUGMAD*, the ECK bible, to help you understand the spiritual reasons behind a problem you are experiencing. The technique works like this:

1. First define the problem. Form a question about something that has been bothering you in your life. The question can be about health, prosperity, love, or any other subject that has been troubling you.

2. Open *The Shariyat-Ki-SUGMAD*, Book One or Book Two, at random. Read one paragraph and then

close your eyes. Sing, or chant, *HU* eight times (eight corresponds to the eight outer initiations) and then contemplate the passage you have just read.

Don't contemplate on your problem or try to establish a bridge between the paragraph and your problem. This is very important. Just contemplate upon the paragraph from *The Shariyat* while chanting *HU*.

3. Open *The Shariyat* at random again and read another paragraph. See how this paragraph relates to the first paragraph, how both offer a new insight and approach to your problem or question.

The usual reason a problem exists for us is that we are afraid to take the next step. Often we can think of four or five solutions to a problem, but we argue with ourselves, trying to decide what the next step should be.

The Shariyat may tell you what the next step is.

You may wish to go through the technique again on the following day to carry the solution one step further or to explore some new question of a spiritual nature.

Twelve-Year Cycles of the Master's Spiritual Mission

This list shows the TWELVE-YEAR CYCLES of ECKANKAR since SRI HAROLD KLEMP became the MAHANTA, the LIVING ECK MASTER in 1981. Future cycles are also listed. The cycles begin on October 22.

Era of Stabilization (1981–93)

In the first cycle, the ECK movement—and all the people in it—needed to learn what was right behavior and what was not. There is a responsibility to living here.

Lessons learned in the first cycle included a code of ethical behavior, a better understanding of karma as a nonretributive part of spiritual law, divine love as the most powerful force in creation, and others.

Age of the ECK Missionary (1993–2005)

The lessons of the second cycle became more evident—namely, how to bridge the gap between the ECK teachings and the spiritual needs of the people in today's society.

A Time for Reaching Out (2005–17)

The creative spirit in chelas awakened to many previously undreamed-of ways to reach people ready for the wonderful teachings of ECK (the Holy Spirit). It included the aim of finding seekers but also involved looking more into how to be of service where there are pressing spiritual needs.

First of the Golden Years (2017–29)

We continue our search for Souls weary of illusions and help them return to God. Will you support this mission? If so, then rededicate your heart and hands to the Spirit Divine.

Second of the Golden Years (2029–41)

Third of the Golden Years (2041–53)

Fourth of the Golden Years (2053–65)

Fifth of the Golden Years (2065–77)

Sixth of the Golden Years (2077–89)

Seventh of the Golden Years (2089–2101)

Eighth of the Golden Years (2101–13)

Ninth of the Golden Years (2113–25)

Tenth of the Golden Years (2125–37)

Eleventh of the Golden Years (2137–49)

Twelfth of the Golden Years (2149–61)

The Spiritual Years of ECK

See page 283 for a chart and general definition. Below is a chronological list and description of the twelve spiritual years, along with the corresponding **twelve secrets to spiritual living**.

1. **The Year of Light and Sound** The first year of the spiritual years of ECK. This spiritual year embodies the following secret: **Hearing the Secret Voice of God**.

   The LIGHT AND SOUND, taken together, are the Voice of God, the Holy Spirit. They form a cosmic wave that goes out from the heart of God to the ends of CREATION.

   The MAHANTA, the LIVING ECK MASTER's job is to help SOUL learn to catch that wave which then flows home to God.

2. **A Year of Spiritual Healing** The second of the spiritual years of ECK. It embodies the following secret: **Secrets of Spiritual Healing**.

   After spending many lifetimes in search of TRUTH, the individual is often a bruised and battered wreck.

   Even after having bathed in the LIGHT AND SOUND of God, SOUL needs time to heal. So it is necessary to set aside a time of healing every twelve years for the individual to gather strength for the next leg of the spiritual journey.

3. **The Year of the Shariyat** The third of the spiritual years of ECK. It embodies the following secret: **Secrets of Living Truth Every Day**.

   The SHARIYAT-KI-SUGMAD is the body of spiritual writings that form the ECK holy scriptures. These scriptures cut through the illusions of temporal power and lead SOUL to WISDOM, spiritual power, and freedom.

4. **Year of the ECK Missionary** The fourth of the spiritual years of ECK. It embodies the following secret: **The Power of Mission**.

   Each SOUL has a mission, a purpose. During this annual cycle, one tries to learn, then align, this personal mission with that of God's divine plan for each Soul's return home to God.

   Soul is here to learn DIVINE LOVE. Along the way, Soul learns that Its personal mission also means helping others find their way to it.

5. **A Year of HU** The fifth of the spiritual years of ECK. It embodies the following secret: **Discover the God Sound**.

   HU is the most ancient name for God, not God Itself. HU, the first impulse from the OCEAN OF LOVE AND MERCY, is the original of all motion, force, light, sound, or vibration.

   Singing *HU* opens one to help from the Holy Spirit.

6. **The Year of Giving** The sixth of the spiritual years of ECK. It embodies the following secret: **The Spiritual Need for Giving**.

   The entire reason for SOUL's journey is to learn the spiritual need for giving. A life of meaning is a life of giving. God's love freely comes to all of us, so we must learn both to accept that love and then to pass it on to others.

7. **A Year of Blessing** The seventh of the spiritual years of ECK. It embodies the following secret: **The Power of Blessing**.

   A time to count your blessings. Bless each moment, each thought, each word, and each deed. Let only the pure love of God flow from you and into your own universe.

8. **The Year of Thanksgiving** The eighth of the spiritual years of ECK. It embodies the following secret: **The Power of Gratitude**.

   This year has much in common with A Year of Blessing, which precedes it. We must be willing to let our joy of life show in a spirit of celebration.

   Enjoy the company of your loved ones at special celebrations of your own choosing throughout the year. Give thanks for the gift of life.

9. **A Year of Creativity** The ninth of the spiritual years of ECK. It embodies the following secret: **Secrets of Divine Creativity**.

   God's special gift to the higher forms of spiritual evolution is the gift of creativity. It is a reflection of SOUL's highest nature.

10. **Year of the ECK Teacher** The tenth of the spiritual years of ECK. It embodies the following secret: **Become a Light to the World**.

    This year is opposite on the wheel to its counterpart, Year of the ECK Missionary. First, the missionary finds the SOULS that are ready for the return home to God.

    Later, the ECK teacher, the ARAHATA, as an aide to the MAHANTA, the LIVING ECK MASTER, leads a class of people who desire the knowledge of truth found in the ECK teachings. This is a key year.

11. **The Year of Graceful Living** The eleventh of the spiritual years of ECK. It embodies the following secret: **The Power of Grace**.

    As SOULS unfold, their way of interacting with others becomes more graceful. There is an honest attempt to see the MAHANTA in every Soul, because then a graceful life is found to be the natural life.

    Grace is a balm that makes things run better.

12. **A Year of Consecration** The twelfth of the spiritual years of ECK. It embodies the following secret: **Loving as God Loves**.

    A time to dedicate oneself anew to *being* a CO-WORKER WITH GOD. A chance to tie up loose spiritual ends of the last cycle and prepare for the new one next year.

Historical: The Spiritual Years of ECK 1985–2000

Below is a list of spiritual years up to October 22, 2001 (when the perpetual cycle began). For the current, perpetual twelve-year cycle of the SPIRITUAL YEARS OF ECK, see page 283; also see the appendix on page 354.

Each of the spiritual years of ECK begins on October 22, the ECK SPIRITUAL NEW YEAR.

1985–86	The Year of Spiritual Healing
1986–87	The Year of the Arahata
1987–88	The First Year of the Shariyat
1988–89	The Second Year of the Shariyat
1989–90	Year of the HU
1990–91	Year of the Vahana
1991–92	The Year of Light and Sound
1992–93	A Year of Graceful Living
1993–94	The Year of Giving
1994–95	A Year of Thanksgiving
1995–96	The Year of Blessing
1996–97	A Year of Consecration
1997–98	A Year of Creativity
1998–99	The Year of Giving
1999–2000	A Year of HU
2000–2001	Year of the ECK Teacher

About the Author

Award-winning author, teacher, and spiritual guide Sri Harold Klemp helps seekers reach their full potential.

He is the MAHANTA, the Living ECK Master and spiritual leader of ECKANKAR, the Path of Spiritual Freedom. He is the latest in a long line of spiritual Adepts who have served throughout history in every culture of the world.

Sri Harold teaches creative spiritual practices that enable anyone to achieve life mastery and gain inner peace and contentment. His messages are relevant to today's spiritual needs and resonate with every generation.

Sri Harold's body of work includes more than one hundred books, which have been translated into eighteen languages and won multiple awards. The miraculous, true-life stories he shares lift the veil between heaven and earth.

In his groundbreaking memoir, *Autobiography of a Modern Prophet*, he reveals secrets to spiritual success gleaned from his personal journey into the heart of God. Find your own path to true happiness, wisdom, and love in Sri Harold Klemp's inspired writings.

ECKANKAR's Spiritual Living Courses

Go higher, further, deeper with your spiritual experiences!

ECKANKAR offers enrollment in the Spiritual Living Courses for Self-Discovery and God-Discovery. This dynamic program of inner and outer study unlocks the divine love and wisdom within you. It offers step-by-step advances in enlightenment through spiritual initiations.

From the first day, you can have direct experience with the God Current and begin to meet life's challenges on the highest possible ground.

You will enjoy monthly lessons (also available online) from the spiritual leader of ECKANKAR, Sri Harold Klemp, creative spiritual practices for daily life, and the quarterly *Mystic World* publication. Optional classes with like-hearted Souls are available in many areas.

Here's a sampling of titles from the first course:

- In Soul You Are Free
- Reincarnation—Why You Came to Earth Again
- The Master Principle
- The God Worlds—Where No One Has Gone Before?

How to Get Started

For free books and more information about ECKANKAR:

- Visit Eckankar.org;
- Call 1-800-LOVE GOD (1-800-568-3463) (USA and Canada only); or
- Write to: ECKANKAR, Dept. BK 167,
  PO Box 2000, Chanhassen, MN 55317-2000 USA.

To order ECKANKAR books online, you can visit ECKBooks.org.

To receive the Spiritual Living Courses, along with other student benefits, go to AdvancedSpiritualLiving.org. You can also call ECKANKAR at (952) 380-2222 to enroll. Or write to the address above, Att: Student Services.

For Further Reading and Study

ECK Essentials

Harold Klemp

Whether you are taking your first bold steps into the God worlds of your being, or you are a seasoned traveler in the ways of ECK, these essential truths and touchstones will serve as a ready spiritual compass.

Each precept, law or parable, key or contemplation seed, holds a myriad of truths for Soul, relevant to your life today!

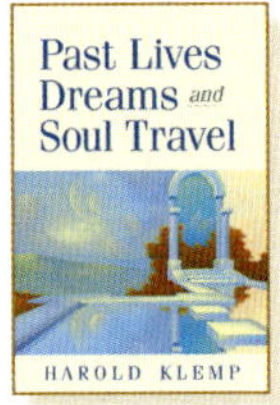

Past Lives, Dreams, and Soul Travel

Harold Klemp

These stories and exercises help you find your true purpose, discover greater love than you've ever known, and learn that spiritual freedom is within reach.

Book 18

The MAHANTA Transcripts Series

Harold Klemp

The MAHANTA Transcripts, books 1–18, are from Harold Klemp's talks at ECKANKAR seminars. He has taught thousands how to have a natural, direct relationship with the Holy Spirit. The stories and wonderful insights contained in these talks will lead you to deeper spiritual understanding.

Autobiography of a Modern Prophet

Harold Klemp

This riveting story of Harold Klemp's climb up the Mountain of God will help you discover the keys to your own spiritual greatness.

Youth Ask a Modern Prophet about Life, Love, and God

Harold Klemp

What am I here for? How do I find lasting love? When will my karma be finished? Do these questions sound familiar? The youth of today aren't afraid to voice these important questions, and many more, to Harold Klemp. His answers are candid and wise with practical solutions. You will find great value in this book no matter your age.

The Shariyat-Ki-SUGMAD, Books One & Two

The "Way of the Eternal." These writings are the scriptures of ECKANKAR. They speak to you directly and come alive in your heart.

The Spiritual Exercises of ECK

Harold Klemp

This book is a staircase with 131 steps leading to the doorway to spiritual freedom, self-mastery, wisdom, and love. A comprehensive volume of spiritual exercises for every need.

ECK Wisdom Temples, Spiritual Cities, & Guides: A Brief History

Harold Klemp

You can use this eye-opening guidebook as creative inspiration for your spiritual exercises. Explore the Worlds of ECK and compare your travel notes with the user-friendly charts, descriptions, and color illustrations to help you recognize your firsthand experiences in the Temples of Golden Wisdom.

Available at bookstores, from online booksellers, or directly from ECKANKAR: Eckankar.org; (952) 380-2222; ECKANKAR, Dept. BK167, PO Box 2000, Chanhassen, MN 55317-2000 USA.